The Anxious Parent

Freeing Yourself from the Fears and Stresses of Parenting

Michael Schwartzman, Ph.D.

with Judith Sachs

A SKYLIGHT PRESS BOOK

Published by Fireside Books

A Division of Simon & Schuster

New York London Toronto Sydney Tokyo Singapore

FIRESIDE
Simon & Schuster Building
Rockefeller Center
1230 Avenue of the Americas
New York, New York 10020

Copyright © 1990 by Skylight Press and Michael Schwartzman Ph.D.

FIRESIDE and colophon are registered trademarks
of Simon & Schuster Inc.

Designed by Karolina Harris
Manufactured in the United States of America

1   3   5   7   9   10   8   6   4   2
1   3   5   7   9   10   8   6   4   2   Pbk.

Library of Congress Cataloging in Publication Data
Schwartzman, Michael.
The anxious parent: freeing yourself from the fears and stresses of parenting /
Michael Schwartzman with Judith Sachs.
p.   cm.
"A Skylight Press book."
1. Parenting—United States.   2. Parent and child—United States.
3. Anxiety—United States.   I. Sachs, Judith.   II. Title.
HQ755.83.S38   1990
306.874—dc20   90-9513
                                                         CIP

ISBN: 0-671-67920-1
ISBN: 0-671-75578-1 Pbk.

Published by arrangement with Skylight Press, 166 East 56th Street, 3-C,
New York, New York 10022

For Joey who gave me my parental anxiety,
and for Lisa who gave me Joey.

...M.S.

For Mia and Bruno, who have taught me the
great value of cosmic humor.

...J.S.

Contents

Acknowledgments

Most of what follows comes as a result of what I have learned from the parents and children I listen to every day. I thank them for sharing with me.

I want to thank my editor at Simon and Schuster, Bob Bender, for his enthusiasm and support. Thanks also to Meg Schneider and Skylight Press for sharing ideas and guiding me in this enterprise.

It has been my privilege to work with Judith Sachs. From the beginning she has understood what I wanted to say and has put my ideas into clear language. In so doing she has helped me to refine those ideas. It has been a pleasure to work with her.

Most of all I want to thank my wife and fellow psychologist Lisa Weiss for all the assistance and support she has given me throughout this project. She listened, offered examples, criticized, and extended her own writing and editing skills. I could never have done this without her.

Preface

Recently a mother of two who was in my office with her husband for marital therapy asked during a pause in the session whether she could discuss some concerns she had about the development of her older boy. She could see that there were no overt signs of pathology, and she did not think the problems in question were really "serious"; nevertheless, she was troubled about various conflicts she confronted on a daily basis as she raised her children. She felt she could not go to a professional to talk about issues that were, in her words, so mundane. "They probably seem minor and insignificant to you," she said apologetically, "but sometimes, when these incidents happen, I just can't seem to think straight."

On the contrary, I told her, these issues are the very ones that trouble all parents as they care for their growing and developing children—and they can be very difficult to deal with. The issues often prove so provocative that parents feel emotionally overwhelmed by them and find themselves acting in ways they know are inappropriate because their own thought processes and emotions are compromised by anxiety.

Faced with this kind of situation, a distressed parent will do what he can to stop the painful feelings he is experiencing. He will try to "turn off" the anxiety. But this may serve only to allow the anxiety to grow or spiral to the point of real panic. As soon as the parent feels out of control, his capacity for effective parenting will be greatly diminished, and both he and his child will suffer the consequences.

As parents we are all aware of the anxious thoughts and feelings that creep up on us as we try to do our best for our children. Who hasn't felt distressed when, sleep-deprived ourselves, we try to help a baby learn to sleep through the night? Who hasn't felt a twinge of guilt and rising panic while handing over our child to a new babysitter before leaving the house for a much-needed evening out? And who hasn't been overwhelmed with mixed feelings when leaving a clinging, tearful child for the first day of school or at a friend's home for a first play date?

The fact that we all experience these feelings and anxieties makes a great deal of psychological sense. They are natural emotional reactions to the real and imagined consequences our actions may have for our child. They are born of our personal psychological and emotional history and occur along with the day-to-day and moment-to-moment decisions we must make as parents. This is a normal process. A problem crops up only when these emotions and anxieties are so powerful as to interfere with our judgment and behavior—when they prevent us from "thinking straight."

We often consciously try to dismiss these unsettling feelings, only to have them return and linger and perhaps claim more and more attention. Anxiety escalates, compromising our ability to think and act. The more emotion we feel in relation to our child, the more anxiety we are likely to experience, and it is difficult to imagine anything more emotional than caring for young children.

It is at times like these, when we are caught in a web of anxiety from which we cannot extricate ourselves, that a sense of perspective is needed most; this is where the balance afforded by two parents' reactions can be invaluable. With luck, our spouse does not have the same anxious reactions to the same situations and can aid by responding appropriately to our child's needs. Sometimes just watching our spouse react in a calm way allows us to establish sufficient distance. Talking out a problem together can allow us to move on so that next time, possibly, we will be able to act in a more reasoned and less anxious way.

If you ignore your anxiety, it will hurt your ability to care for your child, and this, in turn, can mean severe consequences in terms of your child's development. But if you are able to recognize the fact that you feel anxious in certain situations and you have some understanding of why this is the case, then you will be well equipped to meet the challenges of parental caregiving.

In my clinical practice I have found that many of the parents who have sought my assistance were quite capable of handling parenting problems on their own once they understood the nature and source of their anxiety and the ways in which this self-knowledge could be used to enhance their parenting. Though there are many excellent books that provide good, solid advice on specific issues such as feeding and toilet training, what I have found most meaningful to parents is helping them to find their *own* ways to deal with problems. In order for them to accomplish this, I encourage them to see exactly how anxiety is hampering them in their parenting efforts. I lead them to discover the roots of their own feelings so that they are able to free themselves from acting thoughtlessly, guided only by the quickened heartbeat and caught breath of anxiety. They learn to use their anxiety as cues to the complex nature and myriad nuances of their thoughts and feelings. When they are able to separate their own issues surrounding a particular event from the event itself, they can then direct their thinking appropriately toward helping their child.

By writing this book I hope to share these techniques with you. The program for change that I describe can help you to understand your own emotional reactions to many of the major child-rearing issues you confront. I hope that with the ideas presented in this book you will be able to work through your feelings and use them instead of pushing them away. Of course, if you find yourself unable to use the program successfully with a particularly troubling issue, you may want to consult a professional. A single consultation with a psychologist is often sufficient to help parents clarify their feelings and move on.

There are no simple, straightforward solutions that work for everyone. However, when you have learned to locate the sources of the anxieties that color your feelings and behavior, you will be able to meet new situations more calmly. You may experience a coherence and security in parenting that has eluded you before. You will be able to help your child in different ways, *before* problems develop. When you learn to see yourself, your spouse, and your children more clearly, you can put your anxieties to work for you, and ultimately help your family grow stronger.

MICHAEL SCHWARTZMAN, Ph.D.
Malden Bridge, New York, 1989

1
What Is Parental Anxiety?

Paul and Elena never anticipated the struggles they would experience while trying to get their new baby, Katharine, to sleep at night. No matter how long they rock her or walk her, she screams the minute she's put into her crib. Paul can't stand the sound of his child in pain and feels he must leave the house, but instead he paces the floor wondering what he's doing wrong and lets Elena handle the baby.

Margot's three-year-old, Timothy, has always been wonderful about staying with sitters. But when Margot went back to work and hired a capable, qualified woman to stay at home all day with Timothy, he lost his toilet training and started having the worst tantrums. Now Margot doesn't know what to do. How can she go off to the office each day feeling so unsettled by her child's misery?

As soon as four-year-old Melissa saw her new baby brother, she screamed that she hated boys and wanted her mother to throw him in the garbage. Now her parents, Jake and Alice, are fighting constantly about how to deal with Melissa. Jake bends over backwards to make sure their daughter still feels loved; Alice ignores her whines and screams. Both parents feel their daughter's antagonism is eroding their marriage and family life, but they haven't a clue as to how to turn this difficult situation around.

Some of these scenarios may sound familiar to you. This is because they represent just a few of the daily, very common difficulties most parents experience with child-rearing. You may worry that you can't seem to handle situations that should be routine but aren't. You may be anxious that something is going wrong between you and your child, or you and your spouse, but you can't quite put your finger on it. Whatever the issue, the prevailing feeling is that you don't know what to do. Perhaps, you hope, it's just a phase your family is going through that will disappear on its own. But then days pass, weeks go by, and the problem doesn't disappear. Instead it starts to seem overwhelming. It may even color everything else in your life: your job, your marriage, your feelings about yourself as a person.

If you have ever experienced a heart-stopping fear about some element in your life that destroyed your ability to think rationally and coherently, a kind of panic that paralyzed you emotionally and physically, you were experiencing *anxiety*. As a parent you have hundreds of moment-to-moment opportunities to feel anxious. The anxieties you feel for your child might be provoked by stories from other parents, things you've read, and perhaps most significantly, similar experiences from your own childhood that left their indelible mark. Whether you're the kind of person who ignores things, hoping they'll go away, or the type who frets endlessly about the possibilities of disaster, at some time or other in your young child's life you have probably been aware of how powerful a hold anxiety can have on you.

If it seems that you are constantly fighting with your son about eating, sleeping, or toileting; if you and your spouse can't manage to agree on methods of discipline or ways to help your child get along with other children; if you can never quite settle down and feel comfortable about caring for your child, then something's wrong. It's time you began exploring in a deep and personal way what is happening to you as a parent, as a spouse, and as an individual. When you can examine what is really going on, you'll be able to make some positive changes in your relationships with your child and your spouse, and you will be better able to manage the many demands of your own personal life.

What, exactly, is anxiety? Imagine that you're driving down a dark road at night; your child is asleep in the backseat and a thunderstorm is raging outside. The road is slick and twisty, your vision obscured by sheets of rain. You're blinded by the headlights of a car coming in the opposite direction. Suddenly you feel your control slipping as the car begins to skid. Your heart is pounding, and you desperately want to turn and look at your child one last time but know you have to keep your gaze focused ahead of you. You grip the wheel and steer in the direction of the skid. You manage to get the car back on course again. Safe!

Four weeks later, on a beautiful, sunny afternoon, you and your child are driving down that same road. There's no traffic and conditions are perfect, but as you approach the spot where your car first started to skid, you can feel your palms getting damp. Your respiration quickens, your pupils dilate, your stomach tenses, your adrenaline is pumping. You experience all of the physical symptoms you had when confronted with real danger. Although nothing *real* is happening to you and your child, you feel just as frightened as you did when that frightening nighttime event took place.

Anxiety consists of present and past experiences and appropriate and inappropriate reactions that meld into one another. It is a sense of dread and foreboding that is attached to an event that took place in the past, the remnant of a former experience or set of experiences connected with current concerns as well as with long-buried fears.

Anyone can and will feel anxious in a variety of different circumstances, and many people who had breezed through life suddenly find themselves concerned and worried about lots of different things when they become parents. Why? For one thing, we're all completely unprepared for having a child. The most organized, well-adjusted, controlled individual may be overwhelmed when confronted with the responsibility of a new baby. You get trial runs for most other significant life experiences: school prepares you for the career you eventually select, a high school crush prepares you for falling in love and making a lifetime commitment to another human being. But the only training you have for being a parent is what you learned from your own parents, from their style of caring for you when you were a child. Babysitting, taking care of a younger sibling or an elderly parent or even a pet, offers only a small taste of what is in store for you.

When you take on the new role of parent, for the first time in your life you have someone else completely and totally dependent on you for survival. All the chores you do for a baby—feeding, diapering, dressing, bathing—are colored with your overwhelming feelings of responsibility, nurturing, loving, protecting, plus a nagging sensation that even though you're doing everything, you're not doing enough. If you're a new parent, it's understandable that you might often be troubled by anxieties about your infant's safety, health, sleep, feeding, and development—not because you're doing anything wrong but because you just don't know which direction to take and also because everything you do is so evocative of another time when your own parents did the same for you.

Everything you hoped for and never got from your parents, what your friends had that you missed out on, what you saw on *Father Knows Best*—all these go into your conception of what it means to be a mother or a father. Your fantasies and insecurities about doing as well as or better than your parents did with you can spark a lot of anxiety. And why shouldn't they? If you *weren't* anxious about embarking on this extraordinary experience, there'd be something wrong.

These worries you're having aren't new; most anxieties you feel as an adult have roots in your childhood. Take the case of Mary Ann whose father used to slap her when she misbehaved. She doesn't consciously remember the way she felt at the time, but she's undoubtedly going to be hypersensitive about discipline and punishment. She may ignore her child's tantrums without understanding that she can't comfortably deal with rage and fury. Mary Ann's *unconscious* will try to block out the memory of her father's rage because, if she dared to acknowledge it, she might feel acute hatred for a man she cares deeply about.

In the normal development of the psyche, your childhood fears dissipate as you gain more life experience and become more expert at dealing with inner phantoms, but the remnants of fears you once had remain in your unconscious mind and grow as you grow, changing, festering, and taking on all kinds of new meanings. Searching for the roots and meanings of these fears and beginning to understand how they affect you is the key to dealing with your present-day anxiety.

THE MANY FACES OF ANXIETY

Fear comes in many colors, and anxiety is just one component of the different unpleasant feelings we've all had at one time or another. Some of its related aspects are sadness, depression, jealousy, envy, and anger. The most deeply rooted of all human fears is *annihilation,* or a terror of becoming nonexistent, being eliminated. A nine-month-old may scream when his mother goes away. This is because he's at the stage of development where he feels there's a real bodily connection between them, and without her he may no longer exist.

Another group of anxieties comes from a fear of *abandonment.* A child who is sent to her room for a time-out may cry bitterly because she fears she has done something terrible that has driven her mother away.

Other anxieties come from a fear of *physical harm.* If your child does something that makes you furious, she may live in terror that you're going to retaliate and harm her physically.

Because these three types of fears are the significant human responses from which all others emanate, it is important to understand their sources so we can continue to function in the world and not be crippled by them.

THE HIGH PRICE OF ANXIETY

Human beings survive by learning to adapt. As a species we've grown and flourished by learning to make minute physical and psychological adjustments to our surroundings. But the only way we as individuals can gauge our behavior is by experience. Children simply haven't lived long enough to have sufficient experience, so they depend on their parents to help them adapt.

Let's say your child runs and falls. He pauses, more surprised than hurt. You start screaming and rush to help your baby, and only then does he start to wail and carry on! Anxiety is very transmittable; your child can easily "catch" it from you.

It is perfectly natural for you to get caught up in heady emotions when you're feeling a lot of conflict over an issue with your child. You can get so involved that all the various parts of the problem may start to run together. Suddenly you can find yourself in the middle of an anxiety spiral where one anxiety triggers another, paralyzing you so that you can't act on any one concern. You can easily get locked in old thought processes, repeating rigid patterns or ignoring your real concerns, and then it can be much harder to deal effectively with yourself and your family. If you ignore your anxiety, you may be overlooking a significant warning signal; the worries you have are telling you something about your style of parenting or about your child.

Suppose we take the case of Larry whose parents emigrated to America from Greece. They ran an old-style ethnic restaurant and never really bothered to learn English. Larry was determined not to be like them. He worked at a radio station while in college, volunteered for a literacy program, and learned five new vocabulary words a week. When his son Ben was born, he bought vocabulary flash cards so that by the time Ben turned two, he could "read."

Ben played outside every afternoon with neighborhood children, and at the age of four he naturally started mimicking a lot of what the older kids did—including bad language.

Larry began haranguing Ben about his poor speech, but restricting sweets and television every time he misused words didn't seem to stop Ben's new habit. One afternoon Ben, who was working on a puzzle, said aloud, "I ain't never gonna get this sucker." Larry walked over and smacked his son. He was horrified by his own behavior and became terribly anxious when Ben refused to speak to him for the rest of the weekend.

Communication between father and son was reduced to curt greetings in the morning and evening—and Larry became frantic, desperate to change the situation but confused as to what to do. Of course the real reason for Larry's problem with his son was his own inability to adapt. He had never acknowledged his anxieties about speaking properly—which to him meant being an assimilated American—and he transferred his own fears to his child.

If you understand your anxiety—what it looks like, where it comes from, why it's there—you can do something to establish new patterns and change whatever you're concerned about. If you ignore the anxiety, it may not go away. Your child's adjustment to whatever fear you have is directly dependent on your being able to tune into your own anxiety and deal with it.

THE ROLE OF THE UNCONSCIOUS

The unconscious is the part of the mind in which remnants of past memories, hopes, dreams, and fears are stored. In order for an individual to learn to process events in a complete and rational manner, he must have sufficient cognitive development and life experience. A child, still in the growing stages both physically and psychologically, will turn the elements of an emotional event around to suit his particular emotional needs. So when a problem arises, the child may fantasize about it or deny it, but without help he won't be able to work out all of its component parts.

Let's take the case of Jane, a young woman who grew up in an extended family comprised of her parents, grandparents, and two older sisters. They weren't poor, but they frequently talked about money problems. Because she adored her mother, Evelyn, and felt very protective of her in front of friends, she never complained about the fact that she always had to wear her sisters' hand-me-down clothes. Although unconsciously she did feel cheated and was angry about feeling like an afterthought in her family, she never revealed these hostile feelings for fear of hurting her mother.

Jane put herself through college, got her M.B.A., and went to work on Wall Street. She married Harry, a wealthy stockbroker, had a son David, and went right back to work. It was important to her that she help support her family.

Jane planned a large second birthday party for David, and Evelyn came to help. When she walked in the door, she hugged her grandson and handed him a gift. Inside was a blue polyester playsuit with a huge pink elephant with big metallic silver ears on it. "Ooh, Gram!" David exclaimed. "Shiny elephant!"

"Isn't it great?" Evelyn said to Jane. "Your sister wanted you to have it. Her little Sammy just outgrew it, and I knew it would be perfect for David."

Jane ripped the suit out of David's hand. "That's perfectly awful—it's garish. I would never dress my child in anything like that."

David started crying. "Want Gram's present!" he wailed. "Mommy, you mean! Give my present back!"

Jane felt her head spinning. Her mother was looking at her, devastated with embarrassment, and her son was staring at her as though she were an ax murderer.

What made Jane, a characteristically rational, reasonable person, become intolerant, nervous, and short-tempered? She probably had some real concerns about relating to her mother differently now that she had a child of her own, and she was tense because of all she had done in preparation for the birthday party. But a variety of unresolved issues were also at work here. *Consciously* Jane was thinking something like: "I'd never buy my child anything that overdone." *Unconsciously* she had a feeling something like: "I'm not going to let my mother do to David what she did to me."

Jane doesn't remember how angry she used to feel when her mother presented her with her sisters' hand-me-downs, but when Evelyn offered David a gift his cousin had outgrown, she saw red. All the anxieties that she had as a child about not being loved enough came to the surface. Jane's unconscious mind had stored these memories, preserved them and added to them, so that now, when she confronted a situation in the present with her own son that was similar to something she went through in the past, she reacted in a completely emotional, almost automatic and unthinking way. It was not that she hated her mother's taste in clothes or was jealous that her son loved Evelyn more than he did her. She was reliving some deeper issue about her feelings for her mother and was reacting to the present moment because of things that happened to her in the past. Only when Jane was able to separate her emotional state into its various components could she begin to understand where her fear and outrage were coming from.

THE ANXIETY SPIRAL

When you feel anxious, you sense that something isn't right. Anxiety is a cue, a signal that you must pay attention, find the source of your discomfort, and do something to relieve it. If you avoid the painful feelings or try to run away from them, if you don't stop to think about what's actually happening at the moment, you may become overwhelmed by anxiety. The combination of real concerns and unconscious ideas can create cyclical thinking that is as unproductive as it is difficult to control.

Anxiety builds on itself, fueling the fantasies that have caused your initial uneasiness. It can spiral into a cacophony of dissonant, barely relevant feelings. A typical spiral for Jane might be like this: "My mother is really getting on my nerves. If I let her come to help with the party, it'll turn out all wrong, and I'll spend so much time fixing the things she messes up that David will never get properly taken care of. He could get sick right before his birthday. And I'll be so worried about that, I'll perform poorly at my job and get fired. Then we'll have to sell the co-op and move, and David will grow up without any of the advantages, just the way I did."

Jane has to break her anxiety spiral before it gets this far. She must identify what is really bothering her, get in touch with her unconscious fears, pinpoint the real issues, and begin to act to relieve her own anxiety while dealing with her mother and her child.

TUNING IN: ANXIETY AS A TRIGGER

You can't make your anxiety vanish, but you can control it. One of the best ways to banish cyclical, irrational thinking is to talk out your fears—no matter how strange or upsetting they seem—with your spouse or a good friend. Another ear can always hear your thoughts better than you can. Talking about your fears—like talking about your nightmares in the daylight—is the most effective way to tame them.

When you can recognize the cues that anxiety has provided, you are better equipped to understand and control your own emotional reactions and to act positively and constructively in the situation. If you feel capable of handling a difficult situation, you'll present a calm, comforting face to your child, who is naturally going to feel better because he has a parent who is in control of her emotions. If you know that certain events are bound to make you anxious, you can prepare yourself in advance. Anticipating what might happen can help you face the unknown, look at the reality of the moment clearly, and use your anxiety to your own and your child's advantage.

Anxiety should trigger your thought processes, acting as the spur to start some personal investigation. Like a divining rod roaming over dry ground, it should point you toward whatever is really going on under the surface. The anxiety you feel can help you recall memories of the past and recent events that have been distressing you. It can show you just how these various pieces fit together and influence your parenting decisions. When you're able to claim these uncomfortable feelings as your own, you can begin to deal with them.

Anxiety Questionnaire

The following is not a typical true/false questionnaire but, rather, a way for you to start checking the *sources* of some of your central concerns. See how the statements below make you feel. Those that evoke an emotional response will indicate areas that may be particularly anxiety-provoking for you.

1. I recall the everyday events of my childhood with pleasure.
2. I remember a particular instance or instances in my childhood that caused me considerable distress.
3. My parents and siblings were always there for me.
4. My family dealt openly and honestly with difficult issues.
5. My parents showed me a lot of physical affection.
6. I am a physically demonstrative person.
7. I don't worry much about my health.
8. I enjoy living in the area and the home I currently have.
9. I feel secure in my job, and my spouse is secure in his (hers).
10. I sleep well at night.
11. I maintain a healthy and well-balanced diet.
12. I was never worried about the childbirth experience.
13. I planned my children and am happy to be a parent.
14. As an adult I enjoy visiting my parents and having them visit me.
15. I generally believe that people like me when they meet me.
16. I have good, close friends.
17. I easily mix parenting with my career.
18. I have no problem leaving my child in the care of another trustworthy person: my spouse, a parent or in-law, or a sitter.
19. I am not unduly worried about physical survival on this planet, either personally or as a species.

The feelings these responses generate, the positive and negative memories and thoughts they evoke, will give you a general idea of what you consider emotionally easy and difficult and how you approach some of the primary areas in your life.

Don't be concerned if your responses indicate that you're more anxious than calm. This simply means that you're really tuned in to your emotional life. Anxiety exists as long as uncertainty exists, and nothing is certain about parenting. No matter how much anxiety you feel on a daily basis, if you can get in touch with it, you'll be better equipped to deal with your uncomfortable feelings. Recognizing what these feelings mean to you will give you the key to a better understanding of yourself—as a person and as a parent.

Shaping Your Parenting Style

Before you can make any sense of your parental anxieties, it's helpful for you to understand exactly what makes you the kind of parent you are. Once you have a basic comprehension of how you developed the feelings, beliefs, and reactions that are inherently part of you, you can develop new ways of relating to your child. In order to put the Program for Change into action and use your anxiety effectively, you need to discover what it is that shaped your particular parenting style.

Each person, each parent, has a different physical and psychological makeup that contributes to his or her nurturing abilities. Some have the gift of being able to handle babies—able to read the most obscure requests by instinct and infinitely patient with feeding, diapering, and lack of sleep. Some are better with toddlers, enjoying the wild mood swings and endless demands of children who are becoming independent and autonomous. Others prefer the verbal stage when they can interact with a child whose distinct personality is emerging.

You've evolved to become the parent you are today—funny or compassionate or strict or organized—because of three main factors: your family background, your social sphere, and who you are today as a person.

THE FAMILY BACKGROUND

History teaches some wonderful lessons. It's always useful to consider the past, particularly when strong emotions, such as those we feel as parents, are involved. If you can become aware of your own history, you can judge it and see it in the light of present-day circumstances and feelings. Once you've tapped the roots of your early anxieties and understand a little about them, you don't have to pass them on to your own children. If you think about your family history, you'll begin to understand the various influences that made you the sort of person you are today.

Think about your place in the family, how your mother treated you, how your father treated you, the way your parents agreed or disagreed about raising you, how your parents parented your siblings, how you felt in relation to each parent and each sibling, how you thought your mother felt in relation to your father, how you thought your father felt in relation to your mother, and so forth. All of these elements, taken by themselves and in combination, are crucial to the psychological development of each individual.

As children we internalize our family's dynamics, and they become part of us. What you remember about your childhood and your parents' parenting is inevitably changed and distorted by the passage of time, but if you can become aware of the family dynamic you grew up with and how it affected you, you can separate yourself from your children and relinquish the need to repeat or correct the past.

Did your parents love each other? Did they love your sister more than you? Did they worry about money? Did they fill you full of anxiety about achievement? You probably have very specific answers to these questions, and yet your sibling might have a completely different response to the same questions.

The family tree is important not because of what actually oc-curred but because of your personal memory of what occurred. "I always loved our family Christmases, and I want our daughter Marian to have the same terrific experiences I did," one mother, Virginia, said. "Mom, Tanya, and I trimmed the tree and cooked the day before, and the house smelled wonderful. Christmas morning, all the aunts and uncles came, and later we had dinner and sang carols and opened presents together, and I helped Tanya set the table and put out the goodies. It was so fabulous!"

Her sister Tanya, however, recalls, "Mom woke up crying every Christmas morning because Dad had died around that time of year. It was just morbid, the way she carried on. And then later the aunts and uncles came, and it was like a big wake instead of a holiday. Somehow we got around to opening presents, but Mom was never in shape to serve the meal, so Virginia and I ended up having to do everything. It was awful."

The same experience; two different histories. Virginia has a positive and upbeat view of her childhood, so the warmth of the occasion shines through for her. Tanya, the older sister, was acutely more aware of her father's death and his absence during this traditionally happy time of year. What she remembers most is her mother's grief.

It is a natural human desire to experience *closure* (a sense of completion) about every vital emotional experience. When some-thing is still unresolved from your past, you tend to imagine what you would like to have occurred, to inscribe "The End" on the story that was never finished for you. If you felt that you never received enough attention from your parents, you may con-sciously or unconsciously seek a nurturing, caring spouse who devotes a great deal of attention to your child. But if your own conflict with your parents is not resolved, you may begin to envy your child who is receiving all the "goodies" you never lacked.

The kind of relationship you had with your parents, siblings, and grandparents, if they were close, is a great motivator—pro and con—for your own parenting. If your parents divorced, you may say, "Well, at least I can do better than they did," and develop a staunch determination to make your marriage work. If you admired the way your parents handled equality among you and your siblings, you may try to emulate that in your family. Or, as is most common, you may have loathed and despised many of the things your parents did to you and with you when you were a child and yet still feel that they were superb role models, people whose attitudes and behaviors you hope to emulate.

You may want to rewrite history ("my daughter won't have to wear hand-me-downs") or repeat it ("I want my little boy to have the same wonderful talks with his grandfather that I did"). Naturally, neither is possible. If you find that you're constantly running after the image of the past, either to change it or recapture it, you're going to feel disappointment and anxiety, because no matter how hard you try, you can never get it "right."

Your own past affects your present-day actions most when you become a parent because you are once again dealing with the child in you. As a parent you may experience something so similar to what once happened to you that you instantly identify with your own child. You feel *empathy,* a kind of connectedness and deep understanding of exactly what your child is going through. Feeling what he feels vicariously can sometimes strengthen your emotional bond with him, but it can also revive anxiety because you're standing at a distance from the scene with the perspective of life behind you.

You see him clinging and anxious on the first day of school, and it brings back all those terrible memories of your father just dumping you in your classroom and walking out on *your* first day without even a kiss good-bye. But you don't have to be distant and abrupt as your father was. You can rewrite the story of parting and make both the child and the parent into heroes.

Your memory of the past tends to be filtered through the lens of your child-self. For this reason there's room for much introspection and distortion. Over time our memory "corrects" the way things actually happened to conform to our positive or negative view of our own past. But understanding that past is vital in getting perspective on what we do with our own children as parents today.

YOUR SOCIAL SPHERE

Our parents are the primary molders and shapers of our person-alities, but we'd never learn enough about the world if we didn't have any contrast, or *differentiation*. By the time a child is three or four he is exposed to other playmates and those playmates' parents, to friends and mentors and settings entirely different from his home. He learns, for example, that Mary has certain toys she doesn't have to share with her sisters, although he is expected to share everything with his brother. And he finds in Mr. Donnally, the gardener, a grown-up friend who doesn't nag him about getting his pants dirty but instead shows him how to dig in the soil and make flowers grow. He learns about the world as others—not just his parents—see it, and this shows him that there are options and possibilities other than the ones he has been offered for the past three or four years.

Differentiation—the ability to contrast, compare, and distin-guish what you have from what someone else has—is a motivating force in child development. In order for a child to absorb and assimilate what he learns in the family, at home, he has to be able to see that his parents are different from other children's parents and his feelings are different from other people's feelings. A child needs a balance of experiences in order to grow. Even when the home environment is strained by death or divorce or parental illness, for example, the child can retain those qualities in himself if he can see that the rest of the world is healthy and whole.

For your child to feel competent and secure on his own, you must give him every opportunity to see that he is separate from you in the world. The more aware he becomes of himself as a distinct person, the easier it will be for him to function indepen-dently.

How wonderful it is the first time a child feels brave enough to let go of his father in the swimming pool and is able to swim all the way to the ladder by himself. In the same way that he masters this kind of physical feat on his own, he must learn to handle similar emotional accomplishments. The first time your child can kiss you good-bye, tell you to have a nice day, and walk into a new classroom or playground, you'll know that you've succeeded in your goal as a parent. You have given that child the confidence to say, "I can exist without you."

WHO YOU ARE TODAY AS A PERSON

The family tree and social sphere begin in your childhood to help shape the adult whom you eventually become and continue to do so even after you are an independent, autonomous individual. But the life you lead now has much more to it. You play many roles now, and each contributes to the kind of person and parent you are.

Do you have a career? Do you consider it integral to your life and personality, or do you consider it just a job? Do you work in an office or at home? Did you work before the birth of your child, and are you now currently taking a sabbatical or a break from your career? For women, particularly, the choice of whether or not to work has a lot to do with who they are and how comfortable they are in their marriage and in their parenting. For a man, the additional financial concerns that come with the birth of a baby can influence greatly the way he relates to his career and whether or not he's on a fast or slow track. The way both parents integrate their work life into their home life has a lot to do with the kind of parents they become.

Your role as homemaker and caretaker is another important factor. Do you like the home you're in? Does it feel like "you"? Did you and your spouse create it together, and are you currently working to make it more beautiful, more comfortable? Is it a nest for your family? Or are you just passing through, waiting until something better comes along—maybe bigger and grander since you expanded from a couple to a family? Do you do family things—church-related events, picnics, country fairs—or do you tend to spend time by yourselves puttering and fixing? Do you have a hobby or interest separate from your spouse that occupies a great deal of your time? Is there something you're involved in together, such as a community theater group or a jogging club, that keeps you close as a couple?

What about your interactions with friends? Do you have mostly married friends? Married friends with children? Did you meet through your children—walking them in the park or running into them at preschool? Do you have more problems dealing with your childless friends now that you're a parent?

Then, at last, there's being a parent, which probably occupies 98 percent of your unconscious life even if you're a busy career person. How do you add that role to your repertoire? It's probable that you'll do it in a similar fashion to the way you handled other significant milestones in your life. If you achieved in school and your career despite self-doubt, you'll probably approach your parenting nervously but determined to succeed. If you waltzed through life, overconfident and brash, you may have no qualms about your new role as mother or father.

Your roles may include homemaker, hobbyist, social participant, community activist, business professional, romantic and sexual partner, as well as a concerned parent. But it may be difficult to meld the person-self with the parent-self because the roles can so often conflict with each other. The need to combine the various parts of you naturally opens the door to a great deal of potential anxiety.

If the major components of a person's life are love, family, and work, then good mental health depends on the ability to keep these three poles stable and move smoothly among them. Your own self should be free to explore and to grow in each area. Very often, though, the parenting role becomes so overwhelming that other parts of the psyche are left unattended. The *person* can be left feeling detached and unfulfilled.

Let's look at Blanche, a successful graphic artist who married when she was thirty-five. A committed environmental activist, Blanche was also a member of the town council, taught yoga at the local exercise center, and occasionally volunteered at a soup kitchen in a nearby church. She had been waiting a long time to get pregnant, though, and when motherhood came, she put aside everything else, taking leaves from all her various activities. Her husband Jim asked her one day if she was completely happy as "Joshua's mom," and she was struck by the implication of that single role. "I think so," she said.

Her son had just passed his first birthday when her boss called and asked if she would like to come back to work. Blanche felt really excited for a moment, and then she remembered who she was, what she had become. "It's wonderful of you to ask," she said, "but I'm just not ready. Maybe next year." She suddenly felt sad, but as soon as she involved herself in play with Joshua, she was fine again.

Blanche evidently had a great deal of ambivalence about her various roles before motherhood that surfaced only after her baby was born. Maybe she had so many activities going on because she wasn't really sure she was good at any one of them. When her child was born, she put aside her other interests and, in an effort to feel better about herself, devoted herself to the most visible of her roles, which was that of "mother." But she is having difficulty integrating herself as "mother" with herself as "person." When will she be ready to go back to being the multifaceted person she was—with the additional bonus of mother? How will she ever know until she tries?

Parenthood changes everything, and perhaps the most striking alteration is in the relationship of husband and wife. As soon as they have a child, they must learn to readjust their roles; this is something many people find exceptionally difficult to do. The conflict over readjustment and shared chores often causes a great deal of tension and anxiety, making a person yearn for escape from at least one of the roles—often the role of parent.

Nicholas, whose wife Joan stopped working when their twin boys were born three years ago, recalls how he dealt with the split between his working life away from the house and his time at home with his family: "I love those boys—God, I'd lie down in front of a moving truck if I saw it coming toward them—but by the end of the weekend, I've had it. Joan has been after me to finish projects I've started, the kids are fighting over a toy, the dog is howling in the backyard, and I suddenly think, What the hell did I get myself into? I find myself yelling at Joan and stomping out of the house, and then five minutes later I think, Where am I going to go? This is where I live, where every significant part of me exists. I mean, I feel trapped in all that commitment, and yet I chose it. I love it—and them. But I will admit that, first thing Monday morning, I jump into my car to go to the office with a very light heart and a heavy foot on the accelerator."

It's perfectly acceptable for Nicholas to "escape" by running to the office on Monday morning. His job, after all, is to provide for the family, and he can legitimately escape the demands put on him in the home by trading them for those he must assume in the office in order to earn a living.

Like Blanche and Nicholas, you, too, may be feeling ambivalent about the various roles you play now that you're a parent. Because you are the chief influence on your young child's emotional life and because anxiety is so communicable, it's essential that you make time to take care of the person you have become. If you remain in conflict over your needs and wants, your child will feel that discrepancy and begin testing the limits you set. But as soon as you can sort out your self as a person and your self as a parent, it will become easier for you to make sense of the world for your child.

Personal History Profile

This profile will ask questions about your past that will help you to see yourself more clearly. Standing back from yourself allows you to gain a new perspective and tap the roots of your self-image.

Your memory of how things happened will not be factual and accurate but rather will be a deeply *felt* rendition of the past. It's the lens through which your present experiences are filtered. And the way you remember what happened to you will have a great effect on the way you deliver what you have to offer to your children.

These questions are meant to be evocative, to recall elements that you may not have considered for some time or at all. The questions may trigger others in you, pertinent to your own past. One method of answering this questionnaire is to have each spouse ask the other a set of questions, then switch. Try not to limit yourself but let one thought run into another. Remember, there are no "right" answers.

What you remember of your past is uniquely yours, and that's precisely what makes it both wonderful and terrible. The memories you have of family, friends, teachers, holidays, vacations, discipline, petty childhood cruelties, and adolescent crushes color what you're feeling today. The clearer you are about these memories and the feelings they evoke, the more control you'll have over the way they influence your behavior today as a parent.

FAMILY

1. What is your earliest memory of your father, your mother, your grandparents, your siblings?
2. Did your parents seem old or young to you when you were a child? Do you think of yourself now as younger or older than they were when you were growing up? How was their age expressed to you?
3. How healthy did your parents seem? Did they frequently complain or did they shrug off illness and pain?
4. What was their attitude toward finances? Did they talk about money frequently? Was there a lot of emotion expressed around financial issues?
5. Did they both work? At what? How did you view their working?
6. What was your relationship to your siblings when you were growing up? Would you have said you were the most or the least favored child? Or do you think your parents were equally fair and loving to all family members?
7. Were your grandparents living? Were they close to your parents? Do you remember them fondly, as a nuisance, or somewhere in between?
8. Were your parents divorced when you were a child? How

did they deal with it? How did you deal with it? How well did you accept your stepparent?

9. Was there ever a death in your family when you were a child? How did you experience grief? How was the death of a loved one handled by the rest of your family?

10. How do you recall the division of power? Would you say Mom or Dad was the boss? Was one much more aggressive; one much more passive? Would you characterize them as emotional and demonstrative or reserved and distant?

RELATIONSHIP TO PARENTS

11. Did you love your parents? Did they love you? How did they let you know?

12. Did you like your parents? Did they like you? Was it friendly between you?

13. Could your parents keep a secret? Did you trust them with confidences?

14. What special games do you remember playing with your mother? With your father? With both of them together?

15. What was your favorite childhood present? Who gave it to you and for what occasion? Were you surprised?

16. How did your parents behave around such issues as eating? Sleeping? Elimination? Sex?

17. What was expected of you? Did your parents see you as an achiever or a failure? How did this make you see yourself?

18. Did you see your parents as achievers or failures? Were you ever embarrassed by them? Proud of them? Why?

19. Would you say your parents were in control of their lives, or did they seem to be buffetted by every passing breeze?

20. As a child, did you feel confident? Or did you have unreasonable worries about little things?

21. How were you influenced by things your parents said, such as "Hold my hand, you'll be sorry if you lose me," "Do that again and I'll cut off your fingers," "Joey (Peggy) is such a perfect child. Why can't you be like him/her"?

22. If your mother and father were asked, "What was it like being a parent to Susan?" what would they say?

FRIENDS

23. Did your parents generally like your friends or dislike them?
24. Did your parents let you have friends over? What were the rules?
25. Were you generally allowed to do what your friends did, or did you have greater or lesser freedom in areas such as watching TV, having sweets, getting or earning an allowance, staying up at night?
26. If your friends were asked to remember spending time at your house, would they have said: "We could do whatever we wanted there," "There was lots of good stuff to eat," "Her mother was mean," or something else entirely?
27. Did you rebel as an adolescent? Against what sorts of things?
28. What were your relationships with the opposite sex like?

DISCIPLINE AND PUNISHMENT

29. How did your parents handle discipline? What was your father strict about? Your mother? What things were they lenient about?
30. What did you have to do wrong before your parents punished you? Did you get any warnings, or did they just clamp down? Were you always made aware of the rules first?
31. What is your memory of your worst punishment? Your most feared punishment?
32. Were you afraid of your parents? Why? What incidents do you recall that inspired fear?
33. Are there any particular traumas that you recall around punishment or in general?

ADULTHOOD

34. What do you remember about certain significant "good-byes" in your life? How did your parents leave you—at school, at

another relative's house, at camp? Were you allowed closure on these good-byes, or were you just left hanging?

35. Did you have goals that you have not realized? Were they within the realm of possibility or just too hard for you?

36. Did you achieve certain goals that you set for yourself long ago?

37. How have your relationships with the opposite sex changed since you were an adolescent?

38. How is your relationship with your spouse?

39. Was the birth of your child planned?

40. How did you feel about the birth of your child?

41. How does having a family affect you as a person? How does being a parent affect your other roles?

42. Are you different from the "you" you recall growing up? In what ways?

43. Was there ever a time in your life when you felt completely, totally happy? Can you recapture that feeling now? What defines happiness for you?

Parenthood is difficult because you aren't dealing one on one, adult on child. You have yourself as a parent, yourself as a person, and yourself as the bearer of a personal history and family to take into consideration. In addition, your spouse and partner brings his or her own elements to this mix.

The particular balance that two people can achieve in a marriage and a parenting relationship is what gives the unique spin to the ball. If you're dealing with yourself as a child, it may be harder to see what your own child is going through. But if your spouse—who knows you and your many roles well—can add perspective, the two of you together can join strengths and learn to parent well.

The responsibility of parenting becomes much more manageable when you know yourself and you know your spouse. When the two of you use all your roles as fully developed people and learn to share in a balanced partnership, you and your child have the best opportunity for change and growth.

3
Mothers, Fathers, and the Balancing Act

Being a mother or a father isn't an isolated occupation. Unless there's been a death or divorce in the family, it's assumed that there will be two of you simultaneously influencing the growth and development of your child. Becoming a "good parent," as we shall see, depends largely on the balance struck between you—mother and father—over emotional issues.

Neither partner is any more equipped than the other to become a parent for the first time, though, unfortunately, most couples seem to feel that women "instinctively" know what a baby wants and needs. The truth is that instinct and common sense aren't sex-related at all, and men have an equal opportunity to parent well or not so well.

The problem is that most of us come to parenthood with stereotypical images of what motherhood and fatherhood are all about. You get your images from your own histories, from books, the news, the "perfect" neighbors down the block. It's hard to be at peace with what you do as parents because it looks as if there's always someone else doing it better. Only when you can get past the images and start balancing your particular abilities and limitations—really relying on your spouse—can you begin to create a good parenting partnership.

Women and men—mothers and fathers—generally have different anxious reactions to parenthood. Maybe as a new mother you think you're not doing enough and you go overboard: feeding on demand every two hours, scrubbing the nursery to make it germ-free, spending every waking moment wondering if you're stimulating the child properly. Maybe as a new father your wife is spoiling the child rotten and you ought to spend more time with him, but you're too busy working harder to earn all the money you're going to need for college. The two of you disagree on the style of giving to the child—and to each other—and suddenly everything you do ends up in misunderstanding. You're doubly anxious because you know your baby is experiencing your anxiety and being affected by it.

Where do you come by these impulses that lead in so many various emotional directions? The anxiety sparked by parenthood has a great deal to do with the enormous responsibility you're forced to assume. Instantaneously, you're supposed to bond with your child and swear eternal devotion. You're supposed to nurture him in sickness and in health. You're supposed to become "parents" in a moment, although you've never been any such thing before.

THE EXPECTATIONS OF MOTHERHOOD

"The baby is crying all the time," Lucy, a first-time mother, said. "I change her, feed her, rock her, but she won't stop wailing. I feel as though the world is falling apart, especially at 2 A.M. when I haven't had any sleep. Suppose I'm never able to satisfy her needs? What kind of mother am I going to be? I can see the two of us at war when she's a teenager and I'm waiting up for her, and she storms in here and claims I never understand what she wants."

Lucy is a typical new mother. She feels overwhelmed by her inability to soothe her baby but can't see that her own panic may be feeding her child's distress. All she can think is that she must be a bad mother. She's already spiraled her fears as far as her child's adolescence and beyond. She just can't focus on the particular problem: helping the baby to fall asleep. Instead, she has let her anxiety create the rest of their relationship, which she imagines as an ongoing struggle throughout their lives.

What do we consider "a good mother"? How has the concept of a "good mother" changed over time? Why is being a good mother harder today for many women than it was for their mothers twenty or thirty years ago? Precisely because of the role models we've had in the past—models that no longer pertain in many instances.

We've all gotten past the characterization of a woman's place being in the home. A woman's place is anywhere she chooses to be—in a board room, in a factory, in a space capsule—*as well as* in the home. This dual role is precisely what makes motherhood so difficult, and unless the home situation is unusual, it's the woman who will be with her children 75 percent of the time during their formative years, to her husband's 25 percent. But aside from the time factor, why is motherhood different from fatherhood? There are those who would argue today that the roles of father and mother are equal, particularly in two-career families where both parents balance home and work. But there is a crucial difference between men and women in terms of the kind of parenting they do.

Unless a woman's children are adopted, they began life as a part of her body. If she decides to breastfeed, she's continuing the physical tie well into her child's early life. She tends to do more touching and cuddling with the children than her husband and is generally the one her children want when they're sick or hurting.

A woman's strong motivation to become a mother means that she has a stake in doing that job well—as well as she has ever done anything she's attempted before in her life. Many first-time mothers get caught up in old, distorted memories of how perfect their own mother was, though others would love to wipe out any and all connections with the way their mother mothered them.

Naturally these comparisons, in combination with new mothering responsibilities, can spark anxiety.

Mothers tend to set a high stake on making themselves available to their children. By this we mean that as much as they may travel into the outer world beyond the home, they still reserve a part of themselves for parenting. And this may be true even when they're at the office or on a business trip, away from their children. Women very often express difficulty in changing over from the "mommy mode" to the "person mode."

"I was in the middle of this big negotiation," a realtor named Elise said, "when I suddenly remembered that I hadn't told the sitter about the change in my son's medication. He'd developed a rash from the Amoxicillin he was taking for his ear infection, but I'd been too busy the night before to throw the bottle away when I picked up the bottle of Ceclor. I tried calling home, but no one was there; they must have gone to the playground. So here I was, trying to tell the buyers of this house that the seller won't replace the fence in the yard, and all I could think of was Michael's getting a dose of the wrong stuff. I found myself impatient with these people for being so unreasonable about the stupid fence, and I knew my tone of voice made them think I wasn't on their side."

Elise is a concerned parent, but her anxiety about her son's condition is making her a less than effective realtor. She still has to figure out a way of apportioning the amount of herself available for her child and the amount she wants to give to her personal identity.

The mother's domain is the inner world, represented by the home. Even in two-career families where both parents work full-time outside the home, a woman—the housekeeper or preschool teacher or grandmother—is generally in place to assume a mothering role. In most cases the real mother is the one to coordinate and organize the child's life through the intervention of a surrogate caregiver.

But many women today choose to stay at home when their children are young and to place their career on hold for a time. This choice may lead to additional anxiety. The job of mother is hard enough, but when it's contrasted with the excitement of the father's sphere—the outer world, the world of work—as well as the world of couples without children, it can become very disillusioning to be "just a mother."

It requires a great force of will on the part of most women to move fluidly among several worlds. And it also requires the support of a partner who is eager and able to take on the parenting role himself.

FATHERS AND ANXIETY

In the fifties a typical television sitcom father went to work and came home to view the chaos he had left behind in the household. He provided financial support for his wife and children so that they could go about their business without worrying about where the next meal was coming from. The father was generally available on weekend mornings for a ball game with his sons or to teach his daughter to ride her bike. His relationship with his wife was friendly but not passionate. He was, as far as he knew, the head of his household, except that Mom made all the decisions, raised the kids, and managed the money.

In real life, of course, this presentation of fatherhood was considered an exaggeration if not a falsehood. Many new fathers today look back on their own fathers of the postwar era as warm, supportive, practicing members of the family, good role models for the fathering they wish to do. Perhaps the last generation of men didn't change diapers or help with the cooking, but emotionally many of them were just as involved as men are today.

Our culture, however, has grown more sophisticated in terms of the needs of the father and the way he fits into the family dynamic. These days it's expected that the father will coach his wife through her labor and delivery instead of hiding in the waiting room, cigar in hand. It is de rigueur for new fathers to diaper, feed, rock, and play with their infants and to participate in every aspect of child-rearing.

If men today lacked a good image of concerned and connected fathering from their own fathers, they still have another role model to emulate: their mothers. Men, like women, learn how to nurture by remembering the way they were nurtured. A man who grew up standing at his mother's side while she mixed the cookie batter so that he could lick the bowl may be destined to foster a love of cooking in a child of his own. A man who recalls his mother bandaging his cuts and bruises can be just as dutiful a nurse to his own injured child.

How is a man's anxiety different from a woman's? In the first place he lacks the physical bond that his wife possesses, and this may make him more anxious about the child's well-being. The stereotypical image of a father counting the infant's fingers and toes in the delivery room is based on many men's fears that they have not produced a "perfect" baby.

Bob's wife Megan was thirty-six when she conceived, and he lived in fear of a baby born with birth defects, even after the amniocentesis came back normal. "All I could think of," he said, "were those fifteen hundred other things they didn't test for. I knew they were one-in-a-million chances, but that didn't make me feel any better until I actually held my perfect daughter in my arms and saw that she was okay."

It's interesting that men who consider themselves most liberated, with high opinions of their wives' abilities and strengths, tend to become more concerned with their new role as "protector and provider" after their child is born. Remember Nicholas's comment in the last chapter that he would stand in front of a moving truck if it menaced his twin sons? There is a fierce love that comes with fatherhood, and it can be highly physical in nature.

Fathering also changes the way a man sees his relationship with his wife. Suppose that before they became parents *he* was the one who played the role of child. If their relationship was initially based on her taking care of him, he may feel jealous, neglected, even obliterated by the presence of a child. A wife simply doesn't have the time or the inclination to baby her husband at the end of the day after she's been babying a baby.

One of the hardest things about having children is adapting and expanding the marriage and the couple relationship. This involves the new division of labor in the house, but more im-

portant it involves saving time to share together and use well as
a couple.

It's difficult to turn yourself off as a parent at the end of the
day after your child is asleep and turn yourself on as an involved,
caring spouse. Sexual interest often dwindles; romance grinds to
a halt. There's so little time for taking care of yourself—so much
of yourself is spread thin over career and children—that your
primary relationship generally suffers. One of the biggest clues
that something is awry is when "Bob" and "Megan" start calling
each other "Father" and "Mother," thereby confusing the person
and parent roles.

Many fathers claim they feel no anxiety about their role. They
say they're perfectly content with the way their life is running
and depend on their wife to be the one to worry if their child is
having problems. Bob said that he relaxed completely when he
saw that Megan had given birth to a "perfect" baby. He couldn't
figure out, as their daughter Peggy grew into a toddler, why Megan
got so upset over what he thought of as minor concerns.

"I find myself doing things not because I think there's anything
wrong with the kid, see, but because Megan is in a lather over
what I'm *not* doing. There was this night when Peggy was getting
her last molars, and she was a wreck, very cranky and complaining. I said to Megan, Just stop indulging her and put her to bed.
Megan is wringing her hands, saying she's going to call the doctor.
Finally, when I see I can't make her calm down at all, I just go
and give Peg some Tylenol. I don't really think she needed it, but
it made Megan feel better that I had stepped in and done something."

Bob says it's his wife who has the problem, but we can see that
he's pretty anxious himself about how they agree or disagree over
what to do for their child. Luckily Bob is a concerned father,
involved and concerned about both his wife and daughter, and
he wants to help solve the problem.

Some men don't feel this way. It's all too easy for a father to
abdicate, to claim that his wife is the rock of the family anyway,
so she might as well make the rules and uphold them. One way
a man may get rid of the conflict he feels about his wife taking

over is by removing himself from the situation. If he's never present, if his values and ideas don't count, then he can walk away without a scratch, spending more time on his job or household projects because that's what he's expected to do.

Of course what he's actually doing is avoiding his hurt feelings resulting from being shut out as a father. If he becomes a cipher in his own home, he's doing his children, his wife, and particularly himself a vast disservice. One day when the children are grown— now nearly total strangers—he'll look back and complain that he wasn't able to spend enough time with them and now sees nothing of himself in them.

Fathering doesn't happen in that moment when a man takes the infant from the obstetrician's hands and looks into his eyes. Some fathers can relate to their children only when they're old enough to communicate verbally or to share some activity they both enjoy. It takes some men a while to assume the role and *feel* like a father, but it's always worth the wait.

THE FAMILY BALANCING ACT

A balance between father and mother, husband and wife, is what really makes the difference in a family. It can be the deciding factor on how much anxiety there is in a household and how well or badly the various family members figure out new ways to deal with problems and with one another.

A child needs to see herself in relation to two parents—one at a time and both together. When both parents are equally important presences in her life—for routine, ordinary days as well as wonderful, memorable ones—she has the opportunity to contrast and compare her father's reactions to those of her mother. She can gain a sense of emotional balance.

If a child has only her mother around, she gets to see only one set of reactions to her behavior. And if her father happens to be away from home a lot, he may appear on the home front as a "Santa Claus"—the great guy who takes her on trips, brings her treats, and roughhouses with her. If he has missed out on understanding the rules and routines of the household—since he's never there—the child may try to pit him against her mother, the all-seeing, all-knowing boss. If he comes to be the one the child just has fun with, her way of dealing with him will be skewed, and the anxiety between the couple about their parenting will inevitably get worse.

Suppose a mother, left to her own devices, has figured out that denying her four-year-old a snack just before dinner is a good way to make sure that he eats most of what she wants him to at mealtime. But the husband, unknowing because he wasn't there, returns home, opens a jar of peanuts, and gives a handful to his son. His wife explodes, and he's the unwitting victim because he has undermined her authority. He's furious with her for getting unnecessarily upset about a few miserable peanuts. How was he supposed to know there was a new rule? He's been out of the house all day. Exactly, she reminds him, and I'm in charge when you're not here.

Would they be fighting over snacks if they didn't have a child? Maybe their frustration would come out another way, at another time. It's clear, though, that a child can be a catalyst for arguments between husband and wife, whether or not the primary cause. This is why it's so important for parents to learn to manage the stresses of parenting *together*.

HOW PREGNANCY AND CHILDBIRTH AFFECT THE BALANCE

How nurturing does a man want to be? How much of a leader does a woman want to be? How do father and mother in any particular household learn to accommodate to the other's style of doing things? Creating a family together means figuring out ways to use your strengths and weaknesses as people, to complement each other in this brave new world of parenting.

Two people who have made a life together—sharing their work, their friends, their love of cooking or cats or politics—have to take on new considerations and new anxieties as soon as they decide to move from being a couple to being a family. They have to work out new, more flexible husband and wife roles that will stand them in good stead when they assume their father and mother roles.

The very decision to have a child makes for new anxieties in a couple, particularly if one partner wants to rush ahead and the other is holding back. The amount of time it takes to get pregnant and the relative ease or difficulty of the pregnancy all contribute to the couple's need to rework their roles.

A pregnant woman gets preoccupied with her body, its shape and new feeling, its health and growth. She also tends to develop an emotional bond with the child growing inside her. It's as if they're having a private love affair from which the man is generally excluded.

Many men, watching their pregnant wives involved in a world of their own, begin to feel that their only means of nesting is to dig deeper into their careers, building an economic buffer for the future. This frenzied activity outside the home may run completely counter to what the couple needs at the moment, which is a new form of sharing and closeness.

This separation can continue after the birth of the child. When a couple gets lost in the myriad details of diapers and feedings and in-law pacification, when they're so tired from lack of sleep that a romantic life seems impossible, they may find themselves terribly off-balance. Each partner may be so wrapped up in his and her own change of life and relationship to the new baby that their essence as a couple diminishes.

Many of the anxieties that arise after bringing the baby home from the hospital might be dealt with quickly and efficiently if the two people would just take the time to share. But when a new mother yanks the bottle away from her husband, claiming he's feeding the child all wrong, and the new father jumps down his wife's throat for being too protective of the baby around his parents, the couple is suffering. If they don't allow each other room and stay loose in their relationship, they may be setting themselves up for a future filled with criticism and mistrust.

When their child is two or three—or fourteen or fifteen—they may still be second-guessing each other, still trying to live up to some impossible ideals that have nothing to do with their true feelings and central concerns as parents. And as people. Because, regardless of the earth-shattering event that has taken place in their lives, they aren't just parents of a new baby, they still have jobs and friends and hobbies and, most of all, each other.

You have to rely on each other; otherwise you run the risk of creating friction that will color your child's life and your own. The issue at stake is whether you as a couple can handle a change in the focus of your relationship when you become parents. And can you endure the kinds of unpleasant feelings and anxieties that naturally come with the territory?

The truth is that it is impossible to be a perfect parent. Sometimes, no matter how empathic you are with your newborn, you can't stop him from crying. Sometimes nothing you can do will be enough to satisfy this seething bundle of underdeveloped nerves and organs. But you can deal with the anxiety of not being confident and competent all the time when you have someone else to rely on.

STYLES OF BALANCING

Parents sometimes make their balancing act work at the expense of the child. They may handle the situation by passing the hat back and forth so that each can salvage a little private time, or they may "gang up" on the child, joining forces in an attempt to deflect the child's demands. One of the most heartbreaking comments that parents tend to make in unison is "we're doing this for your own good." In other words, both mother and father are presenting the child with an unpalatable choice and even asking to be appreciated for the decision they've made out of the goodness of their hearts. In the meantime, they're denying the fact that it's something *they* want and that they're trying to sugarcoat the pill. The child is made to believe that the early bedtime or the withdrawal of privileges is something he's supposed to like. And this kind of doublethink can cause the child a great deal of confusion, upset, and anxiety.

A better balance is achieved when both parents are honest and back each other up. The mother who is fed up with her son's pestering can say, "I've been with you all day, and I need a break. I'd really be happy if you played with Daddy right now." Then the father can chime in with a request that his son teach him the game that Mommy already knows. When both parties appear to be in agreement, there's less conflict for the child, and when the parents are aware of each other's feelings, there's less danger of allowing their personal anxieties to spill over onto their parenting duties. This is particularly true when it comes to the issue of punishment.

Susan and James had two different styles that often didn't mesh, and it affected the way they handled their daughter Beatrice. James, from a big family, had grown up without much room for negotiation around household rules and was in favor of physical punishment. But Susan, an only child, wanted to reason with Beatrice when she had tantrums and threw things—as her parents had done with her.

"Susan's tactic is to say to Beatrice, 'If you do that again, I'm going to send you to your room.' And five minutes later she repeats the idle threat. Beatrice is never sent to her room and she never gets the message, so she keeps testing our limits."

James finally convinced Susan that he'd come pretty far in his concession not to spank their child, but that meant she also had to move a little in his direction, toward being a stricter parent. The next time Beatrice started throwing toys and yelling, Susan gave her one warning and then marched her to her room for a five-minute "time-out." The child sobbed and wailed throughout the punishment, but when her parents came upstairs to retrieve her, the little girl seemed more impressed with her mother than upset about being sent to her room.

The three of them were then able to discuss the child's mis-behavior rationally and reasonably. Susan got what she wanted out of the situation—to be able to talk to her child; and James got what he wanted—to have the child understand that she was not allowed complete freedom to run wild and upset the house-hold. The couple cooperated on their technique, and it worked.

The issues every parent confronts—what to do about a child's

health, safety, development, separation, discipline, and social relationships—spark anxieties that become increasingly complex
when you consider that there are two people, two family trees,
two personal histories to contend with, not to mention the children's personalities that are developing right before their parents'
eyes.

Each family treats issues in its own particular way, but usually
your choice of how to handle them is a combination of past
experiences and the new customs you want to instill in your own
children. Some issues may mean more to one parent, with their
resolution receiving the other's tacit approval. And some issues
become battlegrounds that never seem to get resolved.

Parenting Profile

In exploring the balance in your own family, it's important to
determine how you feel about each other's style of parenting.
Many of us tend to ignore daily qualms and just go on about our
business, even in areas that are emotionally troublesome. You
learn to live with your anxiety simply because you never bothered
to figure out whether it might be beneficial to do something about
it. And if you don't compare notes with your spouse, you may
fall into habits or patterns that perpetuate your anxiety.

The following questionnaire is intended to help you start sen-
sitizing yourself to how you actually feel while parenting, how
you feel about your spouse's parenting, and how you work together to achieve a balance. It's a kind of wake-up call to your
emotions and may help you realize you want to start breaking
some unquestioned patterns, either alone or between you as a
couple, that may be adversely affecting you and your child.

Fill out the Parenting Profile separately, then compare notes
with your spouse. The information you come up with, alone and
together, may surprise you and point up areas where you're most
in conflict and most in agreement. By bringing these thoughts out
into the open you'll begin to explore the kinds of anxieties you've

been experiencing by *not* communicating. It will also give you the opportunity to think about the areas of your life that are most ripe for change.

Time management. How does your day run? How much time do each of you spend with your children? How much time do you spend together without the children? What do you talk about alone together? About yourselves or the children? About your work or recreation? How much time do you spend on routine chores? How much on special projects or hobbies? On weekends do you take day trips together? Or does one parent frequently end up with one child, the other with another child? How would you like to manage time better together as a family?

Teaching and encouraging. What things do you enjoy teaching your children? How do you teach, formally or informally, when the occasion arises? How does your spouse handle teaching? Do you direct your children toward certain activities? Which ones? Are these activities and interests you have always enjoyed? What do you do if your child asks to pursue an interest that you feel is unworthy?

Setting limits. How do you let the children know—alone or together with your spouse—when they're treading on thin ice? Is your warning in a joking tone or a serious one? How much warning do you feel they should have before you decide on a punishment? What are the issues you have to set limits on?

Punishment. Who decides that your child must be punished? Who metes out the punishment? What does it usually consist of? Who ends the punishment and how? How often would you say your child "needs" to be punished? How do you feel during and afterward?

Power. How much power do you relinquish to each other as parents? How much power do you allow your children to take from you? On which issues?

Control. When do you feel in control? Out of control? What issues make you feel particularly vulnerable? How do you take control when you feel it's slipping?

Privacy. How much do you value privacy? Do you have special times of the day that are yours alone? Other times that belong to you and your spouse alone? Do your children have the opportunity for private moments?

Extended family. Do you enjoy spending time with your spouse's parents? With your own parents? Do you have regular visits to their houses? Do you feel you spend enough time with them? Too much time?

Holidays. How do you celebrate the various holidays? Which traditions from your own past have you kept? Which have you generated as a new family? Who decides which presents are suitable? Who buys the presents? What sorts of presents do you and your spouse give each other?

Vacations. Do you vacation together as a family? Or do you leave the children with friends or relatives and go off on your own? Or do you take other family members or friends with you to share babysitting responsibilities? How do you decide together where you will travel?

Financial matters. Do you worry about money? Does your spouse worry? Who controls the money in the household? How do you explain financial matters to your children?

Sleep. Do you believe in strict bedtimes? Naps? Do you and your spouse agree on when your child should sleep—either when he's tired or when you feel he needs his rest? How do you arrange your child's sleep? How has your child rearranged your sleep? How does this affect your relationship with your spouse?

Eating. Do you eat meals as a family? Or do you feed the children first and save a quiet mealtime for you and your spouse? Do you have rules for mealtime? Are you and your spouse clear on what they are and how flexible they are? Do you allow snacks? Do you require that the meal be eaten completely before dessert is served? Would you say you worry about your children's eating habits? In what way?

Cleanliness. Is having a clean child a priority? A clean house? How does your spouse feel? How do you explain to your children the importance of cleanliness? Or how do you downplay it?

Safety. How great is your concern for your family's safety? Do you have an alarm system in your house or car? Do you explain in detail to your children the ways to handle crossing streets, what to do if there's a fire, playing with older children, talking to strangers? Are you particularly cautious about your child's using unfamiliar playground equipment? Do you and your spouse agree on how to protect your children?

Relationships with others. Are you concerned about your child's relationship with his siblings and friends? How do you explain sharing to your child? What about fighting? Do you stress his individuality in a given situation or his fitting in with a group?

The following chapter is your guide to establishing new patterns in old areas that cause discomfort and friction in your family. The Program for Change, which appears in every subsequent chapter on key anxiety issues, will allow you to take a calmer, more reasoned approach to problems you encounter. But only by understanding your balance as parents to your particular child will this program begin to work for you. Remember that there are no right answers. The only thing that counts is the way you come to your own personal solution.

4
A Program for Change

This program will show you the effective way to *use* your daily anxieties and make them work for you and your family. Anxiety is a cue, a reminder that something with a lot of emotional content is going on. Though problems do exist that require professional assistance and intervention, the daily anxieties that most of us experience are generally manageable. If you can break down the elements of the situation into its component parts, no matter how frightening or difficult they may initially appear, you can confront most issues and work them through successfully.

WHY YOU NEED TO CHANGE

If you always scream at your child when he runs ahead of you to cross the street, if your child consistently disobeys and ends up in a tantrum no matter how forcefully you tackle him at the curb, it's time to change.

If you always downplay your child's fear of dogs and insist that she pet the animal that causes her to quake simply because you were afraid of dogs as a child and got over it, it's time to change.

If you always criticize your spouse for neglecting his diapering and feeding duties but you never give him the chance because you're at the baby's side the moment she cries, it's time to change.

The more you reinforce an old habit, the harder it is to break. If your particular method of dealing with an issue that causes you anxiety is to yell at your child or pull him away or punish him, and if you see the same upsetting behaviors cropping up again and again, you must begin to realize that the tactics you've been using simply aren't working.

Your child figures out that he can upset you by doing a certain thing in a certain way, and he also starts expecting your reaction. He may hate getting punished, and he certainly won't learn anything from it that will make him behave better, but he *will* get your attention, which is, after all, what every child wants from his parent.

Negative attention doesn't help your child learn about the world; all it does is distance you from each other and make communication more difficult. To lessen your anxiety and encourage your child to respond differently, you want to be able to give him *positive* attention. In order to do this, you're going to have to try something new.

The wonderful thing about being human is that we're graced with the facility to gain insight and perspective into our actions by using directed thought and feeling, and this is precisely what the Program for Change aims to do.

You may not immediately resolve the particular problem that's bothering you in your relationship with your child, but if you use this program consistently every time you feel anxious, you may find that the problem you first identified is merely a piece of a larger pattern, one that you *can* slowly and thoughtfully change for the better. By using this program you'll learn to pay attention to one feeling at a time, and this will make it a lot easier for you to deal with difficult situations.

The anxieties you feel may relate to something your child is doing at the moment or to something you remember from your past. Maybe you feel very tense and pressured by family obligations, or maybe you're too hard on yourself and your expectations of perfection are turning you into a frustrated, difficult individual. Maybe something your spouse is doing has set you off. Maybe you're identifying too closely with your son or daughter, expecting perfection from him or her. Whatever the cause, you can establish new patterns by tuning in to yourself as a parent.

KEEP A FORTY-EIGHT-HOUR FEELINGS INVENTORY

It's important to be aware of your feelings so that you can get an emotional handle on a situation when you need it to establish new parenting patterns. We're often so busy with daily trivia and routines that we're completely unaware of our fluctuations in mood. During a typical forty-eight-hour period, most of us will run an emotional gamut from mildly bored to cheerful to elated to annoyed to depressed to sentimental to passionate. Sometimes it's very difficult to tell what's going on inside us—society has programmed most of us to keep a lid on our emotions and just "do."

But for the purposes of tuning into yourself as a parent and dealing in a new way with your child, keep an honest inventory of your feelings for the next two days. Whenever you're in a situation—alone, with your spouse, with your child, or with your friend—that stirs something positive or negative inside you, write it down. Here's an entry from a father of a four-year-old:

> *Monday,* 3 P.M.: At playground with Susie, overheard her comforting her friend who had just been punished for kicking.
> *Feelings:* Smug that my child wasn't misbehaving but also warm and gratified that she had compassion for her friend.

Another, this one from a new mother's inventory:

> *Tuesday,* 10 A.M.: Went to market with Pete. He spit up all over himself and me after doctor assured me the new formula was the best for him.
> *Feelings:* Disgusted, sorry for my poor baby, angry at doctor, and embarrassed to be such a mess in a public place.

You may find a variety of issues that cause you anxiety, or only one. And you'll probably discover that what seemed like random, unconnected worries all center around one or two particular issues. You may find that certain times of day are particularly bad for you—like the rush to get everyone out of the house in the morning or bathtime or drive-time to and from work. Whenever you start getting sweaty palms, a knot in your stomach, or a tightness between your eyes, write it down.

This inventory will help you get to know yourself and will prove enormously helpful as you begin the Program for Change. By zeroing in on one element that bothers you rather than five or ten, you will learn to identify your concerns and think about them clearly and rationally.

After completing this inventory, tally up the happy moments, the frustrating moments, the moments of concern and moments of confusion when you weren't quite certain why you were having strong feelings. What would you say of your balance as a feeling individual? Are there too many "blank" moments when you weren't really interacting with your child or when you let your child continue to do something annoying or destructive because it was just too much trouble to take the reins and be the parent? Can you think back to those moments and decide why you felt you had to turn yourself off just then?

HOW TO USE THE PROGRAM

What you're going to do in this program is break down the numerous elements of any situation into their component parts and look at each one calmly, clinically, putting it into the place where it belongs. You may find that none of your anxieties about this issue, taken singly, seems so threatening and overwhelming and that the terror you felt about going through a certain experience is less intense.

This is not to say that your anxiety is going to vanish after one application of this program; as a matter of fact you shouldn't want it to. Your anxiety points out the problem area and is the helpful clue you need to start your investigation; you can use it to guide you in new strategies. You'll be able to break down and diffuse frightening or unpleasant situations and make them into growing experiences that will help you get closer to your child and to yourself.

Remember that you can establish new patterns together only gradually; sometimes the process is so gradual that it's hard to recognize. The connections between your areas of concern are subtle, and the more anxious you are, the harder it is to see them. Stages of childhood and parental growth are fluid and meld into one another. Some days you're on top of everything; other days everything threatens to overwhelm you.

Let's talk for a moment about the optimum state of mind in which to use the program. In order to break your problem down into its component parts, you have to be able to think clearly.

- If you have an uncontrollable urge to yell at your child even though you're angry at the dog for chewing your shoes, you need to regain control of yourself.
- If everything your child attempts—even the activities you ordinarily approve of—makes you yell "no!" you need to regain control of yourself.
- If you feel overwhelmed because your spouse is out of town for a week and you're in charge of everything, you need to regain control of yourself. In this type of stressful situation, although your feelings are perfectly understandable, you still need to take action.

There are hundreds of other opportunities for anxiety to grip you, and the first thing you must do without even identifying the source is become collected even if you're not calm.

You might try breathing deeply, counting to ten, walking out of the room, washing your face, or having a glass of water. The important thing is to break the interaction with your child just long enough to settle yourself before you start to use the program.

The program isn't designed to be a step-by-step prescription. When you've mastered it, all the steps will go on for you at the same time. You shouldn't expect immediate resolution from it, nor should you expect to be able to put all of the program into practice every time an incident occurs. Time is really essential here—the time to see yourself and your parenting differently. Sometimes just one step of the program will help you over the initial hurdle, but if you can locate the source of your feelings and picture yourself getting beyond the problem you see today, you will be much better able to cope with new and old situations tomorrow.

Program for Change

STEP I. IDENTIFY WHAT'S REALLY BOTHERING YOU

STEP II. CONNECT WITH YOUR PAST

STEP III. GET THE FACTS

STEP IV. UNDERSTAND YOUR CHILD'S POINT OF VIEW

STEP V. GROUND YOURSELF

STEP VI. STEP BACK AND SEE THE SCENE WITH DIFFERENT EYES

STEP VII. ESTABLISH NEW PATTERNS

In each chapter we will offer one or two anecdotes that involve the anxieties of the parents of an infant, a toddler, or a preschooler. The parents in this book have concerns that may be similar to yours, though not necessarily identical. While you read along with their application of the program, you might try to put yourself in their place and put in your own personal questions where applicable. After working through the program completely, we will offer suggestions directed to you, the parent, that you can use as guidelines to stimulate your own thoughts and feelings and generate your own questions regarding parenting.

In order to show you how the program works, we're going to take a typically anxiety-provoking example. Let's imagine that your child is running to the corner of a street—albeit a quiet one with very sparse traffic—without you. By breaking the anxiety and urgency you feel into the seven outlined steps, you'll be able to see that it's possible to react without panic and to use an anxiety-filled situation as a learning experience.

There would be very little time to think out the possibilities of the various steps of the program if you were in the midst of a real situation. This is why you must work the program as an armchair practitioner first, on several different issues, before the need to use this method presents itself in real life. By the time you've practiced by rehearsing what will go on in your mind, you will be ready to collapse time in real life and complete the steps within the seconds or minutes available to you.

STEP I. IDENTIFY WHAT'S REALLY BOTHERING YOU

There generally are a variety of elements that stimulate us in any anxiety-laden experience, and they all tend to overlap and crowd in on one another. But when you enumerate and separate them, it's much easier to see whether they all stem from one or from several central concerns.

You see your four-year-old racing to the corner and don't know whether he'll stop. True, it's a quiet, residential street, but a car *could* come by. *What is really bothering you about your child crossing streets?*

- He's testing his newfound autonomy, and you find that you don't like this hard-to-manage child as much as you did the sweet, docile baby.
- He's growing up so fast, he doesn't need you anymore.
- He never listens to you; your spouse is the only one who can discipline him.
- He doesn't care that you're worried about him.
- If he was hurt while you were in charge of him, your spouse would kill you.

As it turns out, then, your concern is not only about the possibility that your child will get hit by a car; it is also about your feelings of being out of control and inadequate as a parent.

STEP II. CONNECT WITH YOUR PAST

What's really important about our past is not what actually happened but what we remember about it. Let's say you went on a picnic with your parents when you were four, a month before they decided to divorce, and it was on that day you sprained your ankle.

Start by *setting the scene,* remembering the picnic table under the tree and your mother and father putting out the food as you played with sticks and acorns. Think about the weather, the season, whether there were a lot of people at the other tables or just a few. Regardless of how painful the memories may be, try to delve a little deeper to see what you can come up with.

Now that you can see clearly, how did you experience the event? Were they fighting or silent? Was one of them trying to make up and the other critical or difficult? Did they use you as the buffer between them?

Remember how your mother yelled at you for something inconsequential. And when you ran away from them, out of the picnic area and toward the street, you can still recall your mother shrieking at the top of her lungs at your father for not watching you. Was it the loud scream that made you trip and fall so that you sprained your ankle?

Once you've been able to see how the remnants of your memories—the supposedly pleasant day in the country, the friction between your parents, the pain of the sprained ankle—connect with what's going on in the present between you and your child, your current anxiety about crossing streets will start to fall into place.

STEP III. GET THE FACTS

You see your child running to the corner; you see no oncoming traffic. There's a truck parked a few yards from the intersection, and the driver is at the wheel. What are some other reality-based facts that will help you to distinguish your concerns from your emotional reactions?

1. There's a stop sign on the corner; it's the rare motorist who doesn't pay attention to it.
2. A car hasn't come by in the last three or four minutes.
3. The truck driver would notice your child, who is wearing a red T-shirt and is very visible, before pulling out of his space.
4. It's a spring day, and most car windows are rolled down, so that if you screamed to a driver to stop, he'd hear you.
5. Your child has done this often, and he has always stopped at the corner or just off the curb, turning mischievously to see how riled he's gotten you.

STEP IV. UNDERSTAND YOUR CHILD'S POINT OF VIEW

Your child has been testing you lately on all fronts for more independence. He wants to do everything himself, from bathing and dressing to turning off the TV and drawing his letters. Of course you're empathic; you can really feel his need for freedom, his desire to be a "big boy" and do everything himself. At the same time you have sufficient experience in the world to realize that street-crossing is no place to try out that freedom blindly.

When you're both calm, discuss the incident with him, listening to his point of view. What's his view on what just happened? Bring out your child's feelings by talking to him in nonthreatening, noncritical ways, eliciting his responses. By saying, "I know you always look both ways and this is a quiet street, but it's very hard for me to tell when cars suddenly come around the corner. I may need some help crossing myself," you could empower him to take charge of you instead of the other way around.

Act on your child's feelings by doing things with him that will give him limited freedom, such as practicing on dead-end streets or letting him go all the way around the corner by himself and then to you.

Feed back the empathy you feel with his need for independence in such a way that he can understand it, handle it, and accept it. This will give you just the right balance between holding your child back from trying something new and pushing forward into something he's not ready to manage alone.

STEP V. GROUND YOURSELF

Talking yourself down from a spiral is crucial when you're in an anxiety-producing situation. When you put words to your fears, you make them more manageable. While you're in the process of using this program, you may initially have rather negative feelings about the prospects of discovering the real problem and doing something constructive about it. But if you can reframe the scene in your mind and *talk* it out, you can remind yourself that you're already in the process of sorting out your thoughts and feelings so that you can reach some resolution.

Grounding can go on at any point in this program, or it can be used as a quick diffuser, to take the sting out of the situation you see before you. For example:

> *Anxious thought:* Oh my God, he's going to fly right past that corner into the intersection. Suppose some idiot comes bombing through and hits him?
>
> *Grounding thought:* I've watched him run down the street a hundred times, and he always stops and looks back at me when he gets to the corner, no matter how fast he's going. Even if he puts his foot off the curb, I'm close enough now to grab him if I see a car coming. Anyway, cars usually crawl down this street.

You know that your child listens to you when you present situations in a way that he can handle and accept. You know that you're the parent, which means you set the limits. You're also bigger and faster than he is, so you can reach him in time. If you tell yourself all this, calmly and quickly, you can prevent a spiral that may make you panic.

STEP VI. STEP BACK AND SEE THE SCENE WITH DIFFERENT EYES

When you're too involved in an emotional situation, it's hard for you to see the experience clearly. But if you can step away from the harsh reality of the scene and imagine for a moment what you would *like* to happen, you can anticipate the consequences. Take a quiet moment at home and conjure up a scene where your child runs away from you but stops when you ask him to. By creating a plausible ending to a story, you give it a chance to happen. Instead of fantasizing about everything that might go wrong—a car barreling into your child and your spouse in tears in a hospital emergency room—you can try imagining a scene of your child screeching to a halt at the corner, putting up his hands like a traffic cop, and pretending to stop a car that isn't even there.

Imagination is the bridge between fact and possibility. It can sharpen your awareness and give you a window into new perceptions. If you use your imagination to explore whatever is making you anxious and resolve it—not in an unrealistic but in a plausible way—you can give yourself a headstart on dealing with the real thing. Use your imagination to remove yourself from the stressful scene. You create a mental image of yourself reaching the corner in plenty of time. In your mind, make physical and verbal contact with your child, ask him how he's going to figure out whether it's safe to cross, and then allow him to do so as you watch him.

STEP VII. ESTABLISH NEW PATTERNS

As you run toward your child to stop him, you remember that he loves being picked up. In the past, in this same situation, you've screamed at your child to stop and wait for you, but this has only managed to frighten him, even make him start into the street to get away from you. Now, without yelling, you come up behind him and gather him into your arms, crying, "Whee!" as you spin him around in a circle and laugh. He laughs and throws his arms around you. Then you put him down and cross together.

When you've stripped away all the fears, you see that teaching your child to cross a street safely is a task that can be accomplished. Now that the anxious moment is over, how are you going to make this a lesson your child can absorb? A good idea is to make crossing the street something that you practice together. Other parents have offered various suggestions to help a child learn to cross a street safely:

PARENTS' SUGGESTIONS

1. Spend several leisurely afternoons together learning to cross the street. Let your spouse do the same. Pick a quiet neighborhood with very light traffic. Stand aside and let your child tell you if it's safe to cross, then allow him to cross as you look on or cross right behind him.
2. Give your child enough preparation for street-crossing. Remind him that you're coming to a corner, that cars can come both ways or they can turn, that parked cars can pull out into the street, that cars are much bigger than people and travel faster than he can run. Remind him of what he already knows so that next time he'll stop at the corner and look both ways, making an informed decision on his own as to whether it's safe to cross.
3. Practice in the house, allowing him to be the traffic cop. He can set up his dolls or animals on the living room floor and use a flashlight as an improvised traffic light. This will allow *him* the control of telling his animals when to cross.
4. Play red light/green light in the yard with him. Make up a song about looking left and right. Use any creative method that will help to reinforce the new approach to this old experience.

ADAPTING THE PROGRAM TO YOUR OWN NEEDS

Return to the Anxiety Questionnaire you filled out in Chapter 1 (page 25). By looking at your answers you'll be able to recognize your personal areas of greatest anxiety. For some parents, the chief issue is safety; for others, whether their child is developing along "normal" lines; for still others, the conflicts they're having over sibling rivalry. Stop for a moment and make up a hypothetical situation that pertains to this issue, and imagine using the Program for Change on it.

As you look at this situation and try to assess what's happening, you may find that you don't feel as much pressure from anxiety because now you can put it in perspective. The situation that previously seemed impassable and untouchable will become clearer and less confusing. As the experience becomes more reality-bound, less built on anticipation or apprehension, it becomes less frightening and the anxiety surrounding it eases.

Some parents tend to have a low anxiety threshold about everything, and if you're one of them, you'll need to use the Program for Change on a regular basis in many areas. Some parents are relatively relaxed when dealing with their children and will be applying the program to only one or two problem areas. Those families with serious problems such as coping with a divorce, chronic illness, or death will find that they will use the program in a more subtle way—adapting their attitudes rather than their approach.

In each successive chapter dealing with typical problem areas such as your child's health, safety, separation, discipline, and so forth, you'll be able not only to see what other parents do in anxiety-producing situations but also to think about your own reactions and how you might change them. Once you can get some distance from those areas that cause you the greatest concern, you can establish a sense of balance within yourself and between yourself and your child. Together you can learn to change.

5
Anxieties about Food and Feeding

Which of the following statements is true for you?

1. I thought I should breastfeed because it gave me a chance to bond with my daughter even though it hurt and the whole experience made me uncomfortable.
2. When my husband gives the baby a bottle and the infant drinks it all without fussing, I feel jealous that he succeeded where I couldn't.
3. I can't stand the way my wife yells at me every time I try to give the baby a bottle. She's so critical of my feeding, I just don't see the point and end up letting her do the whole thing.
4. When my preschooler refuses to eat, first I negotiate, then, when I'm completely disgusted with his behavior, I scream.
5. I get furious with my daughter when she refuses to sit quietly at the table and eat a meal. All she wants is snacks, and if I don't give them to her, she steals them from the cupboard.

If any of these common feelings sound familiar to you, you are having some anxiety about food or feeding. Maintaining good eating habits is one of the most basic ways to stay healthy. Unfortunately, in your child's life, these habits can be, at best, erratic. Children stop eating and then wolf down the next five meals; they binge on junk food and then fall in love with spinach and fruit salad. But the truth is, they do seem to have a built-in survival mechanism that keeps them from depriving themselves of the nutrients they need. If you find yourself thinking too much about their food and feeding, this may be a clue that you are letting your anxiety interfere with your good judgment and common sense.

It's natural for you to feel anxious about your baby's physical needs, and when you offer the breast or bottle to your infant, you're doing a lot more than just nourishing him properly. Feeding has to do with give and take, with demand and response, with the understanding that develops between what your child needs and what you, the parent, can give. The patterns you develop together at the very beginning will have far-reaching effects on the way your child comes to rely on you and learns to tolerate delays in gratification. It also sets a style for the way the two of you will communicate in the future.

A tense relationship between a mother and her grown son may have its roots in their earliest battles for control waged over food. If, when he was a child, his mother insisted that he finish everything on his plate, monitored what he ate, not just at home but at school and the homes of his friends, and strictly forbade all sweets, he might respond to this controlling style in later life by distancing himself from her.

You want to nurture your child in the very best way you can and as completely as possible. This desire brings with it such loaded feelings that you can easily confuse what you're reacting to on the physical plane with what you're feeling on the unconscious psychological plane. This is exactly what happened to Mary, a mother who was very worried about feeding her new baby.

SEPARATING PHYSICAL NEEDS FROM PSYCHOLOGICAL ISSUES

As Mary fed Jessica during the first few weeks of her daughter's life, she found herself increasingly distressed over the fact that the baby would never take the breast without gagging, spitting up, or turning away. Mary's breasts ached continually, but particularly after the letdown response when her milk started flowing. She became more and more frustrated and annoyed with her baby, and found herself handling Jessica roughly during each feeding. She would sit silently in complete concentration, trying to will the baby to suck properly.

Mary, the oldest child in a family of four boys and three girls, remembered how her mother handled feeding: "The woman was amazing!" she said with a laugh that mixed some envy with admiration. "I used to watch her nursing Ian, my baby brother. At the same time she was reading a story to my sister Peggy and helping my brother Joe with his homework. She seemed so competent; she knew exactly when to give a lot and when to hold back. I just don't seem to be able to do it, even with one." Mary sighed. "My best friend Pat can make business deals on the phone or eat her dinner while she's nursing the baby."

Mary's husband Allan had no difficulty feeding Jessica, and Mary felt jealous, listening to him cooing and laughing while the child finished her bottle of formula, gave a nice burp, and settled down for a nap. "No matter how much it hurt me, I wasn't going to stop nursing because I'd heard that breastfed babies were supposed to get a lot fewer colds and infections," Mary said. "I never told Allan how I felt because he might have thought less of me if I confessed to all the pain I had with breastfeeding. I just have to accept the fact that Jessica is closer to her father already." Mary added, almost too casually, "I'm not a natural mother, and I have to face up to it."

Mary seems to take it as a personal affront that her infant won't accept the breast or bottle easily from her. It's easy to see why this would upset her, but why should it lead her to the devastating conclusion that she's a terrible mother?

The physical act of feeding is the first arena of give and take between parent and child. You want to make your new baby feel secure and loved. The baby gurgles happily, and you know you're doing a good job; you've gratified your child, and her warm response is her way of giving back to you. But sometimes, whether the feeding has gone well or not, the baby may continue to cry—not necessarily from hunger but because he's wet or tired or cranky. A mother who feels insecure about her nursing might misinterpret her infant's upset in her desire to do what she thinks is the essence of mothering. When she offers the breast or bottle every single time her infant cries but the baby continues to fuss, their interplay becomes a vicious cycle. The mother's spiraling anxiety will prevent her from syncronizing with the baby's needs. Her feelings of insecurity and helplessness will prevent her from acting naturally with her infant.

The way you feed your infant, the tone of voice you use as you offer the breast or bottle, will contribute to the way the baby reacts. When mealtime is tense, it's easy to attach all kinds of emotional meanings to the physical act. A parent such as Mary, who is personally offended when her child won't accept the meals she provides, can't see past her own problems to the rather simple exigencies of helping her child take a feeding.

CONCERNS ABOUT FEEDING AT DIFFERENT CHILDHOOD STAGES

The amazing thing about a parent-child relationship is how immediately it develops and how subtly it can change over time. Parents have to learn to be flexible when it comes to feeding. The experience of cuddling a nursing infant is entirely different from offering food to an older baby or a preschooler because of the way a child regards food and mealtime changes at different stages of life.

By the time an infant is six months old she will be moving

away from her mother. She is beginning to sit up and look around and doesn't depend so directly on her parent for every stimulation. She may be ready for weaning now. When a child gives up the breast for the bottle and starts experimenting with solids, food becomes more than a means to physical satisfaction—it's a plaything. This is the first good-bye for most parents, and it is hard for some who have enjoyed a close, easy relationship with their cuddly, nursing baby who is now suddenly eager to explore the world.

When your child is a preschooler, from two to four, he will undoubtedly change his demands again about the kinds of foods he will and will not eat and when he will eat them. It's up to you, the parent, to stay flexible and avoid mealtime battles. When our babies turn into toddlers, some of our expectations for parenting are naturally going to change and expand. Even if it means allowing some trouble to brew around food and eating, it's crucial that you allow your child enough space to make his own mistakes. You simply have to trust that he can skip a meal one day with no ill effects. If you can learn to use humor and ingenuity with a preschooler who always says "no" and let him win a few battles, you can still keep control over the major aspects of mealtime.

Children may use food as a way to gain approval, as a way to express independence, as a way to manipulate their parents. They also go through new developmental stages of eating that may surprise and confound the parent. A toddler who would always eat his beets and spinach may become the preschooler who says he will eat only bread and jam. Toddlers must test their parents in order to find out what the limits are. They must make mistakes in order to learn how to do it the right way.

THE PICKY PRESCHOOLER

Nick and Joan's son Peter suddenly turned into a picky eater at the age of three. He refused all vegetables, demanded sweets and starches, and stopped drinking milk. He was not a particularly active child and was in the ninetieth weight percentile for boys his age. Joan, who came from a large family, took his new eating behavior in stride, whereas Nick saw it as a personal failing he had to correct.

"I'd been overweight myself as a kid, and I didn't want Peter to have the same problem," Nick said. "Peter always wanted to know how many bites of dinner he was expected to eat in order to be rewarded with dessert, so I'd negotiate. When that didn't work I'd start screaming. Dinnertime became a horror show, with Peter having a tantrum every night before he'd sit at the table. He always had some excuse: he had to go to the bathroom or draw another picture or pet the dog. I was so fed up one night, I just walked out."

Food has become a battleground in this household, an issue over which Peter and Nick are not communicating at all. Joan has refused to take a stand, making the situation uncomfortable for all of them. Undoubtedly Nick's anxiety about his own past as a plump child is making him transfer some fears of his own inappropriately to his son. Even the way he expresses his anger— "fed up"—underlines the deep connection he must feel with this issue.

How can Mary and Nick get a handle on their anxiety about their children's eating problems? In order for either of them to deal with their upset feelings, they have to recognize that they are anxious and identify what their anxiety consists of and where it's coming from. They'll do this by using the Program for Change, below.

Your Program for Change

Now you're ready to begin the Program. Take a moment to reflect on food-related moments with your child that seem to cause you discomfort. Chances are, you already realize it's not simply an issue of a fretful nursing baby, one too many cookies, or a week of no green vegetables. This program will help you to realize why you are upset. By recognizing your particular areas of concern, you will be better able to temper your feelings with clear-headed thinking and positive action. For a complete description of how to use this program effectively, see Chapter 4, page 61.

STEP I. IDENTIFY WHAT'S REALLY BOTHERING YOU
STEP II. CONNECT WITH YOUR PAST
STEP III. GET THE FACTS
STEP IV. UNDERSTAND YOUR CHILD'S POINT OF VIEW
STEP V. GROUND YOURSELF
STEP VI. STEP BACK AND SEE THE SCENE WITH DIFFERENT EYES
STEP VII. ESTABLISH NEW PATTERNS

STEP I. IDENTIFY WHAT'S REALLY BOTHERING YOU

There will undoubtedly be many troubling elements going on at once in every situation involving food and feeding, but there is generally one *central issue* (different for each person) that makes each person feel close to losing control. If you stay with your anxiety a moment and listen to what's causing you to feel so deflated, upset or tense, or on the brink of a spiral, you will have pinpointed the first clue in your investigation. What you're aiming for is to be able to look past the obvious in the upsetting situation and determine what's *really* going on for you. You might want to try to put yourself in Mary's or Nick's place as you work through the program along with them.

Let's think about Mary, whose baby cries whenever she feeds her. *What is it about this experience that's really bothering Mary?*

She seems to be giving an awful lot but getting little in return from her baby. Is she feeling rejected? Other mothers she knows have no problem with nursing, but Mary feels stiff and unnatural when she holds Jessica to nurse. She's even unable to talk to her baby while she tries to feed her.

Mary sees that her husband Allan gets a great deal of gratification from feeding the baby. Is she afraid she's doing something wrong, something that's hurting her child? Is she afraid that her milk isn't "good enough" for her child? Is she afraid that her husband will take over, become the favored parent? Mary's primary concern seems to be that everyone does it better than she does, that she's simply no good at something that's supposed to come naturally to a new mother.

A parent of a preschooler is going to have different concerns about feeding. Let's narrow down the possibilities for Nick and his son Peter. *What is it about the mealtime experience that's really bothering Nick?*

First of all, he seems concerned about his son's newfound autonomy. Is he worried that his child's refusal of good food is a sign that he is becoming more independent in other areas as well? Peter's challenge to Nick's authority makes him anxious, and Nick seems to fear that his child will grow up unable to abide by any rules.

He himself was heavy as a child and uncomfortable with his physical image. He worries that Peter may have inherited his tendency toward overweight and the social problems that entails. Then, too, he's worried about how he and his wife sort out problems together. Joan doesn't seem to care what Peter eats or whether he eats at all, or maybe she doesn't feel Nick's concerns are justified. But having avoided asking her how she's feeling, he begins to look at Peter and Joan as united against him.

Nick is evidently anxious about a few things: the breakdown of his relationship with his wife, the fact that he was overweight and his son takes after him physically, and the fact that the dinner hour is always disrupted. But he seems most distressed over parenting an older child—without his wife's support and cooperation. When every moment becomes a judgment call, he feels as though he has to be the disciplinarian, the bad guy that his son wants to avoid at all costs.

Now that you've had a chance to look at Mary's and Nick's particular issues in this area, it's time to look at your own—those that stem from your present-day concerns and past history. The questions and possible answers below by no means cover the entire emotional gamut, but they will undoubtedly inspire your own thoughts and feelings about food and feeding.

What's Really Bothering You

Some of the major parental issues about food and feeding have to do with the following:

- discomfort with your own physicality
- concern with physical image
- concern about doing enough or spending enough time with your child
- feeling that your child has rejected you
- feeling that you've lost control
- discomfort with your child's assertion of his own autonomy

If you're experiencing anxiety over your own expectations about food and mealtime, you might want to look at the following questions that relate to some of the above concerns:

1. Do you ever feel awkward or in pain when you breastfeed your child?
2. Do you ever worry about sterilizing the bottles properly so that your infant won't pick up any infections?
3. Do you feel concerned about the quality of processed baby food but find that your work schedule is simply too busy for you to grind up and prepare homemade baby food?
4. Do you worry that your child accepts food from your spouse or another caregiver but not from you?
5. Do you worry that your child doesn't eat enough? Eats too much?
6. Do you think your preschooler binges too often on snack foods?
7. Are you upset with your child's sloppy eating?
8. Are you concerned that your child's poor eating habits will contribute to his later physical appearance (too fat, too skinny)?
9. Are you concerned that your preschooler always seems to fight with you about what and how much he will eat?

10. Does your child fight with his siblings at the table instead of eating?

What other investigative techniques are helpful? Think about an offhand teasing comment your spouse made the last time you were in the midst of a difficult feeding, or how your friend bragged about her success with nursing, oblivious to your difficulties. Now that you have a handle on the way all these thoughts and feelings about food come together, the central issues may begin to come to light for you.

Your anxiety in one arena of your life may very well relate to that in another arena. If you're a mother who sterilizes baby bottles over and over in an attempt to get them perfectly clean, are you also an administrator who can't get a report off your desk because you always feel it needs more work? By understanding the underlying issue you will be better able to decide whether your concern is realistic or whether you might be loading the scene with a lot of inappropriate emotion.

STEP II. CONNECT WITH YOUR PAST

One of the best ways to begin dealing with your current anxiety about food is to find out how your reaction connects with your past. Some of your memories may be difficult or unpleasant, but the hurt you feel that is associated with your past and with food may be exactly what is making you anxious now with your child. Recognizing this is one of the key factors that will allow change to happen.

Mary: Mary remembers sitting at the table watching her mother "manage" the meal. She always seemed able to juggle feeding and paying attention to the younger ones. Mary, the oldest, was always expected to look after herself. Is she worried that she can't match her mother's abilities?

Nick: Nick recalls that each night when his father came home from work, the entire family descended on the table together and "chowed down." Nick can really identify with Peter's craving for sweets because when he was a kid he never felt full unless the meal ended with dessert. When he got older he was very hard on himself about his looks, his ability to fit in with others, his need for self-control. Is he worried that Peter might also get picked on for being a fat kid? Does he think he has to impose restrictions on his son's eating because Peter isn't yet old enough to have developed his own self-control?

How You Can Connect with Your Past

Begin by preparing a mental picture of yourself as a child at mealtime, surrounded by the people and physical environment you recall from that time. Work your way slowly through questions that will deepen your perception about what might have been going on at that childhood table. Think, finally, about any personal difficulties that mealtime used to provoke. Use the questions below as a guide to stimulate your memory and to think of others.

SETTING THE SCENE

1. When you were growing up, where did you sit at the table?
2. Did you always have a set mealtime? Or were you and your siblings fed separately and your parents ate later?
3. Was dinner always a sit-down meal? Or did you often snack, standing around the kitchen?
4. Did someone serve you, or were you expected to serve yourself?

Now that you can see clearly, how did you experience food and eating?

Some typical memories that many parents recall had to do with:

· being pressured to perform
· food being more emotionally than physically filling
· self-consciousness about physical appearance
· the style of eating counted more than what you ate
· being ostracized by parents

The following questions that relate to some of the above concerns may evoke useful feelings about your past.

5. Was there always too much food on the table? Was there never enough?
6. If you were served, did they give you portions you could manage?
7. Did your parents make you feel guilty or punish you if you didn't eat? How much food was enough?
8. Did you try to please your parents by eating when told to?
9. Did you eat when you were unhappy, to make yourself feel better?
10. Did you feel that your parents made a connection between food and appearance? Did you get the message that by eating too much you'd be fat and ugly, or by eating too little you'd be thin and scrawny?
11. Did your parents always discuss heated issues such as money or job problems at dinner?

After thinking about these questions for a while, you may remember some of your own difficulties around food and eating when you were your child's age. It's likely that these uncomfortable feelings are reemerging for you, but now from the parent's rather than the child's point of view. It's possible that you are replaying the past while you go through it in the present with your child.

STEP III. GET THE FACTS

Your next goal is to collect the factual information that will let you think practically about your problem with food and feeding.

> *Mary:* The first thing that occurs to Mary is that she holds Jessica differently at feeding time than she does at other times because of her physical discomfort. She sits stiffly, presenting the breast to her daughter as though it's a mechanical device. She's trying so hard to do it perfectly that she doesn't give the baby the chance to find

the right fit. But when she bathes or changes the child, her body feels light and free, and the feeling of her baby's skin next to hers is a delight. She sings, laughs, and shares secrets with Jessica.

Just to be sure that the child is doing all right physically, she brings Jessica to the pediatrician. The charts and scale prove beyond a doubt that Jessica is thriving, putting on weight, and growing as she's supposed to.

Finally Mary decides to share her problem with Allan and ask what he thinks. His perception is that she seems to be in pain when she feeds the baby. Mary has to agree that this is the case. She decides that switching to bottle feeding and trying to recreate the easy way she reacts to her child when it's not mealtime might make things better for everyone.

Nick: Nick asks Peter's teacher what goes on at preschool during mealtime and finds out that Peter and his good buddy Sam used to make a game of throwing food away. The teacher handled the problem by separating the two boys, and now Peter eats his lunch without fussing.

Nick asks Joan if anything occurs right before he comes home from the office that might contribute to Peter's difficulties at mealtime. She admits that she's been letting Peter browbeat her into a predinner snack in front of the TV.

Nick, also concerned about Peter's binges, picks up a childcare book and discovers that preschoolers' taste buds are very different from adults'. Children develop a preference for sweets during a period of life when they truly need extra calories to help them grow. Their increased sensitivity to smells and tastes often makes them reject foods that adults find mild and palatable as "too spicy" or just plain "yukky."

With some simple, verifiable facts firmly in hand, you, too, can check out the realities of your problems around food and feeding. The following questions will give you guidelines to begin your own factual investigation.

Consider All Your Facts

1. Do you think your child is really malnourished or overfed?
   Take your child to the pediatrician's office and get him weighed.

Look at any child care book to find out the expected amounts for an infant's, a toddler's, and a child's normal daily consumption.

2. Is your baby colicky? A childcare book or your pediatrician will help you decide. *A colicky infant is one who spits up or gags at the breast or bottle, has difficulty sleeping and eliminating, and seems to be fussy and difficult more of the time than not. One explanation is that the child's developing digestive system is not large enough to accommodate big meals or his internal clock is off, making him want to sleep at mealtime and eat at sleeptime. Medical science is still divided as to whether colic is a purely physical or partly psychological state.*

3. Is your infant's crying related to the scheduling of meals? *You may be too fixed in your idea of how often and how much to nurse or bottlefeed.*

4. Is your baby crying about something other than food? *Experimenting with other physical elements in his life—naptime, diaper changes, rocking or swinging the upset infant—may tell you something significant.*

5. Is your older child coming down with some illness? *A physical problem might take away his appetite.*

6. Is your child simply not hungry? *Some days your child will be hungrier than others, some days less hungry—just as you are.*

7. Are you concerned about your older child going on binges? *Preschoolers often go on eating jags where they refuse all but one food. This may be physical—because of changing taste preferences—or it may be one way to exert independence from parental choice. Ask your doctor the best way to sneak in additional foods to ensure a balanced diet.*

8. Do you have a lot of rules at the table for the way the food is eaten? Do you come down hard on your child about messy eating or wild dinner table behavior? *Sometimes a child will become resistant and stop eating if you apply too much pressure around the issue of his manners.*

Once you have the facts and have placed them against the backdrop of your own past experience and present-day concerns, you are well on the way to putting the puzzle together. You'll be better able to stay flexible in the areas of food and eating. Remember that just as soon as one stage begins, another ends, and the three-year-old who refuses to try anything new may be happily experimenting with rutabagas and artichokes one year later.

STEP IV. UNDERSTAND YOUR CHILD'S POINT OF VIEW

Your own feelings are not all that you have to consider here. You, your spouse, and your child create a dynamic together around eating that's particular to the three of you, and you must elicit your child's point of view. When you're empathic, you'll be able to see the scene the way he sees it and understand why he's having trouble with mealtime and food.

Mary: What clues can Mary pick up from her preverbal infant? What can she learn by watching Jessica's body movements? She watches the baby shut her eyes tightly when she holds her close and sees that Jessica squirms more when she feeds her than when her husband feeds her. Jessica reaches toward her father but turns away when Mary holds her to nurse. It really does seem to come back to Mary's physical position. Jessica is *telling* her without words that she's uncomfortable.

Nick: In Nick's case, he asks some direct questions about dinnertime when he and Peter are getting ready for bed later and are playing happily with trains. "You know," he says, "when I ask you to start putting things away, like this train set, because it's near bedtime and we have to clean up your room, you're so helpful. Why can't we eat dinner together the same way?"

Peter is noncommittal at first, avoiding a difficult issue. Nick persists. "What is it you don't like about dinnertime?" he asks.

"I hate that old dining room," Peter tells him. "It's dark and yukky. I'm gonna take the caboose—you can't have it!" He goes back to the trains and turns his eyes away from his father.

Nick pulls back a little. "Yeah, maybe we could use some more lights in that room. Your mom likes a dinner with candles, but it's sort of hard to see that way."

"Yeah, and we always have to eat right as soon as you come in from work. You never play with me before dinner."

Nick thinks back to all those evenings he dragged himself in the door, exhausted, with scarcely a hello for his wife and son, and just sat down at the table.

"Hey, I have an idea," he says quickly. "Maybe we can have a picnic in the dining room tomorrow night. We'll put on the overhead lights and pretend they're the sun. Could you help me decide what foods we'd take?"

Peter grins and eagerly agrees. "We should bring popcorn, potato chips, cheese doodles, cupcakes, and ice cream for dessert!"

Nick nods and says, "I like how you want to plan the menu, but you've left out the main course. Why don't we bring some broiled chicken and carrot sticks, too, to go with the chips? Maybe you can help me set the table as if we're having a picnic. We'll use paper napkins and plastic forks. That dessert sounds great, by the way."

In allowing Peter to have a choice and in changing the atmosphere of the meal, Nick has picked up on two of the elements that are causing his son the most trouble. He also realizes there has to be a more gradual transition for his preschooler from the excitement of seeing his father after a long day away from him to dinnertime.

Bringing Out Your Child's Feelings

You want to have a dialogue with your child, so try not to ask anything that will elicit only a "yes" or "no" answer, and if your child can't speak, be attentive to what's going on with his eye contact and body movement during feeding.

It's essential to be empathic and to try to put yourself in your child's place; for example, you want to find out whether he throws food on the floor because he's sick of carrots or sick of the way you insist that he eat them. If he feels that you truly respect his needs and wishes, he'll probably be more willing to give you his real point of view. You, in turn, will have a better understanding of what's going on. Some parents have found statements similar to these useful:

1. "Lots of kids don't feel hungry when they're tired. Did you have a nap today?"

2. "What did you have for lunch? Did you eat so much your stomach's still full?"
3. "It's very hard for many kids to enjoy their meal if they have to go to the bathroom (need a diaper change). Would you like to see if you can go now?"
4. "Why don't you choose what you'd like in your lunchbox today: tunafish or ham and cheese?"
5. "You ate a few string beans yesterday, but you haven't touched these carrots. Do you like beans more than carrots?"

Acting on Your Child's Feelings

Now that you have some crucial feedback from your child, you can use action to communicate your willingness to compromise while still getting across the point to your child that meals are there to be eaten.

1. Try to accept the fact that a verbal child may ask for certain things, such as dessert, just to be sure he has your love, not because he's gone off all other foods. Try a good long hug and a quick book or puzzle before dinner.
2. It's sometimes helpful to explicitly offer breaks in the rules. One day you might suggest that your child doesn't even have to taste the one thing on her plate she truly dislikes. This will underscore how rule-making is just one teaching tool and is not the goal of sharing meals as a family.
3. One parent found that it was helpful to explain the purpose of different foods to his child, saying that while sweets tasted good, they were good only for the mouth. The bones and muscles needed vegetables, meats, cheese, and milk to grow strong and straight.
4. A surprise treat in a lunchbox or on the dinner plate shows your child that you take his preferences into consideration when preparing meals.
5. A book or song may be the best way to start a dialogue with your child. Three of the most enlightening in the area of food and feeding are *Gregory, the Terrible Eater* by Mitchell Sharmat,

The Berenstain Bears and Junk Food by Stan and Jan Berenstain, and *Bread and Jam for Francis* by Russell Hoban.

STEP V. GROUND YOURSELF

When anxiety is sweeping over you, threatening to spiral out of control, grounding can help you interrupt the spiral. By putting words to your fears, by talking out what's going on, you will not rid yourself completely of the anxiety, but you will be able to bring it down to manageable size.

> *Mary:* Mary could tell herself that she's learning to be a mother in her own particular way, not like Pat or her mother or her husband. As she gets more experience in mothering, Jessica is going to feel more comfortable with her. And since Mary adores her baby and wants to help her feed calmly, she'll eventually be able to make that happen.
>
> *Nick:* Nick can tell himself that Peter cares enough about him to want them to play together before dinner. He can watch how eagerly his son helps him set the table or mix the salad, and realize that he can help Peter relate to meals better if he stops concentrating on the content of every mouthful and starts thinking about making the mealtime experience better for both of them.

Other parents have used the technique below to ground themselves. It may seem artificial at first, but these statements can act as quick diffusers on uncomfortable feelings and help you use the anxiety you feel in a calmer manner.

> *Anxious thought:* He's not eating his dinner. This is the third day in a row he's refused it. He's going to waste away to nothing!
>
> *Grounding thought:* He had an apple for lunch and celery with peanut butter as a snack. Look at him: he's active, cheery, and healthy.

> *Anxious thought:* I knew I shouldn't have taken him to a fancy restaurant just because my mother-in-law insisted. He probably dropped his hamburger on the red carpet just to spite me.

Grounding thought: He eats calmly and happily at home. Maybe this place isn't appropriate for him; we don't ever have to come back here.

Anxious thought: My baby won't try a cup. Will she be going to first grade with a bottle?
Grounding thought: She's very advanced in other areas, and the bottle gives her a lot of comfort right now. Maybe I could try a straw or a cup with a spout.

STEP VI. STEP BACK AND SEE THE SCENE WITH DIFFERENT EYES

You can take a quiet moment in the day, while you're fixing a meal or taking a break at your desk, to use your imagination and conjure up scenes, playing with their elements as you choose. By allowing yourself and your child free rein in your mental pictures, you may find it easier to be flexible when the real situation occurs.

Mary: Mary would like Jessica to take the breast or bottle more calmly, without fussing and squirming. How does she imagine that might happen?
She steps back and sees her body as loose and relaxed. She recalls the way she plays with Jessica's toes when she changes her: she tries to recapture the soothing tone of voice she uses when putting her into her crib at the end of the day. She imagines herself recreating that good feeling as she holds her close and encourages her to take the bottle.

Nick: Nick would like Peter to eat a little of everything on his plate. He'd love the evening meal to run smoothly. What does he imagine?
He steps back and remembers how he and Peter enjoy being together when it's not mealtime. He thinks about the meal as a whole experience, not just an opportunity for feeding. Maybe if Peter can get into his new way of participating—by setting the table or pouring himself a glass of milk—he'll feel more included in the family experience.

Imagine What You'd Like to Happen

Try to suspend reality briefly. Step back from the stressful scene and figure out what you would *like* to happen. Your goal is to have a relaxed meal where your child is nourished and where you, your spouse, and your child are able to share a pleasing and comfortable experience together. Naturally you should try to be realistic and flexible in your expectations. Don't paint the scene as perfect, or reality will disappoint.

STEP VII. ESTABLISH NEW PATTERNS

After you've explored the other steps of the program, you may feel closer to what's actually bothering you, or it may take a while and several applications of the program over different issues to have it make any sense. Still, once you feel more competent in using your anxiety as a tool, you'll see that there are options you haven't considered.

Mary: Mary made a big decision: to stop breastfeeding. She was so relieved at the lack of physical discomfort that her body immediately became calmer. She picked a comfortable chair by a window the first time she gave Jessica a bottle. She put soothing music on the stereo and sang along with it. Every time Jessica turned her head away or began to fuss, Mary removed the bottle and talked to her child easily until she had her attention again. She stopped comparing herself to her husband, her best friend, and her mother. And though it still wasn't easy, she noticed that more feedings were going well than not.

Nick: Nick and Joan decided together to postpone dinner half an hour. When Nick got in from the office, the first thing he did was spend some time alone with Peter, and then the two of them would go in and help prepare the meal. Peter became an expert at salad mixing and would pick out for himself, with his parents' supervision, the amount he felt he could eat at each meal. Joan gave up on candles for dinner and turned on all the lamps in the room. In the summer the family ate outside on the deck.

PARENTS' SUGGESTIONS

The following ideas will trigger new thoughts that will guide you
in establishing better eating patterns with your child:

1. Let your infant give you cues about his hunger. If three and
   a half hours have passed and he's crying, it's probably hunger.
   If one hour has passed, it's something else. If he pushes the
   breast away, maybe it's your position. Try moving him around
   until he's comfortable, talking to him and soothing him with
   your voice.
2. Make mealtimes pleasant. You don't have to turn the event
   into a circus, but you can make it more enjoyable by including
   your preschooler in the conversation and making sure that the
   food is the right temperature and that there's not too much
   or too little of it on the plate.
3. Serve the food so it looks appealing. You might try cutting it
   with cookie cutters or putting it on colored or patterned plates.
   You might let your preschooler eat with chopsticks instead of
   a fork and spoon, or suggest funny alternatives that spark your
   child's imagination. Pretending that the broccoli spears are
   trees and the mashed potatoes are mountains of snow could
   be the refreshing change you both need.
4. Don't use food as a reward. "If you eat your vegetables (or
   clean up your room or give me a kiss), I'll give you a treat for
   dessert" is a common inducement but a wrongheaded one.
   The vegetables should be presented as okay on their own; the
   room being clean is a separate issue, and affection should never
   be achieved through bribery.
5. Don't use food as a punishment. One of the worst ways to get
   a preschooler to eat is to tell her that if she doesn't, she'll get
   it back at the next meal, and then the next. This cruel method
   will only turn a child against all foods.
6. Don't serve filling snacks before dinner: a carrot can tide your
   child over if he's about to eat the furniture and your spouse
   isn't home yet.

7. Stop associating food with love. Just because you decided to crack down on bad dinner table behavior and told your child he must leave the table if he's not eating doesn't mean you've set him against you for life.
8. Don't get overly upset if your mother buys your child an ice cream cone in the middle of the afternoon. Candy and sweets are fine as an occasional treat; if you prohibit them entirely, you'll make them too precious in the child's mind. Forbidden fruit always tastes better.
9. If your child goes on a hunger strike, don't panic: a child will not starve himself. He may be angry at you for something you did or didn't do; he may be coming down with flu or a stomach virus; he may just not be hungry. Be sure that he's taking fluids while he refuses food.

When your new patterns start working, it's tempting to want to lock into them, but the most effective change happens when you can stay flexible. If you're going on an eight-hour car ride with your child, giving in on the amount and kind of snacks you offer will make the trip much more pleasant for everyone involved. You can put your new rules back into action as soon as you get to your destination.

Establishing new ways of dealing with food and mealtimes will happen slowly, as you put the pieces of this program together to work for you and your family.

6
Anxieties about Cleanliness

Which of the following statements is true for you?

1. I felt I had to change my infant's clothes five times a day just in case. I couldn't bear the thought of her being dirty.
2. It gets me so mad when my husband feeds the baby and doesn't notice that formula is dribbling down Joe's chin. I have to wipe it off the second I see it.
3. Without fail my toddler goes and plays in the mud right before my mother-in-law shows up. What she must think of me!
4. I'm panicked at the amount of dirt my preschooler must ingest. He usually drops half his meal on the floor and then scrambles down off his chair to get it before the dog does.

If you find that some of the above statements pertain to you, you're certainly not alone. Our society values cleanliness, and cleanliness promotes health. Though it's important for parents to teach children healthful habits, much as they teach good eating habits, it's also helpful to remember that adults and children look at the issues very differently. A one-year-old who dumps a bowl of oatmeal on his head or a three-year-old completely wrapped up in making mudpies has no idea why mom might discourage these activities or insist on a bath right afterward.

Being clean is one way a child can learn to feel good about himself, and as long as his parents don't have any fetishes about body odors, bathing, and tidiness, the child will eventually learn that caring about his body is one way to care about himself. But a child has other priorities. When he reaches toddlerhood, he feels good when he feels effective. A toddler knows the world by acting on it, touching and poking it and giving it his own semblance of order. He's only going to find out about the world by getting wet, sandy, and dirty, by experiencing new environments on his own terms. If you restrict his exploration, you're cutting him off from a vital avenue of learning. If you make judgment calls on what he's doing based on messiness or cleanliness, it's going to have consequences in terms of how free and entitled he feels about playing. Your lack of conflict about this issue can determine whether your child takes his daily bath in stride, fights it, becomes obsessive about cleanliness, or turns into a sloppy person.

How clean or dirty our child is reflects on us and often the way others view our caretaking, so someone who is preoccupied with hand washing and pristine clothes isn't just anxious about herself and her child. This preoccupation is indicative of the way she wants her family, her neighbors, and even strangers to view her.

KEEPING AN INFANT CLEAN

How dirty can a baby get? She spends most of the day swaddled in a blanket and is in someone's arms unless she's being changed or bathed. Yet many parents are very nervous about their baby's cleanliness, mostly because they fear that *germs* will contaminate their infant's surroundings and make her sick. And then, too, cleaning obsessively can be one way to stay constantly involved with the baby, even at times when the baby doesn't need anyone.

Sondra was incredibly fussy about her infant, Laurie. "I couldn't stand the idea of anything bad ever touching her," she said. "As soon as I found out I was pregnant, I immediately found foster

homes for our two cats because you know you can get toxoplas-
mosis from the catbox.

"I kept the baby's room practically sterile, even though Dan,
my husband, thought I was going a little overboard about germs.
Each day I changed the bedding in the bassinette and everything
Laurie wore, even if she'd had them on for only a couple of hours.
You just never can tell—anyway, I wanted her to look nice. I
was scrupulous about scrubbing her in the bathtub, too, particularly if she'd spit up or had a really dirty diaper.

"I showed Laurie off to visitors, but I never offered to let them
hold her because of contamination. Also, Laurie had really sensitive skin, so it was important to keep her clean. Whenever Dan
gave her a bottle, it was ludicrous! I mean, he didn't know how
to hold her or burp her, and he didn't want to listen when I
explained it to him. The worst was when he let formula run down
her chin. I told him that could give her a rash if he didn't clean
her up right away, but he never listened. We used to fight about
it all the time."

Sondra is terribly anxious about the baby's picking something
up—a cough from a visitor or a rash from her husband's lack of
attention. Her fights with Dan over the issue of Laurie's cleanliness
indicate that the problem has extended to the marriage. But what
is she really concerned about? She seems to have a need to shelter
her baby from everything and everyone else—just the way she
did when the baby was inside her body.

A desire for complete cleanliness may really be a mask for
something else. If Sondra can begin to connect with her feelings
of protectiveness, perhaps she'll be able to see that germs are not
the enemy she's warding off.

WASHING JIMMY'S HANDS—AND REWASHING THEM

An older child has much greater opportunity to get dirty, of
course, and he can do it all by himself. Battles between parents
and children over keeping clean very often relate to struggles
they're having over autonomy. A parent whose child never enjoyed playing in the mud before may be astounded to find him

filthy right before a visit to Grandma's, after she specifically told him to stay clean. With an older child, too, there's the issue of competition. Parents who find it necessary to compare their child to the "perfect" child down the block very often zero in on cleanliness as a big issue of controversy.

Think about Amy, a divorced, single mother who insisted that her son Jimmy's hands and face had to be clean almost all the time. "It seems as if I'm always dragging Jimmy to the sink. I have him wash before meals, after play, after he goes to the bathroom, when he wakes up, and before he goes to sleep. He can spend the afternoon outside with his best friend Sam, and Sam will walk in looking bandbox fresh; Jimmy looks like a Welsh coal miner. I told him that being filthy breeds germs, and germs make you ill. But that doesn't seem to stop him!

"One Sunday he and Sam were riding their tricycles past the church on the corner. Jimmy's steered a little crooked, and he fell off the bike into a puddle just as the service was letting out. Practically everyone we knew saw him pick himself up from that mud puddle. Sam looked clean and neat; Jimmy was covered from head to foot. He's not a malicious kid; it wasn't as if he did it on purpose to embarrass me. But I was mortified."

What is it that really concerns Amy about keeping her son clean? Is she really worried about germs? Or is she terribly insecure about people's reactions to her and her son? She unreasonably feels that Jimmy is in competition with Sam for the "best kid in the neighborhood" award.

She also seems to be a person for whom everything must be exactly right all the time. You can make a pretty good assumption that she demands perfection in other areas, not just cleanliness. She may need her child to look perfect and *be* perfect in order to show the world that she's a perfect mother—certainly more perfect than Sam's mother. It's possible that she feels she has to be above reproach because she believes that people always love to talk about divorcees. But her unreasonable expectations about the way she wants Jimmy to look are clearly hurting their relationship. How can he possibly know why she's always looking at him with a scowl on her face? He lacks the experience to understand why his mother is so tense about his getting dirty; he may think he's done something wrong and has to make it up to her all the time. He also can't understand that when she scrubs him roughly, she's not touching him this way because she dislikes him but because she dislikes dirt.

She just can't see that Jimmy gets dirty because he's become a great explorer, charting new territory for himself, gaining a sense of mastery over his world. Amy can't appreciate how much fun he has at play, or that he needs to mess so that he can really grasp whatever it is he's involved in. One way for Amy to become aware that her reactions to dirt are inappropriate is by following the Program for Change. Once she has identified her real concerns about cleanliness, she can act to do something about them.

Your Program for Change

If you're a person who is genuinely turned off by mess, you are going to have to do a lot of searching to find the underlying reasons why it upsets you so much. (For a complete description of how to use this program effectively, see Chapter 4, page 61.) Neatness is an acquired habit and an acquired taste, and most parents resign themselves to mess and dirt once they have children. But by recognizing your particular areas of concern around cleanliness, you'll find it easier to deal with everyday problems that arise.

STEP I. IDENTIFY WHAT'S REALLY BOTHERING YOU

STEP II. CONNECT WITH YOUR PAST

STEP III. GET THE FACTS

STEP IV. UNDERSTAND YOUR CHILD'S POINT OF VIEW

STEP V. GROUND YOURSELF

STEP VI. STEP BACK AND SEE THE SCENE WITH DIFFERENT EYES

STEP VII. ESTABLISH NEW PATTERNS

STEP I. IDENTIFY WHAT'S REALLY BOTHERING YOU

Many people with concerns about cleanliness truly believe that they get anxious only because they're afraid of having their child infected with dangerous germs. By examining all facets of the problem, along with Sondra and Amy, you'll be able to see what is really troubling you in each particular situation involving cleanliness and neatness.

Let's think first about Sondra, who is nervous about keeping her infant completely germ-free. *What is it about this experience that's really bothering Sondra?*

She doesn't really trust anyone around her child, even her husband. The animals had to go even before the baby was born, and visitors are asked to keep their distance. She says that her husband can't appreciate the dangers inherent in the germs in their environment, and she implies that she knows better. But what gives her the right to be so critical of his caregiving abilities? She has no more experience taking care of babies than he does. Sondra seems anxious about every external element—formula, cats, strangers, and Dan—that might interfere with her special bond with the baby.

Amy isn't worried about Jimmy being tainted by the outside world, but she, too, is overly critical about his getting dirty. *What is it about Jimmy's propensity for messing that really bothers Amy?*

She seems to feel that everyone is watching and judging her. As a single parent she knows she's overly conscious of the way people regard her, and by making her son an extension of herself, she makes him blameworthy when he doesn't look the way she thinks the world expects him to. It's as if she sees him as a reflection of her failures.

She also compares him to Sam frequently. Sam follows Jimmy's lead, but being more timid or less curious about life, he stays on the outskirts of trouble and never manages to get dirty. To Amy this is the right kind of behavior, the kind that doesn't draw comment or attention. Is she worried about being too different, too noticeable? She admits to feeling guilty about not being able to offer Jimmy the advantages of having both parents at home, so she overdoes it, trying to be both mother and father to him. Does it also concern her that her son doesn't match up to the goals and ideals she always held for herself, that he's not a carbon copy of his mother?

What's Really Bothering You

By examining Sondra's and Amy's troubles with cleanliness, it may be easier to look at your own and identify your major areas of concern. Some typical ones are as follows:

- thinking you can never clean—or do—enough for your child
- connecting your child's messiness with your anger
- seeing your child as a reflection of you
- associating cleanliness with being good, and dirt with being bad or unlovable

If you're having any anxieties over cleanliness, you might want to look at the following questions that relate to some of the above concerns:

1. Do you ever feel you haven't washed your baby well enough? That you have to scrub him harder?
2. Does it upset you to see formula on your baby's chin during or after a feeding?
3. Are you turned off by spit-up food on your clothes?
4. Do you worry if your preschooler misses his bath every once in a while?
5. Are you insulted if someone makes a comment about your child's neatness or cleanliness?
6. Does it upset you if your spouse hasn't bathed? Do you think it reflects on you?
7. Does it upset you if you have to deal with people before you've had your daily bath or shower?
8. Do you tend to worry more about dirt from outdoors, about

dust and grime in your house, pet hair and waste products or the products of your child's messy play—crayon shavings, glue, glitter, Play Doh, sand, and so forth?

Are you a person who entertains a lot for your own business or your spouse's? If you keep a high premium on making your surroundings lovely, it may be harder for you to accept the messes that come with babies and children. Think about other times when you've been particularly hassled by a need to clean or organize. Could they have appeared at times when responsibilities as a parent seemed overwhelming?

If you're a tired businesswoman who likes to come home from the office to a house that's sparkling but the first thing you see when you walk in the door is your son with jam all over his face, it may be hard to switch gears and give him all the affection you truly feel. You may overemphasize your annoyance with his dirty face simply because it doesn't meet with your preconceived notions of home and hearth.

STEP II. CONNECT WITH YOUR PAST

Undoubtedly there are more than a few vivid memories you can resurrect from your childhood of the way your parents reacted to you when you were clean or dirty. Many parents in the 1940s and 1950s seemed to judge their children's "goodness" or "badness" by their ability to keep their hands and face clean. When you begin to remember the feelings you had then, you'll be closer to discovering the bases of your current feelings about cleanliness.

Sondra: As an only child Sondra was close to her mother, a hypochondriac, and became very protective of her. She was rarely allowed to have friends home from school because it "aggravated her mother's nerves" to hear kids playing loudly. She was also very concerned about anyone bringing germs into the house that might make her "sicker," so Sondra and her father had to take their shoes off before coming into the hallway.

Sondra was a B+ student in school, but that wasn't sufficient for her mother. She wanted her daughter to be the best, and Sondra always had the feeling that she had never done enough to please her mother; no matter what her academic or extracurricular triumph, she felt she could have done better.

Amy: Amy was four years older than her sister Kate, a real tomboy. She could recall her piano recital when she was twelve. Kate had slipped her some M&Ms just before she was to play, and her hands bore traces of chocolate when she sat down at the piano. The teacher, standing next to her, stopped her and insisted on wiping her hands before she could begin her piece. Amy never heard the end of it from her mother—how disappointed she was, how she expected something like that from Kate but not from her. And in front of all those people! She never mentioned that Amy had played really well that day.

How You Can Connect with Your Past

Think back to your childhood and see if you recall any memories relating to cleanliness or neatness. Start by setting the scene: remember your physical surroundings and the people you dealt with, and gradually work your way into questions that will provoke more thoughtful perceptions about your past. The questions below can serve as guidelines for your own particular investigation.

SETTING THE SCENE

1. What did your house look like most of the time? Like it was ready to be photographed for a magazine spread or like a cyclone just hit it?
2. What did your house smell like? Does the memory have more to do with cooking odors, household cleansers, or perfume?
3. Were you expected to keep your room neat? Were you supposed to cooperate with a sibling to keep it neat?
4. Did your parents give you household chores to do? Did you ever take out the garbage? Clean the bathroom? Clean the kitchen? Clean the catbox?

Now that you can see clearly, how did you experience cleanliness? Some typical memories that many parents recall had to do with the following:

- the ways your parents responded to you, clean and dirty
- your perceptions of what your parents thought was neat
- your perceptions of how important or inconsequential cleanliness was to them
- how much stake they held in others' opinions

The following questions that relate to some of the above concerns may evoke certain useful feelings about your past:

5. Was your mother always cleaning? Did your mother never clean?
6. Did you have a housekeeper? Was the message that "other people, not us" do menial labor such as cleaning?
7. If you got dirty, were you expected to clean yourself up, or did someone do it for you? Was it done roughly or gently? Were you ever punished for being dirty? How?
8. How frequently did you take a shower or bath? Did you feel grubby if you had to wear an outfit two days in a row?
9. Did you enjoy the feeling of being dirty? The smell that went along with being dirty?

The thoughts that come back to you as you ask yourself these questions may give you some clues into the problems you're having now with your own child over the issue of cleanliness. The instances that occurred in your past, your parents' attitude, and your own feelings of being "clean and polished" or "dirty and soiled" may relate quite strongly to your current-day anxieties.

STEP III. GET THE FACTS

There are certain basic facts you can gather relating to cleanliness that may help to clarify some of your thoughts and feelings about this issue.

Sondra: At her husband's urging, Sondra called her pediatrician and asked about her fears that Laurie might pick up some disease from the environment. The doctor first assured her that there are germs everywhere but that Laurie's own antibodies were good protection against any harmful bacteria or viruses that are floating around. It's good to keep Laurie healthy by changing bedding, clothes and washing floors and woodwork, he said, but a baby isn't much more vulnerable than a child in terms of picking up disease from other people. It's actually beneficial to put the child in a limited social setting since the more people a baby is exposed to, the more protective antibodies she can build up.

Amy: Amy, too, consulted her doctor about Jimmy's propensity for getting filthy. The pediatrician explained to her that Jimmy was learning to be independent by creating a physical environment he could control. It was useless for her to compare Jimmy with his friend Sam because each child is different. Because she was so concerned about what other people might think, Amy asked her good friend and neighbor, Sue, whether she had heard anyone in the neighborhood criticizing her or Jimmy. Sue assured her that she hadn't heard a thing and that it was her feeling Amy was overly concerned with Jimmy's being viewed as the perfect child.

Consider All Your Facts

1. Do you think your child is really exposed to dangerous germs in your home? *If you and your husband didn't get sick prior to the birth of your baby, it's likely your infant won't pick up anything either. Also, if you are breastfeeding, you're giving your child a lot of protection since he's getting your antibodies against infection through the milk.*
2. Will formula on the baby's chin really produce a rash? *It takes constant and prolonged irritation for a rash to develop. A daily bath washes away all surface grime.*
3. Are pets' habits dangerous to your child's health? *A dog's mouth is ten times cleaner than a human's because saliva flows more readily between canine teeth, carrying bacteria out along with it. Dogs and cats who have been immunized against disease cannot transfer anything to a baby.*

4. What happens if your child eats something that has fallen on the floor? *The human body is extremely resilient. We can all ingest (and excrete) quite a bit of dirt, grime, pet hair, grease, and dust before any damage is done to our systems.*

5. Are you insisting too much on bathing with a recalcitrant toddler? *Toddlers go through a stage where they are terrified of the bath. This has to do with their changing perception about their size; if the soap bubbles can go down the drain and vanish, maybe they can too.*

6. What happens to infants and children who don't bathe regularly? *If your child has a cold or fever or is exhausted, it's perfectly all right to skip the daily bath; this will lessen the possibility of tension between you if you don't fight over it.*

7. Are you right to be concerned about cleanliness in your child's day-care facility or school? *Certainly, because the more children you have together, the greater the possibility of spreading disease or illness. Two health-related problems that may occur where many children play together are* giardia, *which is an intestinal parasite spread through ingestion of fecal matter, and* head lice. *Your child's school should be regularly inspected by the local health department for optimal sanitary conditions.*

Having a little knowledge about the effects of dirt on the human body may help you understand that you may be loading the issue of cleanliness with some powerful emotional concerns. If you can keep a sense of humor about dirty paw prints on the staircase and the food mustaches that children like to wear at least part of every day, you'll be better able to cope with your anxieties in this area.

STEP IV. UNDERSTAND YOUR CHILD'S POINT OF VIEW

If you were to ask your child why he got dirty when you specifically told him not to, he would probably respond that he wasn't doing anything but playing. In order to work out a reasonable set of expectations, it's crucial that you spend the time finding out what your child thinks about cleanliness.

Sondra: The next time Sondra gives Laurie a bath, she pays close attention to her child's body language. The infant moves frequently on her sponge mat, which makes Sondra grab her more roughly to keep her in place. The bath takes longer, and the child's skin becomes red and irritated-looking. Laurie nearly always urinates and defecates after her bath, which usually makes Sondra rush to get her out of the tub and onto the changing table, at which point she has a hysterical baby. But this time Sondra makes a big effort to collect herself. She gently lifts Laurie out of the tub and wraps her in a towel, clasping the baby to her body. Sondra talks to Laurie in soothing tones as she puts a fresh diaper on her. Laurie starts gurgling and her body relaxes. This makes Sondra consider that her frantic methods of bathing and dressing may have been provoking her infant.

Amy: Instead of yelling at Jimmy the next time he comes in from a playdate with Sam covered with dirt, she ushers him into the kitchen to discuss it with him.

"Jimmy," she begins, "you must be tired after playing so hard. Would you like to sit down with me and have some milk and cookies?"

Jimmy looks at the shining kitchen floor. "Do I have to take off my shoes?" he asks sullenly.

Amy is about to say yes but realizes she has to give a little if she expects her son to do the same. "I tell you what. You can leave your shoes on if you'll wash your hands first."

He nods and drags a chair over to the sink. "With soap?"

"With soap." She nods approvingly.

Jimmy finishes washing and selects two cookies from the jar. He grins at his mother. "Now the cookies smell soapy."

"Is that so bad?" Amy asks, playing dumb.

"Nah." He licks his fingers. "I guess they taste better clean than dirty." His face suddenly falls, and he puts the cookie on the table. "I look pretty messy, don't I, Mom? You know, Sam's a wimp. He doesn't climb trees or dig holes."

"You like doing that, don't you?" Amy says.

"Yeah, but—" He looks away from her and mutters, "You like Sam better than me because he doesn't get messy."

Amy gets up from the table and goes over to put her arms around Jimmy. "I don't like Sam better. I love you *and* I like you. I get mad at you when I've asked you to stay clean and you don't listen, but that doesn't mean I don't love you. People who love each other get mad, but then they make up. Sometimes they give in a little on the way they do things to make the other person happier for a while."

"You mean, I shouldn't dig holes?"

"You can dig holes all you want when you're wearing play clothes and we don't have to go anywhere afterward. But when we're going to church or to Grandma's, maybe you could think first, before you start digging, and stay clean when I ask you to."

"Can I take my robot into the bath with me tonight?" Jimmy asks.

Amy smiles and nods. "And anyone else you want, too. We'll have a bath party."

By showing Jimmy that the two of them can compromise, Amy is allowing him not to be perfect. By using her empathy she's also finding out that what really upsets him about her urgent need for him to stay clean is that he thinks she approves of Sam and not him. Amy is then able to show him that he's a completely lovable child with one quirk that annoys her.

Bringing Out Your Child's Feelings

Try to put yourself in your child's place when you discuss the issue of cleanliness. This is particularly difficult for many parents because their perspective on dirt, germs, and other people's attitudes in no way matches their child's lack of concern about these things. A child cannot possibly understand, until he is at least six or seven, that he should wash his hands after going to the bathroom so as not to spread bacteria. The concept of looking neat or proper because he is going to have his picture taken just doesn't compute for a toddler. If he has a good self-image, he thinks he looks fine even when his face is covered with jam.

Some parents have found statements similar to those below useful in establishing a dialogue:

1. "It's almost time for dinner. I always feel so much better when I wash my face and hands before I eat. Will you come join me?"
2. "We're going to have our Christmas picture taken at the store today. Would you like to wear your favorite dress and have a ribbon in your hair? When we get back we can both change out of our fancy clothes to play outside."
3. "Do you know that cat pee and poop can be bad for you if you get it on your hand and then put your hand in your mouth? Could you help me clean the catbox, and then we'll both wash our hands at the big sink? You get the soap, and I'll turn on the faucet."

Acting on Your Child's Feelings

1. When your child comes in from playing, challenge him to a race to the tub. "Who can get undressed and into the bathroom fastest, you or your teddy bear?" might be the incentive he needs.
2. Make your child a "slide" for the bathtub out of the rubber tub mat and offer to give him a "ride" into the soothing warm water. If he's negative about it, remind him of the fun he had the previous night playing with all his bath toys.
3. Join your child in a sandbox or let him play in a mud pile. Try to recall a similar feeling you might have had hiking or cooking—when the only thing that mattered was the activity you were involved with.
4. A book or a song can sometimes act as a catalyst for change. Fred Rogers has recorded a wonderful song entitled "You Can't Go Down the Drain," and David MacPhail's book, *Andrew's Bath,* will help you and your child understand some of your feelings about cleanliness.

STEP V. GROUND YOURSELF

A good verbal grounding statement about cleanliness can keep your anxiety under control when the particular incident seems overwhelming.

Sondra: She can tell herself that her worries about keeping her baby pristine stem from the fact that she truly loves her child and wants no harm to come to her. She knows her husband feels the same way, even though his style is different from hers. Laurie has been completely healthy up to this point in her life, so maybe Sondra can give Laurie's system credit for protecting itself. And maybe this comforting thought will help her relax her vigilance about the infectious quality of other people's germs.

Amy: She can tell herself that although she is a single mother she's doing a pretty good job of it. There are plenty of two-parent households on the block whose children get as dirty as Jimmy does. She can see how Jimmy, after an initial difficult period when his father left, is developing into a happy, well-adjusted child who plays well with other kids. Mothers call her for play dates on a regular basis, so she can tell herself that she must be doing something right.

Many parents have found that self-talk as illustrated below is a good method of temporarily easing the anxiety they feel about cleanliness and making it more tolerable.

Anxious thought: The baby just spilled the entire contents of her dinner plate on her head. I can't stand to look at her! I can't finish the feeding—I have to give her a bath right away.
Grounding thought: She's hungry now and she's eating well. Food really seems to be something she has to experiment with right now. When she's finished she'll be much more amenable to taking a bath, and I won't have to hurry to get through it.

Anxious thought: My toddler hasn't had a bath in five days! All I have to do is suggest one, and he starts screaming bloody murder.

Grounding thought: I've been washing his bottom with wipes, and his hands and face with a washcloth every day. The rest of him isn't particularly dirty anyway.

Anxious thought: Everyone's looking at my filthy child. What must they think of me!

Grounding thought: If they don't like my child the way he is, they aren't true friends anyway. Most people understand that kids at play are bound to get dirty. If they don't have children of their own, they certainly see enough ads about it on TV and in magazines.

STEP VI. STEP BACK AND SEE THE SCENE WITH DIFFERENT EYES

Imagine various scenes having to do with cleanliness that realistically are possible for you and your child to achieve. The more creative you are in the construction of these imaginary mental pictures, the more you'll be able to use your anxiety creatively when you're confronted with the real situation.

Sondra: Sondra would like her baby to be healthy and happy. She'd also like to have her husband participate more in making sure that the child's environment is safe.

Sondra steps back and remembers how delicious Laurie smells just before bed—she has that sweet, warm baby smell, unlike any other odor in the world. Sondra imagines Dan holding Laurie as he feeds her, cooing to her, paying so much attention to the baby herself—as opposed to the bottle he's holding—that it doesn't really matter whether a little formula drips on her chin.

Amy: Amy would like Jimmy to stay clean when there's a reason to go someplace looking nice, and she has asked him to try extra hard not to get dirty.

She steps back and remembers how much fun Jimmy had catching grasshoppers and making dirt houses for them in the yard last summer. It was really the first time since the divorce that he was happily involved in an activity that really riveted his attention. She imagines her rough-and-tumble preschooler coming in from the yard with Sam and remembering to take off his muddy shoes at least every *other* time without having to be reminded.

Imagine What You'd Like to Happen

If you can suspend reality as Sondra and Amy have done, it may be easier for you to think about your need for cleanliness in a new light. Naturally you care enough about your child to be concerned with germs, and if you are a person who is genuinely upset by odors, filth, and grime, you want to keep your environment as clean as possible. But if you can soften your expectations about how clean or sterile you'd like things to be, you may get even better results than you anticipated.

STEP VII. ESTABLISH NEW PATTERNS

Sondra: Sondra decided to let Dan or the babysitter give Laurie her bath every other day. In effect she proved to herself that nothing would happen to Laurie when other people with different attitudes toward cleanliness were responsible for her daughter's physical state. She also let Laurie stay in the same outfit for the whole day unless a major mess occurred. She could see and smell at the end of an average day that the clothes looked almost as good and clean as they had when she first put them on the baby.

Amy: Amy began watching Jimmy and Sam at play. Rather than compare the two boys, she began to notice Jimmy's extraordinary abilities—how dexterous he was, how imaginative and creative. She discovered that she liked Jimmy because of who he was and what he was becoming, and this made her less preoccupied with the way his behavior reflected on her. Amy allowed herself to stop reacting to her own need for perfection so that her son could develop in his own way, coming to understand that people didn't think of him as part of her. She was able to see that his need for her had evolved from a baby's dependency to an older child's craving for experience.

PARENTS' SUGGESTIONS

1. Think about ways you can get messy and then clean up with your child in a controlled environment. Let your three- or four-year-old help in the kitchen. You can have him wash and tear vegetables for salad, mix meatloaf with his hands, crack and beat eggs, put together cookie dough and drop it on cookie sheets. The experience you have of getting messy—and later cleaning up together—will be invaluable.

2. Gardening, cleaning up the yard, and washing the car are other ways to get dirty and clean together. If you live in a city, parks and playgrounds may provide similar opportunities.

3. You can investigate the various toddler "messy play" programs given by Y's and play schools everywhere. In a controlled environment, children are allowed to explore water, sand, mud, Play Doh, cooking materials, and a variety of other items you might not want to touch but that are *vital* exploratory tools for your child's development.

4. Make bathtime appealing to an older child. He may resist the bath simply because he's too busy enjoying life to be bothered with something so mundane as cleanliness. There are wonderful bath aids for children around: children's bubble bath, bath goop to paint the tub with, and endless different kinds of bath toys suitable for different ages.

5. If you have a girl with long hair, you might consider washing it every other day so that you don't have a daily battle over getting out the tangles. It might also help to connect the combing with something exciting, such as being able to put her long, beautifully groomed hair into French braids.

6. If it's important to bring your child to your mother-in-law's looking as though she just stepped out of a magazine ad, start well in advance of the time you have to leave. If she wants to play after she's dressed and ready, suggest an indoor rather than an outdoor activity, a puzzle rather than fingerpaints. A

three- or four-year-old eager to identify with his dressed-up parent on this special occasion will also respond to your suggestion that it will please *you* if they stay clean just this once.

SEPARATING PHYSICAL EVENTS FROM EMOTIONAL ONES

It's evident that a clearheaded approach to what is going on physically about the issue of keeping children clean can make sense of anxieties that are directly related to your past experience or old beliefs about sanitation and health. Cleanliness has made many of us feel anxious at one time or another. It doesn't have to be that way. Your child's adjustment to whatever problem you have with staying neat and clean is directly dependent on your being able to tune into your own anxiety and deal with it effectively.

7
Anxieties about Sleep

Which of the following statements is true for you?

1. I couldn't relax, even after my infant started sleeping through the night. I stayed up listening for her to call out.
2. My infant naps blissfully all day and I get a lot done, but then I end up feeling frustrated and incompetent when I can't get him to sleep at night.
3. I rock my toddler to sleep with a bottle every night. I really want her to fall asleep on her own, but I can't figure out how to get her to want to.
4. Our child's been sleeping in our bed since she was born. I'm feeling crowded and want my privacy back, but my husband says she needs us close since we both work and she doesn't see us much all day.
5. Our child has these weird nightmares every once in a while and I try to wake her, but she looks right through me. It's spooky.

Sleeping, not sleeping, fighting sleep, falling asleep, staying asleep—these are all problems you've undoubtedly been through with your child at one time or another. If he doesn't sleep, you don't either, and the pattern can perpetuate itself night after ghastly night. You feel compassion for your child, of course, but sometimes, after a week of impossible nights, you may get irrationally angry at the child who has kept you up or made you vague and distracted at work.

There are really two things happening when you put your child to bed. You want to help him get from consciousness to sleep, yet you realize that the actual process of falling asleep is in his control, not yours. You can pat his back, walk him, rock him, sing to him, give him his favorite toy to hold; when he's older you can read him a story and make plans for the next day. But after that he must do a lot for himself, whether he's four days old or four years old. You can help him approach the gates of sleep, but he must go through by himself; because this involves separation from his parent, it can be a frightening and anxiety-provoking experience. Falling asleep for a child means that the world he's in disappears.

At the same time that your child is hovering on the brink, hanging on to the edge of wakefulness (and some children can seem very wired right before crashing!), you may be despairing that you'll ever get him to wind down. You enter into the same fight the child is having, making going to sleep an ordeal rather than a predictable cycle. After a hard day of caretaking it's understandable that you want your own private time, and you may be trying to cut the parting short so that you can get on to your own business. But the need you feel to hurry the process along may also involve some anxiety and guilt over leaving your child, and it may make the battle worse.

In an attempt to regain some private time, many parents try to get their child to sleep more than they really need to. "I'll put him down" is a common statement many parents make before taking their child to the bedroom for a nap—and it happens to be exactly the same phrasing a horse trainer uses for a wounded animal. "Putting down" implies putting someone out of his misery, but when applied to your child's sleep, we should really ask whose misery we are discussing—his or yours?

Do you ever tell your child he must get some sleep "for his own good"? It's true that sleeping is beneficial and refreshing, but making a child go to bed can also be one way to get rid of him, like placing him in front of the TV.

But you may worry about just the opposite problem if your child is sleeping too much during the day. Though it's completely normal for infants to spend more hours asleep than awake, it may concern you if your three- or four-year-old has trouble keeping his eyes open or takes several naps a day. An older child may fall asleep a lot because he wants to be rid of you—because you bore him, ignore him, or frighten him. If he's not sleeping much at night, he may be going through a difficult period of adjustment about separation.

A two-year-old who begins to dread sleep may prolong the bedtime ritual or may wake up many times and demand to get into his parents' bed with them. An older child may want to postpone bedtime or do away with naps simply because there is too much to do and not enough time in the day or night to do it. Children go through different stages in relation to their sleep, and it's up to you, the parent, to understand where they are—and where you are—in the process if you wish to effect any change.

Sleeping, like eating, is a physical process. The body and mind need a time to slow down, and sleep is the mechanism for doing that. But we don't shut down when we sleep. Our unconscious mind is enormously active, and our dream life helps to renew our spirit and creativity. When a parent is robbed of that possibility, the very idea of sleep can promote anxiety.

This is exactly what happened to Ben when he brought his infant daughter home from the hospital. He had expected to feel deliriously happy, and he wanted to enjoy every minute with this new person who was part of his new family. But he was so bleary from lack of sleep that nothing about parenthood seemed very good to him after a while. It was only after he was able to sort out his personal concerns about the issue of sleep and relax sufficiently to get some rest himself that he began to put his parenting in perspective. The same process may be helpful to you if you find that you're having trouble sleeping with a new baby in the house.

AN INFANT'S INTERNAL CLOCK IS DIFFERENT FROM YOURS

Ben felt he should be the one to stay up with his new daughter Claire when she was wakeful since his wife Francine took care of the child all day. "When we brought Claire home from the hospital," Ben said, "her internal clock was switched around. She wanted to sleep all day and party all night, which meant I stayed up with her at night.

"During the day I wandered around the office feeling as though I had a wad of cotton candy in my head. My boss was sympathetic, but we both knew I wasn't producing up to my usual standard. Francine kept insisting that she could handle staying up, but I refused—I'd hardly have seen Claire otherwise. So I wandered around the house with her, rocked her in front of the TV, read her *Time* magazine. Sometimes I'd put her in the crib and doze off in the chair beside her, thinking about my dad. When I was fifteen he had gone through a weird cycle of headaches. He was in the worst pain—nothing helped—and I'd hear him moaning every night from my bedroom.

"With Claire it was the same way. Every night I'd put her to bed and then put myself to bed. As soon as I started to doze off, she was up. She demanded a feeding every two hours—sometimes more frequently. She always seemed hungry, but she never took the bottle very well. Then she'd fall right back to sleep, and when she finally woke up for the day, at five or six, she'd be all gurgly and happy, as if she'd had a full night's rest. I was a basket case."

SEPARATING PHYSICAL NEEDS FROM PSYCHOLOGICAL ISSUES

If you have a newborn, it's likely that your sleep patterns have changed. A baby *will* rob his parents of sleep, and the resulting mood changes that occur in his mother and father can color the relationship that is forming among the three of them. Sleep deprivation makes you irritable, takes away your appetite, your libido, and your sense that things will look better in the morning. You can go for longer periods of time without food than you can without sleep, and there is no way to make up those lost REMs. Even when your infant's system begins to coincide with the clock, you still may not sleep. Anxiety about how your child is doing or even about the way he has suddenly changed your life may keep you up for hours.

HELPING THE OLDER CHILD DEVELOP HIS OWN GOOD SLEEP HABITS

Amazing as it may seem, babies organize themselves and finally establish a good physical rhythm of waking and sleeping. A newborn generally spends sixteen or seventeen hours of his day asleep, but he can't concentrate most of his sleeping in one period. By the time he is six months old he can usually sleep through the night—about twelve hours—and refresh himself with two naps a day. When he is one year old he can probably give up one of the naps and may sleep longer at night.

The older child needs less sleep, but when he first gives up his nap, he can be a holy terror because he is still going through a period of adjustment. By the time he is three you have to decide whether enforcing a nap is worth the battle. The annoying corollary is that if you take your three-year-old for a ride in the car in the late afternoon, she'll probably doze right off and then, after a delightful late-afternoon snooze, will resist bedtime at eight.

It's at this transitional stage that many parents become concerned about their child's sleep patterns, such as Joe and Jan whose daughter Nina had always slept through the night before. It was very hard for Jan when three-and-a-half-year-old Nina began coming into her room and waking her every morning about four or five, demanding attention.

"Nina was always wide awake, cheery, talkative, and I was completely confused," Jan said, "having been roused from very deep sleep. I got up quickly so as not to wake Joe and took her to her room to change her diaper and get her back in bed. It usually took half an hour to get her settled again, chase out the imaginary monsters, and assure her that the nightlight was bright enough. By that time I was completely awake, wondering why it had to be me and never Joe in this situation. I'd see Nina's eyes starting to close as she cuddled back into the pillow with her teddy bear, and I'd feel like strangling her. The sky was getting light already, and I'd just grit my teeth—I knew I wasn't going to sleep. Finally I started putting myself to bed at 9 P.M., expecting that I'd have to get up at 4. I was never able to spend an evening with Joe or make love to him first thing in the morning, the way we used to. I was annoyed and exhausted, and as much as Joe kept telling me that Nina was manipulating me, I couldn't do a thing to break her of it."

Jan is anxious about dealing with her child's behavior, but she doesn't have a line on the deeper issues that are causing her so much anxiety. When she and Ben can identify the difficulties they're having with their child's sleep and their own, they'll be well on the way to using their anxieties constructively.

Your Program for Change

It's the rare parent who isn't upset over loss of sleep, but each person is going to have a different set of issues, depending on his or her past history and present-day situation. When you're deprived of sleep, emotion tends to take over from thought, and it's difficult to find a way out of the vicious cycle. But by following the Program for Change you'll undoubtedly find a new way to approach the issue of sleep. For a complete description of how to use this program effectively, see Chapter 4, page 61.

STEP I. IDENTIFY WHAT'S REALLY BOTHERING YOU
STEP II. CONNECT WITH YOUR PAST
STEP III. GET THE FACTS
STEP IV. UNDERSTAND YOUR CHILD'S POINT OF VIEW
STEP V. GROUND YOURSELF

STEP VI. STEP BACK AND SEE THE SCENE WITH DIFFERENT EYES

STEP VII. ESTABLISH NEW PATTERNS

STEP I. IDENTIFY WHAT'S REALLY BOTHERING YOU

In determining your own core issue in the arena of sleep, you will probably come upon many varied, unsettling elements. But your real concern may not be as simple as the overwhelming exhaustion or the endless quality of it. As you examine Ben's and Jan's problems, try to put yourself in their upsetting situation and think about your own concerns about sleep.

Let's first consider Ben, whose infant's schedule turned his life upside down. *What is it about this experience that's really bothering Ben?*

Ben is evidently guilty about his wife shouldering the major child care responsibility and wants to participate at the only time available to him. The fact that his baby was staying up at night anyway made him feel as though he was really giving quality time to his child. But no matter what he does in the middle of the night, he can't satisfy his baby. He walks her and rocks her until he's exhausted; then, when she wakes again and he tries to feed her, he feels stymied because she seems too tired to concentrate and suck. And when he sees his bright, well-rested daughter in the morning and contrasts her cheery mood to his own foul one, he feels guilty for his frustration and annoyance with her.

Then there's Jan, whose three-year-old daughter has suddenly begun waking in the middle of the night. *What is it about the experience that's really bothering Jan?*

Jan stresses the fact that this is the first time Nina ever had a sleeping problem. At three a child's increased physical and emotional development usually means a little more freedom for the parent, so it's depressing to go backward. Jan feels betrayed by Nina's new neediness; she's been so independent lately, and now she's reverting to babyish behavior with her fears of monsters and the dark. Jan worries that something she did or said, or some traumatic event Nina hasn't talked about, might have triggered Nina's fears.

Prior to this, Joe and Jan always shared everything when it came to Nina's upbringing. Jan feels jealous of Joe (though privileged that she's the one Nina always wants) because he gets a full night's sleep every night and she never does.

What's Really Bothering You

Ben and Jan both have a variety of issues to consider here, as will you. Some of the major parental issues over sleep are as follows:

- separating from your child
- causing your child a great deal of distress
- your child's lack of sleep affecting his health and yours
- wishing your child would sleep because you need some time for yourself
- having overlooked some problem your child can't yet discuss

If you're having any anxieties about your child's sleep patterns, you might want to look at the following questions that relate to some of the above concerns:

1. Do you find it difficult to listen to your child crying in his crib?
2. Do you feel impelled to go in and check on your child several times a night? Do you leave the monitor on to listen to his breathing while you're in bed?
3. Are you ever concerned that your child sleeps too much? Or not enough? Or at times you consider inappropriate?
4. Is naptime and/or bedtime always the occasion for a fight?
5. Do you worry that your spouse or another caregiver never has any problem putting your child to sleep and you generally do?
6. Do you blame your child for the poor quality of your sleep?
7. Are you ever worried about your child's sleep behavior, that is, rocking, head rolling, or head banging?
8. Are you ever concerned by the sounds your child makes when he sleeps, that is, snoring, moaning, crying out?

9. Are you troubled by your child's nightmares or night terrors?
10. Do you ever attribute your child's irritable daytime behavior or moodiness to his sleep patterns?

Bedtime problems tend to get so ingrained that they are difficult to sort out at first, but by discussing the changes that both you and your spouse have noticed, you'll gradually start to become aware of how much of your concern relates to purely physical matters and how much spills over into the emotional arena.

STEP II. CONNECT WITH YOUR PAST

Your present-day reactions to your child's sleep habits and your own may be closely connected with your past experience. In summoning up memories of your childhood you will undoubtedly feel a mixture of comfort and distress. These feelings can help immeasurably in enabling you to realize what is currently making you anxious about your child.

Ben: Ben's memories of his father are vivid and sharp, even now. Whenever he heard his father cry out at night, he'd wake up instantly, sure that something awful was about to happen. He'd just lie there, wondering whether his mother was up, too, wondering if he should get the ice bag for his father. Some nights he'd keep himself awake, thinking he might be needed.

Jan: Jan's father was a traveling salesman, and when he was on the road she and her sister would climb into her mother's bed to read or talk. It was a wonderful time. Sometimes their mother would allow the girls to stay with her for the night.

When their father came home from the trips, however, the girls were banished from their parents' bedroom. Jan always resented the abruptness with which her father would hustle the girls into bed, without even a story or a good night kiss. She recalled feeling rejected and shut out, and grew resentful of the times when her father was in the house. Does she think she'll be hurting Nina— as her father did her—if she doesn't spend the time putting her back to bed?

How You Can Connect with Your Past

Think back to the time when you were a child ready for bed or lying in bed, waiting for sleep to claim you. Imagine a complete mental picture, starting with the physical surroundings and working your way slowly toward questions that will evoke provocative issues about sleep. Use the suggested questions below to trigger your imagination and provoke particular memories you might have had.

SETTING THE SCENE

1. Where did you sleep? Think about your childhood room and where the bed was.
2. Did you think of your childhood bedroom as a special place full of wonderful possessions and dreams or something to be avoided?
3. Did you sleep alone, or were there siblings in the room with you?
4. Did you have a set bedtime, or did it change with the night and the family's activities?
5. Was the room warm or cold? Silent or noisy? Dark or light?

Now that you can see clearly, how did you experience going to sleep?

Some typical memories recalled by many parents had to do with the following:

· wanting to be close to your parents
· feeling pushed away and abandoned
· escaping into a comfortable, soothing world
· fearing nightmares and dreams; lacking the ability to let go

The following questions that relate to some of the above concerns may evoke certain useful feelings about your past:

6. Who put you to bed at night? Was it a long, comfortable ritual, or was it very short and abrupt?

7. Did you fall asleep right away, or did you stay awake thinking and listening? Did you ever have anxieties about the next day at school?

8. Did you ever wake up in the middle of the night to the sounds of your parents' fighting or making plans in which you weren't included?

9. Do you recall whether you used to dream a lot? Did you have nightmares? What were they about?

10. Did you ever wet the bed? How did your parents react? Were you ever punished? How?

11. Did you awake rested and refreshed? Or were you tired, as though you hadn't slept at all?

These questions and the scenes they evoke in your mind will probably bring back memories about sleep that may go far back, to when you were your child's age. As you consider them now, from a parent's perspective, you may be better able to see how much of your own past you are replaying as you go through similar experiences with your child.

STEP III. GET THE FACTS

It's now time to collect some hard, factual information that will make your particular area of concern about sleeping a bit easier to comprehend and deal with.

Ben: Ben decided to make a chart of Claire's typical sleep patterns for an entire week. He noticed that she got up at 5 or 6 A.M., took a catnap of about twenty minutes at about 10 A.M., and then after her lunchtime feeding took a nap that could last an hour or two. She was usually up until 4 P.M. and then fell asleep for three or four hours, waking after Francine and Ben had finished dinner. She would be terribly cranky, and it was almost impossible to prepare a feeding for her fast enough. She generally stayed up until

11 and then fell asleep again, but she would wake several times for a feeding.

Ben called their pediatrician and described her day over the phone. The pediatrician reassured him immediately by saying that their child would sleep through the night when she began napping less and at better-timed intervals during the day. Rather than allow her to chose her own schedule, her parents were to choose it for her, gradually changing her waking and sleeping hours. They would at the same time be changing her feeding schedule to make it more regular so that she wouldn't be as tired or as ravenous when she took her bottle.

Jan: Jan also decided to keep a chart to figure out Nina's sleep schedule. She kept bedtime at precisely 8 P.M. for the entire week and put the baby monitor back into Nina's room so that she could hear how long it took her daughter to put herself to sleep and at what time she woke up.

She read several good child care books on the older child's sleep patterns and discovered that a preschooler who is toilet trained for daytime but not night may be waking herself up when she urinates in her diaper. In fact, the books explained that most children in training pants will rouse themselves from sleep in order to get up to go to the toilet—something they generally won't do if they are given the safety net of a diaper to wear. Jan figured out that Nina might be waking because she was wet. Humiliated to find herself in this babyish situation, she needed Mommy to get her back to the comfort of her bed. Perhaps if Jan let Nina sleep in underpants, the child would feel grown-up enough to go to the toilet by herself.

Consider All Your Facts

1. Do you think your infant is not getting the proper amount and type of sleep? *Make a chart of his naps and nighttime sleep, indicating the number of hours he sleeps and the intervals between sleep periods, how long it takes for him to put himself to sleep, how long he stays asleep, and what kind of mood he's in when*

he wakes. Once you have actual numbers you can call your pediatrician to verify that your child is getting a normal amount of rest. Some babies simply need less sleep than others, the same as some children and adults.

2. Are you concerned about your infant's restlessness during sleep? *A thorough book on children's sleep patterns will explain that the developing brain goes through a variety of cycles during the night, and these cycles change from month to month. A new-born will have longer periods of REM sleep than a child and will appear to be twitchy or fitful in his crib. As the child gets older, his periods of non-REM or "quiet sleep" lengthen.*

3. Does your infant/child have a special toy that gives her a lot of comfort, that might make the separation with you or your spouse easier? *From the age of six months or so, when a child can hold on to and relate to a stuffed animal, you should let him select one and keep it with him at naptime and bedtime. This soft, fuzzy creature, imbued with the warmth and smells and feeling of "Mommy," can tide the baby over emotionally until he falls asleep. The toy begins to represent the absent parent and can comfort the child even when the parent leaves the room.*

4. Do you worry if your child won't go right to sleep at bedtime? *Most experts say that children react best to bedtime if they have a ritual to follow, a quiet period of winding down at the end of the day. It's useful to have both parents alternate giving the bath, reading a story, singing a song, and preparing the nursery for the night.*

5. Are you concerned that some event during the day is causing sleep problems? *A change of caregiver, a move, a new sibling could all make a child restless at night and scared to be without you.*

6. Does it bother you that your child really resists bedtime and wails when you leave the room? Do you feel that you have to stay with him until he's asleep? *It may be necessary for you to let your child cry for several nights—without your being present in his room to soothe him—in order to help him learn to get himself to sleep. Naturally you should go to him if the crying accelerates and your child is in real distress because no learning*

can be done under that kind of duress, but in order for your child to establish a good pattern for falling asleep, he has to be able to accomplish it by himself.

7. Are you concerned because your child is scared of the dark? *This is one of the most common childhood fears, beginning at about age two and continuing off and on throughout childhood. A nightlight will help, of course, and there are stuffed animals that light up when you squeeze them. Check the child's room in the glow of the nightlight to be sure that the furniture doesn't cast too many strange or unsettling shadows.*

8. Do you start to panic if your child appears to stop breathing during sleep? *The condition known as sleep apnea can cause SIDS (Sudden Infant Death Syndrome) in infants, but today there are professional monitoring devices you can rent to ensure your child's safety. If you notice that your baby is experiencing a disrupted breathing pattern, call your pediatrician at once. He will have you hook up your child to a machine that will gently rouse the baby and start him breathing again. Sleep apnea in older children is rare and causes the child to snore loudly each night during restless sleep. The cure for this is usually removal of enlarged tonsils and adenoids.*

9. Are you worried when you notice your child "rocking and rolling" during the night? *Children often develop a pattern that mimics being rocked in a parent's arms as a soothing method of putting themselves to sleep. This rhythmic movement can go on even during sleep and occasionally may appear violent, as when the child bangs his head into the pillow or mattress.*

10. Why do you have so much trouble waking your child from a nightmare? *He may be experiencing a night terror instead. A nightmare is a scary dream during REM sleep from which the child will wake and call out, remembering many details. A terror is a partial arousal from deep, non-REM sleep where a feeling of fear is present but no dream can be reported. The child will generally fall back to sleep on his own and should not be roused or questioned.*

11. Are you anxious about your preschooler being a bedwetter? *Your four-year-old son is not a bedwetter if he is recently toilet*

trained and has accidents about once every two weeks or so. The term should not be applied to any child under six who urinates in his sleep. Being physically ready to stay dry through the night is more difficult for boys than for girls, and many parents choose to keep their children in diapers or training pants at night for nearly a year after they are toilet trained during the day.

The actual facts you can garner about your child's sleeping patterns will put your past experience and present-day concerns into a clearer light. When you understand some of the intricacies of the sleep process, it will be easier for you to make accommodations for your child's fears and desires, and establish new patterns for good sleep habits.

STEP IV. UNDERSTAND YOUR CHILD'S POINT OF VIEW

Going to sleep, for a child, means a separation, entering another world that his parent can't be part of. At certain stages of development this can be very frightening. It's important that you try to discover your child's perspective on sleeping and see the issues from his point of view. When you use your empathy to discover how your child really feels, you'll be much better equipped to handle any problems that sleep produces.

Ben: At Francine's suggestion Ben came home from work for lunch several times over a few weeks so that he could see Claire asleep during the day. He was there in time to give her a lunchtime bottle and then get her settled for her nap. He left her awake in her crib and listened outside her door. He could hear the baby's sounds, at first excited, then settling down into chirps and quiet gurgles. Then he heard a few sighs. When he tiptoed in he saw her completely relaxed, lying on her stomach with her head turned to one side, her toy lamb near her cheek. It was as if she were telling him, with her body position, that she was comfortable and sleeping soundly. Each day Claire was more alert as she was aroused from her naps and took her bottles better at each feeding.

Jan: When Jan, Joe, and Nina were having breakfast, Joe asked whether Nina had gotten her mother up that morning.

"Uh huh," Nina said, nodding. " 'Cause when I wake up I think maybe there's a monster under the bed, so I have to come get Mommy."

"Well, sweetie," Joe interjected, "that could just be a dream or a thought you're having—not a real monster. Tonight we'll check your room together *before* you go to sleep."

"No, only Mommy!" Nina insisted, near tears. "I want Mommy! I never see Mommy!"

Of course Joe and Jan know this isn't true, but Nina seems to need her mother more right now. Maybe Jan, assuming that her daughter is getting more independent, just hasn't been paying enough attention to her.

From the depths of her exhaustion, Jan said, "Honey, you're such a grown-up girl now, I wonder if tonight you want to try sleeping without a diaper. We could go to the mall together today and buy you a real nightgown to wear to bed instead of your sleeper."

"Then I could go potty in the middle of the night?" Nina asked eagerly. "All by myself? Could Pooch come with me?"

"Sure," Jan said, smiling.

Nina reached down and scratched Pooch's head. "Daddy, where do we go when we dream?"

"Nowhere," Joe said. "We're still in bed, even if it looks like we're flying to the moon. Dreams are just thoughts we have when we're asleep."

"But why can't you or Mommy be there with me if I have a bad dream?"

"We're right there, sweetie," Jan assured her with a hug. "If it's really too scary for you and Pooch to handle, we'll be there in a second."

Nina sighed and nodded. "Pooch, you sleep in my room tonight, and you and me can scare the monsters if they come."

Jan and Joe have elicited a lot from their daughter in this conversation: first, that she's confused about the difference between dreams and reality; second, that she misses her mother who hasn't been spending a great deal of time with her; and third, that she's really ready for another step toward independence—having a sleeping garment she can get out of easily in order to go to the bathroom by herself. She still wants the protection of a parent substitute (the dog), but having Pooch in her room may mean that her mother will be able to get a full night's sleep.

Bringing Out Your Child's Feelings

Sleep brings up dozens of questions in toddlers and preschoolers, and some of them may be too frightening to ask. It's going to be your job as a parent to elicit some of the feelings your child has about falling asleep and staying asleep. It's crucial that you find out from your child whether she hates bedtime because she hates the color of her blanket, whether she doesn't feel like winding down from a day of playing and socializing, or whether she is having difficulty separating from you.

By respecting your child's needs and wishes you will encourage him to participate with you in delving into whatever is bothering him. Some of the statements below are those that parents have used to start a dialogue about sleep with their children. They will undoubtedly inspire some of your own that are pertinent to your child's special problems with sleep:

1. "I know you're not really tired and don't want to take a nap, but we'll be able to have even more fun playing this afternoon if you take a quiet time in your room."
2. "If we talk about the things that went on in your nightmare together, maybe it won't seem so scary."
3. "Let's have ten more minutes of running around the house together, then you can change into pajamas and we'll pick out the clothes you're going to wear tomorrow."
4. "I remember when I was a little girl and was alone in the dark in my room at night. I used to lie there and tell my pillow a wonderful story, and by the time it was over I was asleep."

Acting on Your Child's Feelings

Once you're aware of your child's point of view you can take positive action that will help to make bedtime a more pleasant experience for both of you.

1. An infant who cries before bed may be hungry, exhausted, or in need of holding and comforting. You might try experimenting with different ways of calming your infant before naps and bed.
2. Listen to your preschooler without laughing or criticizing when he procrastinates. His reasons for not wanting to go to bed—being afraid of the dark, monsters, or because he never sleeps anyway so he might as well stay up—all have real meaning to him.
3. If your child protests napping but it's clear that she still needs to, try an innovative solution such as a sleeping bag on the floor or a nap on a couch that's not in her bedroom.
4. If bedtime has become an ordeal, change it around. You might find a special TV show to watch together just before lights out, or you might suggest that your spouse do the bedtime ritual.
5. If your child is old enough, you might ask if there's any (small) redecorating he'd like to do to make his bedroom more appealing. A new wallhanging or quilt on the bed might make all the difference in attitude toward bedtime.
6. A song or story on the subject can be comforting and can start a real dialogue about your child's fears and apprehensions. There are numerous comforting books about bedtime for toddlers and older children. Margaret Wise Brown's *Good Night, Moon* and Russell Hoban's *Bedtime for Francis* are the classics in the field. You will have to gauge your own child's tolerance for books about nightmares. Maurice Sendak's wonderful *Where the Wild Things Are* and Mercer Mayer's *There's a Nightmare in My Closet* may spark more fears than reassurance, but you might do well with books about the special qualities of dreams themselves. David MacPhail's *The Train,* Cooper Edens's *Caretakers of Wonder,* and Sendak's *In the Night Kitchen* are three of these. No matter what you think your singing voice sounds like, a lullaby crooned by Mom or Dad has been the age-old panacea for helping children fall sleep.

STEP V. GROUND YOURSELF

It's particularly hard to talk yourself down from an anxiety spiral when you haven't slept in days, but this is when grounding is doubly important. By talking to yourself logically and calmly about what's going on, you'll be able to see an end to the difficulties you and your child are currently having about sleep.

> *Ben:* Ben told himself that he had already taken steps toward ensuring Claire's nighttime rest and his own. Knowing that he was in the process of changing his baby's daytime nap and feeding schedule meant that pretty soon her hours would conform to his. He knew that when she was getting more continuous nighttime rest, he wouldn't feel obligated to stay up for her as he did for his father.

> *Jan:* Jan can tell herself that she and her daughter are really developing a very wonderful new wrinkle in their relationship. Rather than treating her as a baby, Jan is beginning to give her some autonomy. She tells herself that she doesn't have to pop up as soon as Nina comes to the doorway of her bedroom because her child has chosen the dog to be a nighttime surrogate parent. Jan reminds herself that she can spend time with her daughter during the day when it really counts.

The suggested thoughts below are examples of different ways that parents have succeeded in grounding themselves. These may or may not relate to your personal situation, but it is hoped they will ease the way toward allowing realities to temper anxiety about sleep.

> *Anxious thought:* This is the fifth night in a row I've been up with the baby. He's never going to sleep through the night!
> *Grounding thought:* He's only three months old and still getting himself organized. Eventually he'll sleep through the night, and I will, too.

Anxious thought: I knew I shouldn't have taken my toddler to that dinner party and put him to sleep in the hostess's bedroom last night. He woke up as soon as we got home and then had a fitful night. Maybe he won't get back on schedule.

Grounding thought: Everybody has late nights once in a while, and everybody returns to the norm when tired enough because the human body craves sleep and can't survive without it. By tomorrow he'll be back on track.

Anxious thought: I had to drive my child twenty miles in the car today before she dozed off for her nap. I'm going to spend the rest of my life driving.

Grounding thought: She's been going right into her crib every afternoon for the past week without fussing. Maybe she just wasn't very tired today.

STEP VI. STEP BACK AND SEE THE SCENE WITH DIFFERENT EYES

If you can picture in your imagination a positive scene having to do with you, your child, and sleep, you'll realize what may be possible for you in reality.

Ben: Ben would like Claire to sleep through the night and would like to believe that she's doing fine so that he can end his vigil.

He pictures himself holding his sleepy infant, placing her in her crib, kissing her gently, and leaving the room. He remembers how she looked in the middle of her nap, completely relaxed. Then he switches the scene and imagines himself lying in bed, drifting off comfortably. Even if he has to get up for her once in a while, he sees himself falling back to sleep right afterward.

Jan: Jan would like Nina to feel confident without her mother at night so that Jan would get a full night's sleep without feeling guilty that she had abandoned her daughter.

She steps back and sees herself participating in Nina's day, really listening to her child when she describes what happened at pre-school or in the playground. She imagines the two of them at the amusement park, where Nina took the lead showing her mother around the climbing equipment. Then at bedtime she imagines Nina drifting off with a smile, sleeping peacefully, "protected by her bear," and having enjoyed her mother's attention during the important moments of the day.

Imagine What You'd Like to Happen

Step back and use your imagination to picture an alternative to the anxiety-driven scene of not sleeping. Your goal is to have your child sleep through the night, to take naps if they are age appropriate, to have a pleasant bedtime and a good waking. You also want the night to be a time when you can stop worrying about your child and get some much-needed rest yourself. Perhaps you can also fit in a little intimacy with your spouse that may have been missing since the birth of your child. Remember to keep your scenarios within the realm of possibility—you can be positive but realistic.

STEP VII. ESTABLISH NEW PATTERNS

The combinations of elements that lead to sleep problems are many and varied, but once you've identified your own areas of concern you'll be ready to think about establishing new patterns. Remember that they will be slow in evolution, and there may be a good deal of backpedaling while you get closer to your desired goal. But good, restful sleep on a regular basis for you and your family is definitely worth the wait.

Ben: Ben realized that he had been loading a physical problem— his baby's irregular nap schedule—with a variety of psychological issues, such as his need to spend more time with his child and his remembrance of difficult nights not being to help his ailing father. Now that he's been able to distinguish his anxious feelings, he has a much better fix on how to parent Claire. He won't feel obligated to knock himself out trying to take care of things that she doesn't really need him for.

Each day he and Francine shortened Claire's naps a bit more and spaced them out better during the day. Ben found that he was now able to put Claire to bed at night and fall asleep himself, secure in the knowledge that she'd be resting calmly for at least five or six hours at a stretch. He could see that a full night's sleep was only a short distance ahead.

Jan: After buying Nina a new nightgown and installing Pooch's dog bed in her daughter's room, Jan herself was infected with Nina's excitement about the new sleeping arrangements. On the first night Jan woke as soon as she heard Nina get up. She heard the child talking to her dog, a little later the toilet flushing, and then Nina padding down the hall to come and wake her.

Jan restrained herself from popping up and instead, feigned sleep. In another two minutes she heard Nina telling Pooch that it was time to go back to bed. After this there were several instances in which she did wake her parents, because of a bad dream or some other difficulty, but by the end of three months Nina either put herself back to bed or slept through the night. So did Jan.

PARENTS' SUGGESTIONS

1. If your child has a favorite toy or blanket—perhaps one that you've played with together—let him take it into his crib or bed. This can serve to keep Mommy with him even when he's asleep and will help to make a good separation from you at nap and bedtime.

2. After a suitable time of holding or rocking, you can place your infant in the crib awake, with his toy and perhaps a pacifier. It's wiser not to give a bottle in bed so as not to run the risk of dental problems (caused by milk or fruit sugars remaining in the mouth during sleep).

3. If your child consistently cries when you leave him awake, give him a little time alone to vent his feelings, then return to reassure him that you're there and to say that it's now time for him to settle down and be quiet. You can gradually extend your time out of the room, increasing the intervals until he's able to tolerate your leaving him alone to put himself to sleep.

4. Experiment with both bedtime and naps to see whether your

ANXIETIES ABOUT SLEEP   133

child has outgrown his more babyish routine and is ready to extend his day. Your pediatrician can help you make an informed decision about how much sleep your child needs at this stage.

5. If your child is still in a crib, perhaps it's time to switch to a bed. Giving a mobile child a bed gives him power over when he gets in and out of it. Most parents are surprised to find that when their child is free to move around his own space, he bothers them less than he did when he was incarcerated behind bars and had to plead for Mom or Dad to rescue him.

6. Never use going to bed as a punishment. As much as you may feel your child needs some time alone to think over his behavior, you don't want to make his bedroom seem like a den of horrors. Think about another location for time-outs.

7. Use a timer to allow your child to anticipate his coming bedtime. When the "dinger dings," he'll know it's time to brush teeth and read a story. Make preparations for nap and bedtime pleasant, but be firm about how long they go on.

8. You might try relaxing your rules on the weekend; for example, you can let your preschooler skip his nap, allow him to stay up a little later, or come into your bed to snuggle on a Sunday morning after it's light outside.

9. If your child is a midnight wanderer, be cheery but firm and brief when you put her back to bed. The more you prolong the contact between you, the more she'll believe it's something to be continued.

10. Allow your newly toilet-trained child to sleep without a diaper. You'll need to restrict his liquids after dinner, put a plastic sheet under the mattress protector, and consider doubling everything—plastic, protector, and sheets—in order to make middle-of-the-night bedding changes easier.

11. You can wean your newly night-trained child from rousing you at night by making it easier for him to find and reach the light switch in his bedroom and the bathroom.

12. If you currently sleep in a familial bed, you might begin to think about discontinuing it. Many parents feel that they want

to be close to their child, particularly if they both work and don't see her much during the day. Also, they tend to think it will make their child feel more secure to be physically close to her parents at night. But on a regular basis the familial bed disrupts the sexual relationship of the married couple while it encourages the child to believe that his parents will always be with him, sleeping or waking, for the rest of his life. Every once in a long while, however, sleeping together as a family may not be anything to worry about; it tends to relieve both parent and child at a time of high stress.

THE IMPORTANCE OF SLEEP—YOUR OWN AND YOUR CHILD'S

Sleeping has undoubtedly become more precious to you since you had a child. Think about the helpful ways in which you are coping with your child's sleep problems and try to remember that this is a brief period in your life. If you and your child have established a good groundwork for sleeping, you will be able to regain the capacity for deep, undisturbed sleep once your child is a little older.

As with good eating and cleanliness habits, you can only encourage your child to develop his own good sleeping habits. If you rock your baby to sleep with a bottle every night, you will not give him the chance to learn to put himself to sleep. If you agree to sit with your four-year-old until he falls asleep, you are not offering him the opportunity to separate from you. The bed and bedroom should be a welcoming, safe place, and sleep time should be a way for the child to gain an important kind of privacy he will value for the rest of his life.

Try to keep in mind that a curious, active child who eats a healthy diet is eventually going to be a tired child, and when he's tired, he'll sleep. As we grow older we have less need for sleep, so if you miss a few hours, no irrevocable harm is done. Tomorrow or next week, if it's still important to you, maybe you'll think about going to bed early for a change.

When your child is ill, it brings back the original concern you undoubtedly had about whether your newborn, who used to live all safe and sound inside the womb, could really exist on his own out in the world. During your child's illness it's particularly important for there to be a good balance between husband and wife so that if one is panic-stricken, the other can add a more realistic voice. A child's illness often does seem worse than it is; children typically run higher fevers than adults (though for shorter periods of time), and they're often unable to describe the symptoms or pinpoint the location of the pain or discomfort, so they seem more generally miserable. Also, a parent who is used to seeing her bouncing baby or rambunctious toddler enjoying every moment to the fullest is going to experience a real jolt when the same child acts limp and listless during a bout with a cold or flu.

Illness is not pleasant, but it's a fact of life. We all get sick and then we heal. There is nothing bad in and of itself about your child getting sick—but if your child is often ill, it's possible that something emotional may be going on that he can't handle by himself. He may be reaching out to you, in some way trying to regain that special mommying he had as an infant. This is not to say he isn't really sick: children can produce real physical symptoms when they're feeling emotionally troubled. If you're the type of person who enjoys reliving that time when you had to do everything for your dependent infant, you may unconsciously encourage your child's symptoms rather than try to cure them. As your child grows older and his emotional needs become increasingly complex, it's sometimes easier to concentrate on his physical aches and pains instead. You may pay too much attention to the concrete manifestations of his body even if there's really nothing much wrong with him because they're simpler and easier to handle than the psychological ones.

The corollary to the parent who is overly worried about her child being ill is the one who worries that her sick child will make *her* ill. It's true: if you have to lose work time to stay home, you may tend to shy away from your sniffling toddler or treat your chicken-poxed child as though she were Typhoid Mary. Needless to say, this attitude isn't good for either of you. The way a parent cares for her baby is at least as important as the medicine or treatment the child needs to get well. A distant, uninvolved mother who looks at her son's flu as an inconvenience is giving the boy a message that she doesn't really love him in sickness and in health.

Illness is a fact of life, and it happens to all of us. When you're ill and your child is well, you may have another form of anxiety to deal with. Children don't like to see their parents as fallible or human, and it may be hard to convince a demanding toddler who wants you to play that you must get some rest. It's at a time like this that balance in the family is crucial: a spouse, grandparent, or neighbor really must step in. Kids have to learn compassion, and they have to know that you need a break every once in a while. Though it's best to try and get this point across when you're perfectly well, you'll do a lot for the give-and-take aspect of your relationship with your child if you can assure him that while Dad or Mom may feel awful right now, he or she will recover in time.

The more typical experience of anxiety over illness takes place, however, when your child is ill and you feel desperate to make him feel better. This was the case of Jennifer whose son Johnny had a series of ear infections after his first birthday.

DO YOU SEE YOUR CHILD AS WELL OR ILL?

Jennifer, who had always been treated like a fragile flower by her own mother, began to think of Johnny as a sickly child because of his recurrent ear problems. "I couldn't be too careful," she explained. "I kept him bundled up all winter and rarely let him play with other children for fear of his catching something, and still he had these awful bouts with pain and fever. The antibiotic would clear him up, but it seemed as though two days after his checkup he'd start crying again, pawing at his poor ears, and back we'd go to a doctor. I never trusted any of them, so we switched around a lot, getting second and third opinions. Finally my mother suggested we go to her family doctor. He recommended shunts, so that's what we did.

"I'll never forget that day. I was in tears, my mother was yelling at the nurse, Johnny was hysterical—it was like bedlam. He must have cried himself to sleep in the car and slept for about six hours after the procedure, while I watched over him, crazy about what we'd just done. Suppose it was a mistake?

"Well, amazing as it might seem, he didn't have any more ear infections after that. It's not that he's really recovered, though— he always looks pale to me. Watching him playing with other kids, you see that he doesn't really join in because he doesn't have the strength. My husband says I treat him like a baby, but of course he is! I wouldn't be a good mother if I didn't keep him home and spoil him a little when he comes down with the sniffles."

It's going to take some thoughtful probing into Jennifer's attitudes to change her mind about Johnny and about her anxieties over his well-being, but it's crucial to their relationship that she do so. Regardless of how prone they may be to physical illness, children do tend to heal better and faster if their parents give them the message that good health is the norm.

HEALTH CONCERNS WITH AN OLDER CHILD

When your toddler or preschooler is ill, you not only have a child care book or your pediatrician's recommendation to rely on, you also have the child's own verbal cues. An older child can tell you that his tummy hurts or his throat is sore; he can also generate a lot of complaints in the hope of getting some much needed attention from Mom and Dad. Some of the "excuse" aches and pains can be just as legitimate as the physically caused ones, of course, and shouldn't be ignored. Many children of this age are fascinated by their negative fantasies about illness, and it may take a good deal of sleuth work before you can figure out why a sneeze or a sore provokes so many frightened questions.

An older child will rankle at having to stick around the house and "do nothing," perhaps taking naps he hasn't taken in a year, perhaps being restricted to a special "yukky" diet until he's well.

Caring for a sick four-year-old can be a real challenge to a parent in terms of diagnosis, treatment, and recovery.

Helene and Pete's daughter Mandy had hardly ever been sick. "When it was time for her four-year checkup, she got very excited about seeing her pediatrician, Dr. David, again," Helene said, laughing. "I think she remembered he'd given her a lollipop the year before. Anyway, at the exam Dr. David asked if Mandy had been to the dentist yet. I think I made a face and said, 'Why would we want to subject her to that?'

"Well, he said we had to go, so I made an appointment with the dentist that Pete and I always went to. I can't tell you how I hated bringing my child to that place! As I'm sitting in the chair, having my teeth cleaned, I could see Mandy's face crumpling. I didn't know whether she was just bored or if something else was the matter.

"Anyway, when I was done the dentist scooted me out of the chair and lifted Mandy into it, and lo and behold, she burst out crying. She claimed she had a stomachache and wanted to go home. I tried talking to her about it but became frustrated, telling her she had to have her teeth cleaned and as soon as it was over she could go home and lie down. I told her that if she was just pretending to be sick to worm her way out of the dentist's chair, it wasn't going to work. But she kept crying and holding her stomach and gagging, so I thought, Oh, my Lord, the poor kid really is sick. I raced her out of there. That evening she was running a little fever, and she hardly touched dinner. I let Pete put her to bed. I was so fed up from this wasted day and so baffled as to what was wrong with Mandy. Maybe she had really been brewing something, and I'd ignored it. Maybe bringing her to the dentist and asking her to do something she didn't want to do had made it blossom. The next day she had a full-blown stomach bug, with vomiting, diarrhea, the works. Then I felt like a terrible mother because I'd accused her of malingering and hadn't helped her when she really needed me."

We have several elements to examine here. First, did Helene simply ignore the fact that Mandy was coming down with something because she wanted to get the appointment over with? She lets comments slip that indicate she doesn't really feel comfortable in the role of mother to a dependent, sick child, which is unusual behavior for Mandy who is always at the peak of health. Second, does Helene bring some emotional baggage to the dentist's office that she doesn't bring to the pediatrician's office, and is Mandy picking up on this? Is physical health or emotional health at stake here, and how are they intertwined for the older child?

Jennifer and Helene are going to have to consider why they react in such an anxious manner over their children's health. If their goal is to have children who take illness in stride, who recover and go on from there, they're going to have to identify where their concerns come from and see how they may be infusing a physical situation with underlying emotional issues.

Your Program for Change

STEP I. IDENTIFY WHAT'S REALLY BOTHERING YOU

STEP II. CONNECT WITH YOUR PAST

STEP III. GET THE FACTS

STEP IV. UNDERSTAND YOUR CHILD'S POINT OF VIEW

STEP V. GROUND YOURSELF

STEP VI. STEP BACK AND SEE THE SCENE WITH DIFFERENT EYES

STEP VII. ESTABLISH NEW PATTERNS

STEP I. IDENTIFY WHAT'S REALLY BOTHERING YOU

Try to look at the issues of illness in a concrete way, fixing on each individual element that upsets you rather than focusing on the general feeling that everything about the subject is awful. If you can identify your own special problem involving your illness and your child's, as Jennifer and Helene did, you'll probably be better able to see past the upsetting current situation and unlock the meaning behind your anxiety.

Let's think about Jennifer who is overly worried about her son's susceptibility to illness. *What is it about this experience that's really bothering Jennifer?*

Although Johnny has already outgrown his early susceptibility to ear infections, Jennifer can't get over the feeling that at any moment tragedy might strike. She keeps him away from other children, inhibiting his ability to socialize properly, and she infantilizes him because the infant stage of his life was the one during which she had the most control.

The way that a parent handles her child's illness teaches the child how to handle it. Jennifer's chronic anxiety whenever she perceives something wrong with Johnny, her inability to pick a pediatrician she considers suitable, her feeling that Johnny could get sick at any moment will all contribute to making Johnny feel that he's somehow not all there, not all right, unless his mother is taking care of him. Jennifer seems to have an excessive need to be the sole source of comfort to her child and is using illness to gain that powerful position.

Helene, whose older child seems fine most of the time, is having trouble dealing with her daughter's sudden onset of illness during a stressful situation. *What is it about this experience that's really bothering Helene?*

First, she seems confused as to whether she's supposed to react to Mandy's stomachache. Although she sees that her child has real symptoms, she blames Mandy for fabricating them just to get out of being examined by the dentist and to gain her mother's sympathy—which really annoys Helene who hates being manipulated.

But Helene realizes that she herself has problems with having her teeth checked and cleaned. Has she transferred her anxiety about dentistry to her child? And is Mandy overreacting because her mother is too wrapped up in her own feelings to help Mandy through this new experience?

Then Helene feels like a bad mother for passing her child off to her husband Pete. Helene has so rarely had to take care of a sick child that she feels unequal to the task. First she thought her daughter was lying, and now she has to acknowledge that she's really ill. She wonders if by misreading her daughter's reaction she has made her sicker.

What's Really Bothering You

These two mothers have begun to identify their own difficulties with their children's health. Some typical parental concerns over health and illness have to do with the following:

- a fear that your child has an untreatable disease
- your desire for your child to depend only on you
- your fear that the outside world may infect your child
- your fear that you'll catch the illness and not be able to care for your child
- your overreaction or underreaction to what is going on

If you're having anxiety over any of these issues, you might want to look at the following questions that relate to one or several of the above concerns:

1. Do you worry that you may overlook your baby getting sick and attribute his crying to tiredness or crankiness?
2. Do you ever feel that you're the only one who can take care of your sick child?
3. Do you worry that your doctor may not have enough expertise or be too busy to treat your child?
4. Do you worry that your preschooler makes up illnesses just to get special treatment?
5. Are you afraid that you will do the wrong thing for your child and thereby worsen the illness?
6. Do you and your husband frequently disagree about whether or not your child is really sick? Whether this illness warrants a doctor's visit or medication?
7. Do you ever worry that other mothers won't let their children play with your child if he is frequently ill?
8. Are you afraid that other children may contaminate your child?
9. Are you ever upset by the physical manifestations of your child's illness—vomit, diarrhea, runny nose, runny ears?

10. Is your own health a real issue? Do you or your spouse ever complain of minor ailments? Do you often take sick days? Do you never take sick days?

One of the best ways to identify your central issues regarding health and illness is to compare and contrast your version of the sickness with your spouse's version. If you're always the one who recognizes your child's feverish brow or glassy eyes, are you also the type of person who tends to be self-critical, often dissatisfied with life in general?

When you've begun to uncover your basic issues about health and illness, you'll be better able to distinguish the physical from the emotional elements of your child's illness and be more aware of your reaction to it.

STEP II. CONNECT WITH YOUR PAST

The memories of illness that you may have will undoubtedly evoke mixed emotions. You should allow them all to surface now, as you think back, so that you can begin to piece together the sources of your current anxiety and correlate the way you experienced illness as a child with the way you deal with your child's illness now.

Jennifer: Jennifer's frequent colds and stomachaches were opportunities for her to get her mother to stay home from work, and she relished those times because her mother coddled and pampered her. Because she was physically small she was nervous around bigger children, and her mother confirmed her anxiety that other kids were rough and careless. It's possible that her present-day protectiveness of Johnny might stem from her feeling that if anyone ever hurt him, she'd feel as though they were hurting her—just as they might have when she was a little girl.

Jennifer's usually distant, distracted mother was always there for her when she was sick, but when nothing was wrong with Jennifer, it was frequently difficult to make contact with her mother. She remembers feeling that the only time her mother cared about her was when she was sick.

Helene: The third of four children in a rather poor family, Helene remembers that the only time she went to the doctor was when the school nurse said she was too sick to be with other kids and had to have a doctor's note saying she was well enough to come back. Her parents generally made fun of a child who complained of symptoms, so she learned to suffer in silence.

She didn't have much dental care as a child, either, but remembers one night in college when she had a terrible toothache and the nurse in the infirmary sent her to a dentist in town. He didn't give her enough novocaine to dull the pain, but she was so unused to having a tooth drilled that she assumed any dental procedure was that painful.

Helene's attitude toward Mandy reflects her own stoicism (and certainly her own fear of dentists!) but also her own ambivalence about having to hide her real feelings from her parents. She doesn't want to deal with her child's illness this way, but she doesn't know any other way.

How You Can Connect with Your Past

It will probably be easy to paint a mental picture of sometime in your childhood when you were ill and wanted your parents to come and take care of you. Try to delve deeper into the experience to give yourself new insights about what was really going on at that time—for your parents and for you. The questions below are a guide to stimulate your memories and provoke your own personal journey back in time.

SETTING THE SCENE

1. Do you remember being sick often when you were a child?
2. Do you remember never being sick as a child?
3. Did you enjoy being sick? Did you get special treatment?
4. Did you hate being sick? Were you ignored or ridiculed?
5. Was there a special place that you liked to lie down when you were sick? Your own bedroom? Your parents' bedroom? The living room?

Now that you can see clearly, how did you experience illness? Some typical memories that parents recall had to do with the following:

- how much you felt your parents loved you
- how you felt about being cared for
- how you craved more attention than you ever got
- how self-conscious you were about your body's functions
- how you felt unlike yourself

The following questions that relate to some of the above concerns may evoke certain useful feelings about your past:

6. Did you ever will yourself to be sick on purpose so that you wouldn't have to do something or to go somewhere? How did you feel about "getting away with it"?
7. Do you ever remember being embarrassed because you were ill? Throwing up in school, in public, or in a friend's house?
8. Do you remember fighting your illness or hiding it from your parents?
9. Were you ever ridiculed or punished for being ill? Did it ever seem as though you had inconvenienced your parents?
10. Did one parent seem much more concerned than the other about your health?
11. Did you ever have to be taken to the hospital? Why?
12. Was there ever a time when you or a sibling were seriously ill for a long period of time? How did your parents' attitude change or did it remain the same during this time?

These questions and the intense feelings they may evoke will bring up certain parallels with the way you as a parent currently deal with your child's illnesses. When you're able to recall and evaluate your childhood experiences, you will be better equipped to deal with your current-day feelings about health and illness.

STEP III. GET THE FACTS

Although sickness and health are often relative and depend in large part on emotional states, it's still possible to assemble an array of useful facts that will enable you to examine your problem with illness in a concrete manner.

Jennifer: Jennifer checks in her diary and verifies that Johnny did indeed have six ear infections in an eight-month period. Her notes to herself show that each doctor she saw told her to watch her son carefully, which is exactly what she has done. Unlike many of her friends' children who appear cheerful and unaffected during illnesses, Johnny seems to collapse whenever he gets sick and he heals slowly.

Jennifer looks up ear infections in a child health encyclopedia and discovers that some children tend to have more of these problems at a young age because of their short eustachian tubes and large adenoids. There's more opportunity for infections because fluid accumulates in the tubes and the adenoids block the way, preventing free drainage from the tubes to the throat. Any inflammation such as a cold or teething can start an infection if the bacteria or virus finds its way up the tubes. But often these recurrent infections stop completely when the child gets his two-year molars and lessen as the child grows—and the tubes do, too.

Jennifer can comfort herself with the knowledge that the shunts her family doctor inserted help to equalize the pressure inside and outside the eardrum.

Helene: She calls the pediatrician and asks about Mandy's upset stomach at the dentist's office. She relates the experience and mentions that when the dentist was working on her own teeth, she spit some blood into the bowl. The pediatrician tells Helene that the sight of the blood could have frightened Mandy badly, especially if she wasn't prepared for it. She must have thought her mother was sick or injured. He tells her that some children develop real somatic illnesses in reaction to a traumatic event. Mandy was probably coming down with something anyway, but the nausea, gagging, and fever could have been fueled by the child's insecurity and apprehension.

He suggests that Helene wait at least a month and then take Mandy in to meet a pedodontist, a dentist who deals exclusively with children and adolescents. In addition to having an office decorated with kids in mind, this type of specialist is trained to respect his young patients' feelings. He should also have a bedside manner that a four-year-old can relate to.

It occurs to Helene that the moment Mandy's pediatrician mentioned the word "dentist," she grimaced and made a disparaging remark. She talks to her husband Pete that night about her own feelings toward doctors and illness. Pete points out that she has never trusted a doctor of any sort and that he was the one who found the pediatrician they now see.

Consider All Your Facts

You, too, can compare reality with unconscious or imaginary anxieties by garnering a few basic facts that relate to your child's illness or wellness. The following questions will start you in the right direction for your own factual investigation so that you will be able to think logically and rationally the next time your child is ill.

1. How can you best prepare for the inevitable childhood illnesses that seem to come out of nowhere? *Keep your medicine cabinet stocked with child-formula acetaminophen, a child's medicine spoon with dosages written on the side, a rectal thermometer, nose and ear syringes, saltwater nose drops, and children's cough suppressant.*

2. How do you really know when your child is ill or coming down with something? Dr. Spock's Baby and Child Care *and* Penelope Leach's Childcare Encyclopedia *are two invaluable reference books that you can use as guides to describe your child's symptoms to your doctor over the phone and to alleviate fears of your own about what is actually wrong. If there is real indication of illness, your child's symptoms should be diagnosed by a doctor at his office.*

3. How do you know you're selecting the right physician for

your child? *You should interview several family doctors, pediatricians, and pediatric groups before your child is born. You should also visit the hospitals with which they are affiliated. A group is a particularly good solution for an anxious parent who believes that one doctor is never enough. Optimally, you would like a physician who is warm, wonderful, and funny with your child and forthcoming, informative, and reassuring with you.*

4. Suppose you need an immediate answer about your child's illness? What do you do? *Most pediatricians have a morning call-in service and emergency hot line so that you can describe symptoms to a doctor. He or she will be able to tell you at that point whether your child should be brought in for an examination.*

5. When is it right to get a second opinion about your child's illness? *If your child has been diagnosed with a particular illness and a form of treatment has been suggested that you are uncertain about, by all means get a second opinion. A doctor should be able to explain the illness and its prognosis to you so that you understand and are calm enough about it to explain it to your child. A parent who repeatedly changes doctors, however, and who feels that no specialist can take care of her baby as well as she does is conveying a message to her sick child that doctors are not to be trusted.*

6. Should your child take antibiotics? *This wonderful family of drugs clears up most bacteria, from those that cause ear infections to those responsible for urinary tract infections. Most physicians feel that it's more important to treat the illness quickly and efficiently, and antibiotics do this. On the other hand, antibiotics should not be used for routine colds and sore throats because the body can become resistant, and complications such as rashes, fever, and anemia can occur.*

7. Should your child eat a special, healthful diet to forestall predictions of later cancers and heart disease? *Recent studies have shown that children do not process pesticides sprayed on fruits and vegetables as well as adults, so there is logical concern for their future health. Cholesterol tests done at the age of four show that children can have fatty deposits on their arteries just as adults can. The best advice is to use common sense about*

eating—to stay away from greasy, salty, high-calorie, low-fiber, and processed foods.

8. How do you explain and introduce unfamiliar and sometimes frightening medical procedures to a child? *It's vital to make the experience of going to the doctor an easy, unthreatening one for your child. The man or woman in the white coat should be portrayed to your son or daughter as a good person who knows a lot about making the body well, and the things that person uses in the office should be described as tools specially designed to help kids when they're sick. Children should get used to making well visits on a regular basis so that they have the experience of being in the office and talking to the staff. This way they may feel more confident when they're ill and must be subjected to an unpleasant procedure.*

9. Why are children often more afraid of the dentist than the pediatrician? *Children don't begin to make dental visits until they're three, and after that they see the dentist only twice a year. Today, where AIDS is an ever-present specter in our daily life, dentists wear a mask and rubber gloves as a precautionary measure, and this "costume" can be terribly frightening to a child.*

10. Which communicable childhood diseases should you expect? *With the advent of the measles and rubella vaccines, and one for chicken pox almost ready to be tested, there are few routine illnesses left for your child to be exposed to. Aside from several strains of influenza yearly and many colds and bronchitis—particularly if your child is in day care or preschool—you need worry only about keeping your child home with ear infections, chicken pox, mumps, croup, roseola, and pink eye (conjunctivitis). There are still rare cases of whooping cough and thrush. The prevalent theory these days is that tonsils and adenoids should not be removed except in extreme situations.*

11. What can you do when your child is confined at home to make her feel better? *If your child is feverish or in pain, you can give an analgesic to alleviate it. You should follow, of course, all the doctor's instructions about medication, rest, and diet. The most important factor, however, is the tender loving care that only Mom and Dad can give.*

The facts of your particular situation regarding illness may easily be obscured by your intense feelings. It's therefore doubly important that you sort out reality from fantasy when you want to get your child well as quickly as possible.

STEP IV. UNDERSTAND YOUR CHILD'S POINT OF VIEW

Listening to your child's feelings about his illness or yours will help you to treat him. Many children love to be babied when they're sick; others like to tough it out and can't bear to be torn away from their rough-and-tumble play. And it can be hard to separate fact from fiction; three- and four-year-olds can have some rather bizarre explanations for the way they feel and *why* they think they feel that way. But if you can gauge your child's reaction to being sick, you'll have a partner in your endeavors to help him get well again.

Jennifer: Jennifer usually kept Johnny still and quiet whenever he was ill, having him stay in his crib most of the day and eat lightly. She rarely played with him for fear of tiring him out or getting him overheated. But this time she made a conscious effort to treat him as though he were perfectly fine. She put him down for naps at his regular time and was curious to see that he woke himself up, cheery and ready for play. She didn't overdress him but just made sure that the house was warm enough for him to play in. He ate his usual amount at meals and took his bottles well. She saw that despite his sniffles he seemed alert, his eyes were brighter, and his movements were more deliberate than during other colds.

Helene: Helene was doing a puzzle with Mandy on her third day at home with a stomach virus.

"Would you like to go back to school tomorrow?" Helene asked when Mandy had beaten her for the third straight time.

The child didn't look at her mother. "I don't know."

"Why not? You seem pretty well, and you ate a good lunch today."

"Mommy, I'm still sick," Mandy assured her. "I itch all over and my hair hurts."

Helene controlled her annoyed reaction. She knew now that Mandy really was sick; this was just her way of expressing it. "Well, if you feel this badly tomorrow, maybe we should see Dr. David," she suggested calmly.

"But not that other doctor," Mandy said quickly.

"Who?" Helene asked, playing dumb. She knew that Mandy meant the dentist.

"Where there are bad things and the noisy machine in your mouth that made you spit blood."

"Oh, sweetie, you don't go to a dentist for a stomachache. As a matter of fact, Daddy and I would like you to see a dentist who is just for kids. He has special things in his office that kids like— toys, games—"

"Does he make blood?" Mandy's eyebrows were a worried line across her forehead.

"No. All he does is count your teeth and polish them. Would you like to meet him? The first time we go, we'll just talk, okay?"

"Mommy, I think I have to throw up." Mandy's face was suddenly white.

Helene reached for the bowl that she was keeping by the child's bed and let Mandy spit up a little bile. She wiped her daughter's mouth and eased her back on the pillow. She was very tender with her, and she could see that Mandy appreciated the gentle touch. "Better now?" she asked softly.

"I don't want to go to the dentist," Mandy said suddenly.

"I know, sweetie. But we go to the dentist to be sure we're brushing right and so our teeth don't get sick."

Mandy made a face, then turned away. "I think I want to go to sleep," she said. "We can go to the dentist next week, okay, Mommy?"

"Fine." Helene nodded and pulled up the covers.

By allowing Mandy to make some decisions about dealing with the fear of "bad things" happening, Helene is helping her get control of the situation in her own way. She is also attentive to her illness, which makes Mandy feel that her mother is close and taking care of her at a time when this is important.

Bringing Out Your Child's Feelings

Empathy is always important when you're trying to elicit your child's point of view, but with illness it's probably the key to the issue. When children can talk about their true feelings, it's easier for them to get rid of whatever negative fantasies they may be having about being sick. Remember how lousy you felt as a child being cooped up in a sick room? Think about the way you feel now when you come down with the flu. It's not going to be difficult to convey your understanding to your child. You might want to use the statements below, which some parents have found helpful, to start a dialogue with your child about the way he really feels:

1. "Would you like to lie down on the couch for a while? I know you're too big for naps, but sometimes when you have a high fever, it feels good just to rest. I'll sit with you."
2. "The doctor wants to keep your tummy empty just for a little while so there won't be anything in there to throw up. By tomorrow you can probably eat something such as toast with your favorite jelly."
3. "These dots all over your skin aren't really ugly, they're the way the sickness comes out of you so that you can start to feel better."

Acting on Your Child's Feelings

Your child will let you know what kind of doctoring she really needs. Remember that a sick kid is a cranky kid, and you may get a lot of whining, tantrums, and other objectionable behavior that you don't get when she's feeling fine. It's not necessarily a step backward in her development; don't be too hard on her during the illness. The idea is to act so as to help her feel good about getting well.

1. You might want to set special hours for a sick day—a certain period of time must be spent in bed, but another time block can be devoted to some new library books or a special TV show or game.

2. Consider your own part in your child's illness. Is there some quality time you aren't spending with her that may be causing her to exaggerate her symptoms? While she's still in bed, you can make plans together for a special day or weekend.

3. Books that specifically deal with illness can be very comforting at a time when your child is feeling awful. Stan and Jan Berenstain's *The Berenstain Bears Visit the Doctor* and Fred Rogers's book, *Going to the Hospital*, are two of the many teaching tools available for children.

4. If your child is creating an illness in order to get extra attention, you or your spouse will probably be able to spot it. Point out to your child that sick people need to stay in bed and sleep, and that usually they aren't hungry for snacks. If your child is malingering, he'll demand to get up to play sooner or later.

5. Ask your child how *he* likes the doctor he's been seeing, and discuss the things the physician did to help make him well again. Talk about the scary moments and the funny ones. Try to paint illness and wellness as a natural cycle that everyone goes through.

6. When your child is well, buy her a doctor kit of her very own. This way she can practice on her dolls, animals, and parents when they're sick. This toy will give your child a sense of mastery over the mysterious realm of illness.

7. An illness that requires hospitalization or some unpleasant medical treatment will be frightening to a child who has no experience or knowledge of how his condition must be treated. It is often helpful to use a doll and playact what's going to happen. Allowing the child to give a shot makes it easier for him to get a shot, for example. It's up to the parent and the child's pediatrician to explain things in the simplest terms, with all the love and reassurance they have.

STEP V. GROUND YOURSELF

It's very useful to verbalize your fears about illness and to counter with a quick diffuser that may give you a new perspective on the situation. Remember that grounding can be done throughout the various steps of the Program for Change and will help forestall an anxiety spiral that might make it more difficult for you to take care of your sick child.

Jennifer: She tells herself that her child really doesn't need the kind of smothering she's been giving him. As a matter of fact he seems to be doing better without it. Actually he has fewer coughs and less frequent runny noses thea she has observed recently in several of their neighbors' young children. She reminds herself that Johnny has always healed before and will again, that it didn't really make any difference which doctor they were seeing at the time, and that her son has been thriving since he had the shunts put in.

Helene: She reminds herself how much Mandy likes Dr. David and recalls that just because she grew up with an ambivalent attitude toward doctors and dentists, there's no reason for her child to feel the same. She remembers that Mandy is basically a well child, and when she comes down with something, as all kids do, she needs Helene even more for the special touch that only mommies have. It makes her feel warm and wanted when she thinks about this relationship with her daughter that she never allowed herself to have before.

Some of the suggestions below have been helpful to many parents when they were trying to ground themselves. In the midst of an illness, your own or your child's, it's natural to feel overwhelmed, but reminders similar to those below may help you to deal with your anxiety in a more rational way.

Anxious thought: She's been running a fever on and off for days. High fevers can lead to brain damage. What am I going to do now, in the middle of the night?
Grounding thought: I'll call the doctor's number, and his service will page him for me. He did see her yesterday and reminded me that high fevers are typical in this illness, but it's probably a good idea to check back with him. That way he'll know we're going to bring her in to see him tomorrow if she's still this listless.

Anxious thought: She can't keep anything down. She's so skinny as it is, I'm afraid she'll go right off the charts if she loses any weight.

Grounding thought: When she's well she eats like a horse. I know she's small for her age, but she's wiry. In a couple of days she'll be climbing the furniture again.

Anxious thought: That child in my daughter's day-care group has been coughing every time I've seen her this week. I'm sure my daughter's going to catch it. What should I do?

Grounding thought: I had better tell the head of the center that the teacher is not putting her foot down about when a parent should keep her child home. Of course every kid picks up some germs in day care, but there's no reason for my daughter to be exposed to a really sick child.

STEP VI. STEP BACK AND SEE THE SCENE WITH DIFFERENT EYES

If you think about your underlying feelings concerning illness, your immediate associations may be entirely bad. There doesn't seem to be one element relating to being sick that can be construed as helpful or positive. And yet, if you look at it from another perspective—maintaining *good* health—you may be able to get a different fix on what physical wellness means to you.

Jennifer: She would like to be able to think of Johnny as basically okay and be less concerned with his illnesses.

She steps back and remembers taking Johnny in his stroller on a sunny day last summer. He had just recovered from a cold and was squealing and laughing. His forehead was dry and cool to the touch. She tries to recapture the feeling she had right after he was born: even covered with blood and mucus, he was filled with life. It's not that he was without flaws or perfect, but he could carry on in any situation.

Helene: She would like to help her daughter to form her own good opinions about medical care and to regard physical illness simply as the flip side of physical wellness.

She steps back and thinks about Mandy taking care of her dolls, how she makes sure they dress warmly so they don't get a chill, how she puts them to bed lovingly but firmly when they aren't feeling well. She imagines Mandy and Dr. David together, and she can hear him saying jovially, "Everything's all right now," and Mandy agreeing with him because she, unlike Helene, has a good feeling about doctors. If she could be more supportive of Mandy when she's sick and less insistent that she be well immediately, maybe Mandy would feel taken care of and independent at the same time.

Imagine What You'd Like to Happen

Naturally you would like your child to be in perfect health all the time, but realistically that's not possible. If your child attends a day-care center or preschool where she's exposed to germs on a daily basis, you *know* you're going to have to deal with a variety of coughs, stomachaches, rashes, and mysterious ailments. But if you can see yourself and your child coping with days off from work and school, if you can tell yourself that children recover quickly, you'll be better able to handle the sick days that necessarily become part of your life when you become a parent.

STEP VII. ESTABLISH NEW PATTERNS

At this point in the program you will probably feel a little more secure about using your anxiety over illness as a clue to what is going on in your family when someone is sick. You and your spouse will have a different fix on what it's like to be sick and to deal with a sick child. A good balance of sympathy and clear-headed, practical care can emerge from your talks together.

> *Jennifer:* At her husband's suggestion she joined a play group with Johnny, determined to treat him like a well child all the time. For the first few weeks she was worried about the bigger kids knocking him down and popping his shunts out, but when she finally stopped herself from interfering, she saw that he seemed to be managing well, putting himself in the middle of whatever event was taking place.

Helene: She took some time to ground herself before taking Mandy to the pedodontist. When she got to the office, the doctor's personality charmed Mandy, and Helene took a backseat, watching Mandy establish her own relationship with the new dentist.

A few weeks later when Mandy came down with a high fever and the flu, Helene and Pete took turns staying home with their daughter. Helene realized that the quiet time they spent reading and listening to music together was something very precious. There was an intensity to the connection between them that was never apparent during a busy, active ordinary day. It was a chance, too, for Helene to allow herself to be a softer, more tender person.

PARENTS' SUGGESTIONS

Taking care of a sick child or being sick yourself has probably forced you to come up with innovative ideas to cope in a more comfortable manner. The suggestions below by no means cover the entire repertoire, but they can serve as a springboard for you to take off on your own to establish new patterns in the areas of health and illness.

1. Start by trying to follow a program of good health as a family. This may mean a new consideration of diet, exercise, dressing appropriately for the weather, and getting enough rest.
2. Find a pediatrician or a pediatric group you like and trust, one who is affiliated with a reputable, modern hospital. Referrals from friends with children are your best bet.
3. Preventive medicine is the best kind. Make sure you check with your pediatrician about the immunizations your baby needs and when she should have regular checkups.
4. Learn to ask the doctor for what *you* need. If you're confused about symptoms or treatments and want to call the doctor a second time, assure yourself that this is your prerogative.
5. Keep all medicines—prescription and over-the-counter—in a locked box, out of reach of children.
6. When you are ill and your child is well, don't try to be a martyr and keep going. You can explain simply to your child

that there are a few rules to follow while you're recuperat-
ing—such as no jumping on the sickbed, less noise in the
house, and fewer demands—so that you'll get well and will
be able to play later. If you don't give yourself a break when
you feel awful, you'll end up doubly burdened, which can
only make you a less competent parent.

7. If you or your child comes down with something, arrange
your work and home situation accordingly. If your spouse
can't stand in for you, call grandparents, friends who live
nearby, and several sitters so you'll have a backup at a moment's notice.

8. If your child is about to meet a new doctor, take the time to
prepare for the visit. Find out from the nurse in advance
what kind of special equipment this doctor uses and exactly
what the child will go through at the office. If your doctor
or dentist will agree to make the time, you might want to
bring your child in just to say hello and get acquainted before
the physician actually does anything.

9. If you must take your child to the hospital, be sure to have
your medical insurance card and any necessary forms with
you.

10. Try not to smother your sick child. Some time alone—spent
either asleep or awake—is very important to a young child's
recovery process. A favorite toy or doll can act as a parent
surrogate.

MAKING THE NEXT ILLNESS MORE BEARABLE

Remember that dealing with your child's, your spouse's, or your
own illness is not a one-time event. If you were overly anxious
the last time your daughter was sick for a week and you had to
stay home with her, tell yourself that this time you can function
better because you've had more experience. Now that you've seen
how well she responds to treatment and recovers, you can use
the anxiety in a constructive way to take care of yourself and her
at the same time.

9
Anxieties about Safety and Injury

Which of the following statements is true for you?

1. I can feel a knot in my stomach when I watch my toddler trying to walk. It's so hard to keep from rushing over to help him. I'm sure something's going to happen.
2. I never even think about where my toddler has wandered because my house is completely baby-proofed.
3. I get absolutely panicked when I see a bee come near my child. I'm allergic to bee stings, so I keep him inside most of the summer just in case he is, too.
4. I have a hard time leaving my son at preschool and going to work. I'm afraid that he'll have a terrible accident if I'm not there to watch him every second.

You have probably worried about all of the above accidents occurring—and many more. It's almost impossible not to worry when your little one starts moving around in the world because *you* know (though he hasn't a clue) that he just learned how to walk and is unsteady on his feet. You know that the radiator is hot; to him it just looks painted. You know that he can drown in a shallow pool; all he can think about is splashing.

A hurt child calls forth your animal protectiveness and a feeling of anxiety that can make you overly emotional, less thoughtful, and therefore less competent parents. The element of guilt looms large. You tell yourself that if you worked really hard at it, you could construct the perfect safety bubble for your child, a padded room with no electrical outlets, no heating units, no sharp objects, nothing to climb, no place to pinch. Baby-proofing and, later, child-proofing the home and yard is essential, but no parent can protect his child from every mishap. In fact, no one should try.

The only way a child learns is by making mistakes. As he exercises his newfound physical abilities he grows in his understanding of the world. By trying a knob—jiggling, shoving, hitting, and finally turning it—he learns how to open a door. The ultimate show-and-tell experience is the hand demonstrating to the brain how to think about something in a new way.

Naturally, because you know your own child, you understand how much she can take. Every child needs to be challenged, and it's the parents' responsibility to keep one step ahead of her, realizing her physical limitations, daring her to go up to that barrier, and maybe when she's ready, just a little beyond. The parent who has confidence that her baby can and will learn to walk on her own will give that infant the confidence she needs to try it, fail, try it again, fail again, and finally succeed.

MOBILITY MEANS DANGER—AND LEARNING

You can protect an infant fairly easily from real danger, but you have much less control over your mobile one-year-old who is into everything. Suddenly you are not the center and hub of your child's world. He has interests above and beyond you. A toddler's natural curiosity will make it necessary for him to walk into walls, roll down hills, and throw himself downstairs. As grown-ups we're in the difficult position of knowing exactly what the consequence of our child's actions will be. It's our hard job to let him experience the world without holding him back. Eventually he'll learn to put limits on himself so that he doesn't go out of control. It's up to you, the parent, at this point in your child's development, to be watchful but not smothering.

Injuries do cause pain, but our reactions to pain are primarily learned responses. If you scream when your child crashes to the ground, he's probably going to burst out crying because he thinks he's supposed to. But different children have different thresholds for pain, and if you belittle your child for sobbing over a bruised knee, you may be setting yourself up for situations where he'll injure himself again and again, just trying to get a sympathetic reaction from you.

When accidents do occur it's important to deal with the anxiety they provoke without allowing it to overwhelm you. This was very difficult for Elizabeth, as we'll see, when her two-year-old daughter burned her hand.

NOT EVERY ACCIDENT IS YOUR FAULT

Elizabeth's doctor had suggested that she use a hot steam vaporizer for her cold, but she was naturally concerned about keeping it on the coffee table when Sally was around, so she waited until she had put the child in her room for a nap before turning it on. Half an hour later she got up to go to the bathroom. When she came out she saw Sally, a mischievous grin on her face, making a beeline from her bedroom door to the steaming vaporizer on the kitchen table.

"Sally! No, get away! You'll be hurt!" She lunged for her daughter, but the two-year-old was quicker and made it to the table as though she had won a race, her palm outstretched toward the lovely plume of smoke coming out of the machine.

"Sally was howling with pain; I screamed, I think," Elizabeth said. "I swooped her up in my arms, furious with myself that I'd turned that horrible thing on and let her get to it. What kind of mother am I anyway, that I would care more about my cold than her safety? I felt paralyzed, as though I couldn't do anything for her but hold her and say I was sorry.

"Luckily, my husband Jim was in the next room. He ran the

cold water full blast in the sink and dunked Sally's hand in it.
Then he tried to calm me while he dialed the pediatrician. He
even remembered where we'd put the special prescription cream
for burns, and he stuck Sally's hand right in the jar while the
doctor gave instructions. I wasn't myself for another day; if I
hadn't had a cold, if I hadn't used the vaporizer, if I'd at least
been right next to it when she came into the room, none of this
would have happened. I felt so awful."

Elizabeth became hysterical when she saw her two-year-old
going toward the vaporizer because she knew what harm it could
do and because her preparation for protecting her child from it
had failed. Elizabeth's anxiety pushed her over the edge of control;
she felt too guilty to do anything useful for her child. Luckily she
could rely on her husband to balance the situation. His calm,
methodical caretaking made it possible for Sally's physical wound
to be treated. It's not hard to see that the psychological wound—
Elizabeth's guilt and anxiety—will take longer to heal than Sally's
burned hand.

SAFETY AND THE OLDER CHILD

When your child is three or four and his physical abilities are
more developed, he feels omnipotent, oblivious to danger. A
mother or father who starts worrying a lot about his child's safety
at this stage is often masking his own inability to separate. If you
hold your child back from climbing, running, sliding, falling *for
his own good,* what you're really doing is stunting his growth. Of
course you're going to be concerned because you love him, but
your reactions to his valiant attempts will often determine what
heights he's eventually able to reach.

A parent who screams "No!" when she sees her child about to
burn herself, as Elizabeth did, is reacting out of panic to an
emergency. The parent who yells "No!" when she sees her precious
daughter dangling by her knees upside down from a playground
gym, however, is creating an emergency when one doesn't really
exist. This mother needs to be in control all the time, where she
can anticipate everything that's going to happen to her child. But

what she's doing is affecting her daughter's sense of how safe she is by constantly questioning it. She's also creating a terrible conflict in her child. The girl is curious and is able, but her mother tells her she isn't, that she's going to be hurt. If enough of these problematic events occur, she'll begin to doubt her own abilities and may eventually become fearful of anything new, that is, anything that would displease her mother.

A USEFUL AMOUNT OF FEAR

It is essential, of course, that every child be taught a useful amount of fear. You have to alert her to real dangers—cars, strange dogs, poisonous berries, broken glass—but the rules about not touching and not running out and not eating must be explained so that the child can understand; otherwise the lesson will never stick.

One of the consequences of modern life is that it has become increasingly necessary to warn our children against strangers, whether they are purposely malicious people or mentally unbalanced. It's good, sound thinking to warn your child to stay close in a large public place because it's hard to tell at a quick glance whether the strangers you encounter are harmless or potentially dangerous. But cautioning a mischievous three-year-old who has no idea why you should warn him about something he has no experience with doesn't always work. This is what happened to William, who was in the men's shop in a mall with his son Scott. He had given his standard lecture about staying where he could be seen and not wandering off, and he thought Scott was listening.

"I turned away for a second and he was gone," William said. "I remembered that every time we were in the store Scott would hide in those round clothing racks, and when I called him, he'd come. This time he didn't. The store was crowded. I was sweating. I asked a salesperson if she'd seen Scott, and she began quizzing me on what he was wearing and what other stores we'd gone into together. It was as if she didn't think a father was capable of taking care of his son all by himself.

"I imagined Scott being carted off by some weirdo child molester, the guy handing Scott a lollipop and getting him to walk out without making a fuss. I saw the headlines: FATHER ABANDONS SON IN MALL; KID FOUND DEAD IN PARKING LOT. I couldn't think. I just did what this dumb lady suggested and raced out of the store to retrace my steps.

"I couldn't find him anywhere; I was frantic. About a half hour later I came back to the men's store where I'd lost him. I was haranguing the clerk at the cash register when I heard a little sob. I followed the sound back to the dressing room and there he was. We hugged each other; I was kind of angry, but I was crying too hard to yell at him and he was crying too hard to listen. I recalled those stories people tell about how they died and came back again. When I held him I could feel my heart pounding like a jackhammer."

William panicked. You may feel that his reaction was completely appropriate, given the circumstances, but perhaps if he had stopped for a moment to sort out his fears for his son, he might not have bolted from the store so quickly. He wouldn't have allowed his emotions to override his good sense. And if Elizabeth had given herself more credit for being a responsible parent, she might not have felt so guilt ridden that she needed her husband to take over for her. In order for them to use their anxiety in a constructive way the next time their children's safety may be in peril, it will be useful for them to consider the Program for Change.

Your Program for Change

For a complete description of how to use this program effectively, see Chapter 4, page 61.

STEP I. IDENTIFY WHAT'S REALLY BOTHERING YOU
STEP II. CONNECT WITH YOUR PAST
STEP III. GET THE FACTS
STEP IV. UNDERSTAND YOUR CHILD'S POINT OF VIEW
STEP V. GROUND YOURSELF

STEP VI. STEP BACK AND SEE THE SCENE WITH DIFFERENT EYES
STEP VII. ESTABLISH NEW PATTERNS

STEP I. IDENTIFY WHAT'S REALLY BOTHERING YOU

Identifying your central issue in an incident that involves danger
and injury to your child may be particularly difficult if you are
spiraling. In this case you might want to go directly to Step V
and ground yourself before using each subsequent part of the
program.

Elizabeth was unable to stop her daughter Sally from burning
her hand. *What is it about this experience that's really bothering
Elizabeth?*

The worst thing, perhaps, is that Elizabeth had thought about
the danger and made every attempt to prevent it, but despite her
good intentions and her concern for her child, she was unable
to stop Sally from burning herself.

In one way she was upset because she misjudged her daughter's
abilities and perceptions. She was wrong on every count; she
never figured on Sally being able to get out of her crib, on her
going immediately to the steam, or on her being able to outrun
her to get to the danger.

Does she feel inadequate as a parent? She says that she was
"paralyzed," that only her husband's quick thinking saved the
day. She is almost acting like a child in this situation herself—
she's vulnerable, out of control, waiting for an authority figure
to take over.

What about William's problem with his older child who ran
away from him in the mall? *What is it about this experience that's
really bothering William?*

First, he has been in this situation before and thinks he knows
what to expect from his son. Previously when Scott hid from his
father, he would come when called. But now he was testing his
father's patience and exercising his own newfound autonomy.
William was obviously angry that his son didn't comply as he
used to. Then he was aggravated by the attitude of the sales-

woman. How dare she assume that he was not able to take care of his son on his own? Except that *he* felt he had failed, so her criticism really hit home.

Naturally he was concerned about the unknown factor: other people in the mall. He had no means of controling strangers' access to his child when he had no idea where his child was.

There wasn't anything he could do about unknowns, but if he could stop himself from spiraling, at least he would be able to narrow down his options—somewhat like a detective—by a process of elimination. Once he was able to identify the central issue of his anxiety, he would be better equipped to deal with his son's disappearance and prevent the same thing from happening again.

What's Really Bothering You

What about your particular issues around safety and danger? Some typical parental concerns are as follows:

- fearing that nothing you do is enough
- fearing a loss of your child's dependence on you
- feeling insecure about yourself; unable to protect yourself or your child
- projecting your own fears onto your child's situation

If you are having any anxieties about your abilities to keep your child safe, you might want to look at the following questions that relate to one or several of the above concerns:

1. Are you always on the lookout for dangers?
2. Are you always concerned that your home isn't baby-proofed enough?
3. Do you feel safe at home but unsafe in the world outside, populated by bigger, stronger children, adults, cars, animals, and other unknowns?
4. Do you ever feel incapable of protecting your child from harm? What kind?
5. Do you feel that your child is safer with your spouse than with you? Not as safe?

6. Do you feel pain when you see your child in pain?
7. Do you restrict your toddler or preschooler from new activities he wants to try because they might be dangerous?
8. What makes you nervous about strangers? Their physical appearance? Their mannerisms? The situation in which you've met them?
9. Do you trust your child to obey safety rules you've set down?
10. How anxious do you get about leaving babysitters alone with your child? How well do you screen them in advance?

If you're the kind of person who's always looking over your shoulder and second-guessing yourself, you are probably hypervigilant when it comes to your child's safety. This doesn't mean, however, that you'll be any more successful than the more relaxed parent at warding off danger. Your central issue may not really have anything to do with the threat of injury but may be more closely related to your personal anxiety about separating or your concern that you're not being the very best parent you can possibly be.

STEP II. CONNECT WITH YOUR PAST

It's going to be enormously important now to think back to when you were small and felt that only your big, strong parent could keep you from harm. These will undoubtedly be difficult memories to recall, but they're essential in your exploration of the way in which you're reacting to your child's safety issues right now.

Elizabeth: Elizabeth remembers being pulled into the ocean by the undertow when she was about five or six. Her father grabbed her, gasping and choking, and carried her back to where her mother, frantic at having watched her daughter almost drown, was sitting on the sand with Elizabeth's little brother. Her father began screaming at her mother that she was supposed to be watching Elizabeth. Her mother yelled back that it was all his fault because he'd told her that morning she was big enough to swim in the ocean. He said children had to be encouraged to try things or otherwise they'd be afraid all their lives. Since her father was the one who'd saved Elizabeth, in her memory she cast him in the role of hero, though in reality he was a person who never took responsibility for his actions or his children's well-being. Elizabeth's parents' differences over how to deal with her in unsafe situations left her feeling insecure about herself.

William: William, the oldest of three brothers, was a real daredevil when he was a child. His mother was always warning him not to play too hard, jump too high, or run too far, but he rarely listened and nothing bad ever happened to him. Then one morning when he was seven his baby brother was squirming in his high chair and managed to pitch right out of it, banging his head against the side of the radiator as William looked on.

The child had to be rushed to the hospital, and all that day in school William was certain he was going to come home to learn that his brother had died. Although it was just a concussion, that experience stayed with William. And his mother, understandably, became very upset each time one of the children tried something dangerous. As a child, William associated danger with a lot of confusion and chaos.

How You Can Connect with Your Past

Set the scene by remembering where you were and where your parents were just before some childhood accident or injury occurred. If your parents weren't present, this may have given you even more cause for anxiety. Move along chronologically in your mind until you reach the memory of the frightening situation that is causing you pain. Your recollections will help you to get a handle on the feelings you have now, as a parent with concerns for your own child's safety.

SETTING THE SCENE

1. When you were growing up, how much physical freedom were you allowed? Do you remember climbing on chairs to get things on high shelves? Do you remember sliding down the banister?

2. What was your mother's attitude toward a skinned knee? Your father's?
3. Were you a daredevil? Were you a "scaredy-cat"?
4. Do you ever remember being in a situation where you felt physically threatened? What was it?
5. Did you ever see one of your siblings injured? Your parents?

Now that you can see clearly, how did you experience safety? Some typical memories that many parents recall had to do with the following:

· not being taught how to anticipate things that might happen
· parents' inconsistencies with each other in their care
· putting themselves in danger to get more attention
· being thought of as a nuisance for getting into trouble

The following questions that relate to some of the above concerns may evoke certain useful feelings about your past.

6. Did your parents ever warn you not to do something because you'd be hurt?
7. Can you remember a childhood injury in detail? Did you ever . . .
    . . . fall down a flight of stairs or out of a tree?
    . . . burn yourself?
    . . . cut yourself?
    . . . fracture a limb?
    . . . knock yourself out?
    . . . nearly drown?
8. When you were injured, were your parents sympathetic? Did they agree on how to take care of you?
9. Were you ever punished for having an accident or getting lost?
10. Did you ever try to get hurt on purpose in order to get sympathy?
11. Were you ever injured or lost when your parent wasn't around? How did it make you feel?

Some of what you may recall about getting injured may make you feel strangely proud because, after all, you did attempt something new and survive. Whether this feeling of pride helps to ease your anxiety about your own child is another matter, but it certainly should give you a new perspective on your parental attitudes toward safety and danger. The anxiety or lack of it that you bring to your child as he faces new tasks and challenges will affect the way he approaches them.

STEP III. GET THE FACTS

Physical situations generally happen so fast that it's difficult to tell what's really going on. But there are always specific details you can examine. Think about what happened to your child the last time you were in a similar situation. Have you really watched your son or daughter on that staircase lately? In the playground? In the mall? Are you close enough to catch him if he's in real trouble? Remember that your child's abilities grow as he grows— in spurts—and what he couldn't do last week he may master easily today. Give him a chance to show you.

> *Elizabeth:* Sally's pediatrician quizzed Elizabeth thoroughly on her memory of the event and found, by analyzing the elements, that the only thing she'd done "wrong" was not to unplug the vaporizer when she left the living room. The doctor explained that this experience wouldn't scar the child for life emotionally, nor would she feel that her mother had let her down. The pediatrician pointed out that it was the rare parent who was able to react rationally when she saw her child trying something new and difficult or dangerous.
>
> Elizabeth and her husband Jim read several books on Sally's stage of development and realized that the toddler's curiosity was a vital part of her growth. Elizabeth was also relieved to read that the trauma of the burn would probably make Sally warier the next time she was in a situation where she had an opportunity to touch something hot.
>
> *William:* He called security at the mall and found that they had no specific way of dealing with lost children but that each clerk

in each store had been notified to bring any child unaccompanied by a parent to the central information booth. If William had gone to the booth, he would have been able to use the paging system that broadcasts throughout the mall. Perhaps if Scott had heard his father's voice calling his name over a loudspeaker, he would have come out immediately.

William, too, looked at a child development book to find out why Scott, who had previously come when called, now stayed hidden. The book suggested that this might have been due to a recent argument at home, to new and stricter rules being enforced, to a new fear the child had developed and not talked about, or simply to the child's stronger desire to be independent.

The facts you can garner with relation to your child's safety will make you a more prepared and therefore, possibly, a less anxious parent. This is one instance where you can really use your anxiety to tell you what you anticipate and perhaps to forestall it by physically doing something preventive *before* an accident can happen.

Consider All Your Facts

1. Where can you get approved, baby-proof items? *Subscribe to the catalog "Perfectly Safe," which offers every conceivable item to child-proof your life. Even if you don't buy, the products and pictures will give you a good idea of what you should be doing to make your house and yard safer for a physically inexperienced child. The address is: 7245 Whipple Avenue, N.W., North Canton, Ohio 44720.*

2. How do you protect your child in a car? *By buckling him into an approved car seat before you drive anywhere. It is law in most states that any child under the age of four or weighing under forty pounds must be secured in a car seat. After your child has passed the age and weight restrictions, have him learn to use his seatbelt, and set a good example by using your own.*

3. Is it true that a baby could drown in the bathtub? *Yes, a child who is unable to right himself in a slippery tub could knock himself unconscious on the porcelain and slide under the water. Bathmats*

and specially designed bath rings will support the child, but they are no substitute for a parent on the premises.

4. How do you know that your baby who mouths everything won't choke on a toy? *If you have older children in the house, they must be taught to keep small parts of toys out of the infant's reach. Be careful about dropping loose change or other small objects. Always read the manufacturer's age restrictions on a toy before allowing your baby to play with it. Outdoors, be vigilant about pebbles and unknown plants.*

5. Do you worry a great deal about your dog or cat injuring your baby or toddler? *Domestic pets must be exposed to and allowed to sniff the newborn on a regular basis so they come to think of him as a member of the household rather than a stranger. Some experts counsel getting the animal his own toys so that he won't feel jealous about the baby's toys. Never leave your child alone with a pet no matter how well you think you know the animal's personality.*

6. How can you keep your child from touching a hot stove? *From her first days repeat "Hot! No!" to your baby when she gets near a radiator, stove, or hot appliance. She will still probably try to touch the forbidden object, but the repeated verbal cue will reinforce Mommy and Daddy's attitude for her.*

The facts leave out a very important point: accidents do happen. You'll never be able to keep your infant or child entirely safe, but you can make certain that you've eliminated many dangerous elements if you scout out your house and yard. Make lists of possible occurrences and think logically about what you can do to try to prevent them.

STEP IV. UNDERSTAND YOUR CHILD'S POINT OF VIEW

Showing your child that you understand his need to get into everything will make it easier for him to accept warnings or cautions when it's necessary for you to give them. You can deepen your relationship with your child by showing empathy after an accident—when he needs you most.

Elizabeth: Sally started shying away or running out of the room whenever she saw a stove, a radiator, a toaster—any heating element at all. She also acted fearful with Elizabeth, as though she didn't trust her anymore. Elizabeth wanted to figure out how to make her daughter feel secure when she was with her, so she decided to try a challenging experience she and Sally could have together. On the first nice day she took Sally to the park, but she could see the child shying away from the merry-go-round, the slide, and the swings.

"Could you take Mommy on the slide?" Elizabeth asked. Sally shook her head.

"Is that slide too high? Maybe just the hill, over here." She lay down on the ground and rolled down the hill, while Sally, amazed at her usually sedentary mother, started laughing and pointing.

"Oh, Mommy's having such a good time doing this," Elizabeth said, smiling. "I bet you'd like it, too." And Elizabeth rolled down again. At last Sally scrambled down after her. By the end of the afternoon Elizabeth had persuaded her to try all the playground equipment because she had tried them first. She could see Sally's body unfolding, becoming loose and relaxed, as she started to play and enjoy herself.

William: While William was helping Scott put his puppet theater together one night, Scott picked up a rabbit puppet and put it on. "I'm a big boy. I'm going out to the playground by myself right now," he boasted.

William, who felt a little uncomfortable about talking to Scott, decided to do it indirectly, through a puppet. He put a raccoon on his hand. "I know your Mommy and Daddy would want to know where you are, even though you can do it alone. Why don't you go tell them."

"Uh-uh. They'll say no. They always do."

William wondered whether Scott felt as if he and Ann were sitting on him all the time. The playacting with puppets had allowed the child to protest his parents' treatment of him. Maybe they were remembering him more as a baby than as the child he had become. Maybe it was time to make a few changes.

William took off the raccoon puppet and put on a Mickey Mouse puppet. "Oh, there you are, Rabbit!" he exclaimed. "Your dad's been looking all over for you. He was just saying it was too bad that you weren't around because he wanted to plan a special Sunday with you. But if you're not around, he can't ask your opinion."

Scott frowned and took off his puppet. "I don't want to play this anymore," he said. "I'm not Rabbit, I'm Scott."

"That's right," William agreed, removing his puppet. "And I'm your dad. Scott, I know you're a big boy, and I think maybe Mommy and I should give you a little more responsibility than we have. But that's only when we know where you are and what you're doing. When we go to a mall, where there are a lot of strangers, people we don't know who don't know us, it's important that we stick close to each other and that you listen to what I say. That's not a rule, it's just a fact."

"What could happen to me if I didn't come out when you called me?" Scott muttered. "Could someone bad hurt me?"

William paused. He didn't want to scare the child, but he did want to make a point. "That doesn't happen often, but yes, there are bad people around who aren't nice to kids. The point is that when you didn't come out of hiding, I got worried that I'd lost you, and you got worried that you'd lost me."

"I don't ever want that to happen again, Daddy," Scott sobbed.

"Then we won't let it!" William promised, and hugged his son tightly.

Bringing Out Your Child's Feelings

You don't want to frighten your child with repeated warnings but instead want to elicit his fears and fantasies with pointed questions. Even children who run forward into every new situation tend to have a variety of anxieties about danger and safety that they may be able to articulate to a sensitive, sympathetic parent. You might try statements like the following, which a variety of parents have found helpful:

1. "Those cars are going so fast. You'd better hold my hand and look left and right for me so I'll know when I should cross the street."

2. "Are those the biggest waves you ever saw? If we build our castle a little farther back in the sand, it won't get washed away and we won't get splashed."

3. "Today, Aunt Mary's going to take you in the subway for the first time. Can you repeat the special subway rules about holding hands and not talking to strangers to her, so she won't forget and you won't either?"

Acting on Your Child's Feelings

1. Help your baby learn about new physical situations. If she's just beginning to climb stairs, stay behind her in case she starts to tumble backward, not ahead of her to coax her upward.
2. Tell your preschooler what the smoke alarms in your house are for and explain procedures you would use if they went off. Many preschools and day-care centers feature visits from firemen, and at home you can reinforce the information they give.
3. If your older child is cautious about new playground equipment, you can make it a little easier for her by helping her become familiar with it. For example, you can climb up the high slide with her and send her doll down first. Then let her try it while you hold her finger. Then suggest that she do it while you're a distance apart—always close enough to sweep her away from real danger. This will allow her to assert her independence and at the same time give her a sense of security that her parent is near.
4. Have your child playact a scene in the mall, the subway, or the train station at home with dolls. This will tell you how he'll deal with the real thing.
5. If you've been using a child-lock leash to keep your child close in a public place, you might try a different tactic. Yes, you have physical control, but unless your child knows the rules and can repeat them back to you, you haven't accomplished your mission of keeping him safe because he understands the value of being safe. The leash restraint only tells your child that you don't trust him and that you don't believe he can follow instructions.
6. If you went through an accident together, ask your child what he thinks might have caused it and how it might be prevented

next time. Remind him that things turned out okay and that his injury is healing.

7. There are numerous songs about crossing the street safely and many about remembering your name, address, and telephone number. The Sesame Street books often talk about safety in the playground and at the pool, lake, or ocean. Another series by Dorothy Chlad includes the titles *When There Is a Fire ... Go Outside* and *When I Cross the Street*. A good book that cautions but doesn't terrify children is *The Berenstain Bears Learn about Strangers* by Stan and Jan Berenstain. The companion piece for parents is *How to Raise a Street-Smart Child* by Grace Hechinger.

Some parents feel more anxious with an adventuresome child; some feel more anxious with a less daring child who always seems on the brink of injuring himself because he's not physically agile. The increased empathy you have when you see your child having trouble, however, may make the clinging baby even more clinging. The child who will race full tilt into a tree, pick himself up, and run on laughing may come home bloody but unbowed, regardless of his mother's nerves.

Maybe once, long ago, you yourself were that wild child. Using your empathy will go a long way here. If you can recall the way you felt about daring the impossible and transmit that feeling to your child, you will be able to engender a kind of trust that will make it possible for you to work together on safety prevention.

STEP V. GROUND YOURSELF

There can be no more important step than grounding when it comes to anxieties about your child's safety. If you're starting to panic, try to talk yourself down. It's enormously difficult to keep control of yourself when you imagine your child hurt or lost, but if you keep verbalizing exactly what's going on, you'll have a better chance of thinking logically and perhaps preventing a more serious consequence from the accident that's about to take place.

Elizabeth: She tells herself that the world may be a dangerous place, filled with electric sockets and sharp edges, but she is *usually* very close to her child and will probably react now much more quickly than she did during the vaporizer incident. She can tell herself that a child who has put her hand on a hot stove is going to be much less likely to do it again. She can tell herself that Sally is alive and well, thanks in no small part to her own vigilance in re-child-proofing her environment after the accident.

William: He can tell himself that Scott now has a much better understanding of the difference between playing at home and playing in public and that he has recently developed eyes in the back of his head and is no longer quite as trusting in a strange place as he was before the incident. He can tell himself that he and Ann have started working on giving Scott more power over his own realm so that he doesn't feel he has to hide from his parents.

The following suggestions may give you a hint as to what you might say to yourself in the midst of a difficult situation involving an injury or accident. These diffusers will help you to gain control over your anxiety momentarily so that you can stop a spiral before it overwhelms you and start to think more clearly.

Anxious thought: She's nearly at the top of the stairs! She's wobbling! She's going to fall!
Grounding thought: I'm right behind her, so the worst that could happen is that she'd sit right down where she is. She's wearing a padded diaper, which means it would hurt her less than it would me if I fell.

Anxious thought: He's never climbed a tree before. He's going to fall and kill himself. I've got to stop him!
Grounding thought: He's been watching his older friends climb that tree all summer, and he finally feels ready to try it himself. Look at the excitement in his face; he's really mastering something on his own. That branch isn't very far from the ground if he *does* fall.

Anxious thought: Why did I take him to this circus? There are so many people here, and all he wants to do is run away from me. What if someone grabs him?

Grounding thought: He's wearing a red jacket, and I can see him. We went over the rules together before we came, and he knows that when I yell "Apples!" he has to come right to me. I'll do it now, just to test our system.

STEP VI. STEP BACK AND SEE THE SCENE WITH DIFFERENT EYES

Your imagination probably hasn't had too much trouble conjuring up worst-case scenarios, but this is the time to think up some positive options. When you can imagine what you and your child might do the next time something dangerous happens, you'll be better able to keep your wits about you when a real, distressing situation occurs.

Elizabeth: She would like to be able to care for her daughter in an emergency.

She steps back and tries to imagine another frightening situation: suppose Sally were about to stick her finger in the light socket. She sees herself calling to Sally and diverting her attention from the dangerous element. Then she imagines that Sally ignores her and does get a shock. She pictures herself in control, upset but perfectly capable of wrapping Sally in a blanket and holding her as she calls 911 for help.

William: He would like to give his son a little responsibility, but he also wants his child to pay attention to the necessary rules that will help keep him safe.

William steps back and remembers taking Scott fishing with him a few months ago. It was the first time, William recalls, that he thought of his child as a pal, a person he could share things with. At the same time the child really listened to his father warning him about how to hold the pointed fish hook and how to be careful not to fall off the steep bank. William takes this imaginary picture and transfers it to a scene in a crowded store. Now that Scott knows the rules and the reasons for them, William imagines calling him, then waiting, without getting angry or panicked, to hear the voice from the dressing room.

Imagine What You'd Like to Happen

It goes without saying that you'd like to prevent accidents and injuries from occurring. But life just isn't like that, and you're going to have to handle more than a few mishaps before your child is grown. If you can step back and tell yourself that it's necessary to your child's development for him to dare difficult if not impossible feats, that curiosity may cause accidents but it also promotes growth, you will be better able to handle the unpleasant events that occur in every parent's life. Step back and consider the fact that children's bones are more resilient than adults' and heal more quickly if they break.

STEP VII. ESTABLISH NEW PATTERNS

If you can keep grounding yourself throughout this application of the program, you will overcome the major hurdle—panic—that most parents experience with their child's safety. But none of us can prevent the inevitable, and none of us can be perfect people or perfect parents. Most of our children will experience some trauma before they're grown—and they will heal.

Elizabeth: She didn't push Sally to try new things but attempted to get the toddler to feel more secure in her surroundings. She and Sally enrolled in a baby gym class where they both had an opportunity to master new physical feats under the direction of a sympathetic teacher. As Elizabeth watched Sally gain more confidence in her physical abilities, she stepped back a little more and could feel herself relaxing. Watching her daughter trip and fall and recover was helpful to Elizabeth in overcoming her guilt about not being able to prevent Sally's burn. At the same time, seeing Sally blossom among the other kids, she was able to reinforce her own pride in her abilities as a mother.

William: William and Scott started spending more time together at home and on outings, and William made sure that Scott understood the ground rules before they went anywhere new. William and Ann started giving Scott an allowance for helping to set the table and feeding the dog, and he was told that he could spend the money he earned on toys or save it, as he wished. This new responsibility made the child feel that he was in control of his world, and it was easier for him to understand and assimilate the rules of his household.

PARENTS' SUGGESTIONS

Here are a few of the ideas parents have provided about their own methods of dealing with safety and injury, along with actions they've taken that have allowed them to rest more easily. You may think of more as you begin to consider how they apply to you and your child.

1. It's crucial to be psychologically attuned to safety, but first you must be sure you're physically safe. This means keeping the phone number of your doctor, hospital, police, poison-control center, and ambulance right on each phone in the house and making sure you know where your backup sitters are at any given time.

2. Make sure that your home is really baby- and child-proofed. There should be plugs in all electrical sockets, baby gates in front of stairs (top and bottom), rounded corners on tables at child height, and smoke alarms in the nursery and throughout the house. Medicines should be kept in a locked box, and all cleaning products stored out of reach.

3. Get a baby monitor so that you can hear what's going on in your infant's room when you're not present.

4. Never leave your infant or toddler alone in the bathtub.

5. Keep a first-aid kit stocked with gauze, merthiolate for disinfecting cuts and scrapes, Silvadene cream for burns (available by prescription), and oil of ipecac to induce vomiting.

You might consider taking a basic first-aid course that would teach you how to deal with emergencies.

6. Make sure the territory right outside your home is safe. Check for poison ivy, stray dogs, and so forth, and think about installing a fence with a child lock.

7. Be certain your child has well-fitting play shoes with nonskid soles. Check your child's size every three months at a store that carries children's shoes.

8. Dress your child wisely for activities outside. Soft baby skin needs protective covering on the beach and in hot weather, and should be adequately protected from cold. Older children should be encouraged to dress appropriately to protect them from sunburn, sunstroke, windburn, and colds.

9. Carry "Sting-Away" capsules with menthol-gel (available by prescription) during summer months to reduce the potency of bug venom. If you know from experience that your child is allergic to bee stings, he or she should wear a necklace or bracelet with the pertinent medical information stamped on it. Ask your physician about epinephrine injections for allergic reactions to stings.

10. If you have a swimming pool, never allow your child to play beside it unattended, even if you can see him from the kitchen window.

11. If you go boating with your child, you must have him wear a life preserver that fits. You should, too.

12. If your child is going to ride on the back of your bicycle, he must wear a protective helmet and be strapped into a secured baby seat.

13. Be street smart about city traffic with your child and make sure he knows the rules. Even if you hold hands, be careful at intersections to keep him from stepping down in case a bus or taxi is about to careen around the corner.

14. Check out each new play area before your child begins to play. Look for poison ivy, broken glass, and—though it's unfortunate you should have to think this way—discarded hypodermic needles and crack vials.

THE NEXT TIME THERE'S AN ACCIDENT

If you've recently gone through a scary incident with your child, you can congratulate yourself for getting through it. Accidents happen to *everyone;* their occurrence has very little to do with your parenting skills. Injuries are part of your child's growing experience and education. If he went through his childhood without a scratch, he'd be unprepared to deal with the craziness of modern life.

The physical realm causes anxiety because it seems so palpable and changeable. As parents you're always trying to make the world nice and stable for your tender and untried child, so you probably tend to get anxious when the world doesn't behave the way you want it to. But the way you manage even the most problematic event that touches your child can make a difference in how he accepts the fluctuations and uncertainties of life.

10
Anxieties about Your Child's Development

Which of the following statements is true for you?

1. My daughter still wasn't walking at seventeen months, and it drove me crazy. I was sure she was going to be physically stunted for life.
2. My daughter was this gigantic baby, and it really annoyed me every time someone complimented me on my big, strapping son. Just because she was big didn't mean she wasn't feminine.
3. We felt we'd failed Jason by not being able to convince him to play with dolls. When he was two, we started hiding his trucks and Legos, so he wouldn't be interested in only boy toys. But he never touched the stuffed cartoon figure we bought him, and now he wants a gun.
4. It worries me to think I might be overlooking my three-year-old's speech problem. My mother is always telling me she can't understand a thing my child says, and she's sure there's something wrong with him. I'm not sure if he has arrested speech or slushy speech or if he's just playing around with sounds and words.

When you look at your child, do you see the whole person or do you tend to make comments like those above about how he's progressing? Do you measure your child's achievements against your neighbor's child or the paragon you read about last week in a magazine article? It's really quite natural to want to compare your son or daughter to the blueprint you read about in books, not because you suspect there's anything wrong but because you're convinced there's something very right.

What parent doesn't study her baby's every move, every sound? She knows that her child is spectacular, special, probably solving equations and writing the great American novel in her head right now as she sucks on that nipple! The good thing about a parent who finds her child exceptional is that she will be pleased with any accomplishment and will learn to expect even more. The unfortunate thing about a parent who *demands* that her child be exceptional is that the expectations never end, and nothing is ever good enough. Interest in how your child is developing is natural; deep concern, however, means you're anxious—if there's nothing really wrong.

Development comes in cycles because the new abilities a child gains are matched by the increasing awareness of what that ability can mean. The more he's able to do, the more independent he becomes, but as soon as experience tells him that independence can be a mixed blessing, he may stop for a while. A two-year-old may whiz down the highest slide because he has mastered skills in climbing, turning around, and getting his legs out from under him. A three-year-old may avoid the slide because he has a new appreciation of how badly he could hurt himself if he happened to fall.

INFANCY: THE FIRST MILESTONES

Every infant starts life equipped with certain motor reflexes and with the potential to develop along certain physiological, neurological, cognitive, and emotional lines. You can't classify a child as passive, aggressive, or normal. He's all three at various times of the day and week. He's not necessarily either quick or slow, better at gross motor skills than fine motor skills, easygoing or ill-tempered, placid or physical, very masculine or very feminine. Take any infant or toddler and watch him over a period of a month, and you'll see all conceivable behaviors that fall within the range of his individual personality. And yet many parents get anxious if their child isn't progressing by the book.

Developmental milestones are based on learned behaviors that are biologically rooted. Your child learns the things he's supposed to because he's physically able and emotionally ready. You can't control your child's development any more than you can his personality. This isn't to say that you can't *shape* behavior or development that may be emerging, but you can't force your child to do things he simply isn't ready to do, whether it's mastering Suzuki violin or being nicer to his little brother. What's consequential here is your attitude and your expectations. If you convey the message that what he's doing is fine, he'll progress at his own pace. If you're anxious about where he is on a scale, he'll begin to doubt the worth of everything he's doing.

The minute you begin to despair over your child's lack of progress in a certain area, suddenly he turns around and leaps over the hurdle he was struggling so long to clear. And then, perhaps, something traumatic occurs, such as the birth of a sibling or a parent's illness, and he retreats to childish behaviors. You just have to learn to live with your children's inconsistencies; they're part of growth, too.

Current-day pediatric authorities have done endless research in child development so that there are documented norms for every conceivable milestone. This is useful because it gives you a backdrop of information against which you can measure and understand your child's progress. It's not good, though, if you're constantly comparing your child to the norm and finding that he's always superior or inferior. If you feel pressured to compare in order to be sure your child measures up or if you go to the opposite extreme and feel compelled to ignore all measurements because you're absolutely positive your child is special, different, unique, and so forth, you're being unfair to your child. The important thing is to be aware of the norm and aware of your individual child and see how the two fit together.

This was very hard for Jeff, whose daughter Abby hadn't yet learned to walk at seventeen months. Jeff himself was a workaholic, an overachiever, and he found it very difficult to watch Abby struggling to do something that her peers had mastered months ago. "It was wrong, I know, but I felt as though I'd failed as a parent before I'd even started," Jeff said. "First I had to admit I wanted a boy. You know, someone like me, whom I could relate to. Then, when I was holding Mary Jo's hand in the delivery room and I saw Abby coming out, I thought, 'Hey, a sweet, delicate little girl, that's fabulous!' Only Abby was a nine-pound six-ounce whale of a kid.

"She just didn't fit any of the norms. Girls are supposed to be quieter, more passive, but she was a rip-roaring loudmouth right from the start. And then when all the other babies on the block were crawling, she was just lying there. Maybe it was her size, I don't know, but it took her forever just to learn to roll over.

"I read all the books—I guess looking for confirmation that everything was okay—and it seemed as if she was behind in everything. It was hard for her to crawl, to pull herself up, to scuttle around. She just liked to sit in her walker and talk to herself—always babbling. She passed her first birthday, and there was no sign of walking, no matter how hard I tried to get her going. At fourteen months Mary Jo and I would stand Abby between us and kind of shove her back and forth, trying to get her to use her legs properly. She hated it; she'd just sit down and cry. At seventeen months I took her to the pediatrician and told him he had to do something. I mean, the kid was talking in paragraphs, she was memorizing songs, for heaven's sake, but she couldn't walk."

TODDLERHOOD: EXPLORING THE WORLD OR HOLDING
BACK

Of course, despite Jeff's anxiety, we can see that Abby was moving forward at her own pace. All children do. It's extraordinary—we might even say miraculous—to watch your child growing and developing. As her neurological, physiological, mental, and emotional systems evolve, she masters incredible feats like sitting up, crawling, pulling up, standing unassisted, standing while holding an object, drinking from a glass, self-feeding, walking, and talking, as well as the myriad learned tasks involving gross and fine motor skills. And as she achieves each milestone you can pull back a little more, doing less and less for your more independent, more able child.

One vital lesson of parenthood is learning to leave your child on her own as much as possible to do what she can for herself. When a baby first makes that internal click and realizes that by getting onto her hands and knees she'll be able to move forward and grasp a particular toy, she's learned something invaluable all by herself. No parent should push that moment.

Some children will attempt anything; they have a brash kind of daring that makes them lurch and stagger on jelly legs at nine or ten months. Others are perfectionists and cautiously work on one motor skill before going on to the next. The "decisions" these two sorts of children make are based on their personalities and temperaments, and no amount of prodding will change that.

Jeff wants to make his cautious daughter bold, but why? Just because she's not walking like every other child in her play group is no reason to panic. The girl's physical skills may not be quite up to the task yet, or she may have fallen a couple of times and not gotten the parental encouragement she needed to get right back up and try again. Or she just may not be psychologically ready to strike out on her own with nothing to hold on to. By being so anxious about Abby's late development, Jeff isn't doing himself or her any good. Eventually she's going to walk. And she will run and jump and undoubtedly master many other physically sophisticated activities.

PLAY AND GENDER IDENTITY

It's interesting to watch the gender-based preferences for play that emerge when children are about three or four. Researchers have done a lot of experimentation with nonsexist toys and play environments, but clearly, children of both sexes *tend* to prefer toys that encourage certain interests.

When a three-and-a-half-year-old girl plays with a doll, she tends to make herself the mommy and the doll the baby. This is a time when girls become aware of the fact that their physical body is like their mother's. It's also a time when their mother may actually be pregnant again, which offers the first opportunity for questions such as "Where did I come from?" and "When can I have a baby just like you?" The doll they love to play with is a likely candidate.

A boy of the same age might not have any interest in the new baby to come, but that doesn't mean he might not want to play with dolls. His own interests would turn this play into a scenario about building them a house to live in or putting them into some vehicle such as a truck or wagon and taking them for rides.

Same toy; different use. A child has no preconceived notion of what a thing is for, as an adult does. Kids don't enjoy playing with Legos because they're Legos but because of what they can create with them.

Trying to shape your child's play is generally a losing battle. Children will make a box into a spaceman or a set of spoons into toy soldiers. They'll use their imagination on the item they're given and create their own world with it. The boy who won't play dress-up or put a doll to bed isn't necessarily going to develop into a male chauvinist; he's just not into experimenting with pretending to be someone else or with nurturing right now.

SIZE AND SEX

Despite our "raised consciousnesses," despite the general belief that boys and girls should be equally valued in society, despite our understanding that bigger doesn't always mean better, many parents are preoccupied with concerns about their infant's size and gender. A big baby is assumed to be handsome and boyish; a small, delicate one must be a girl. A large child can be rough-housed and manhandled and treated like a mature person; a small one is often infantalized and treated with kid gloves. In reality we know our children have inherited a certain genetic code and will develop along rather expected physical lines, but what we know and what we'd like don't always match when we're watching our children grow.

It's good to be honest about your own preferences, but it's better to be flexible and admit that though you really wanted a boy because you're a man and have experience you can pass on, the little girl you got instead offers you the opportunity to get to know the other side. Fathers of girls say they are more concerned about protecting their children (from all the nasty little boys who might hurt them!), and mothers of boys tend to worry about their kids having future problems with drugs or violence.

But look at how easy it is to blow these stereotypes apart. The delicate little girl may turn out to be the star Little League short-stop, and the strapping boy may enjoy hours spent practicing the oboe in his room. If your expectations don't make your child anxious about his or her worth and potential, he or she could develop along any line at all.

If you really wanted a big boy and got a small girl or vice versa, you have some rethinking to do. It's also a mistake to blame your spouse's side of the family for attributes that bother you and claim that "if she'd just been born with my looks and your brains, she'd be wonderful." You can't turn your actual baby into the one you imagined. Your child will have unique and special qualities that may have nothing whatsoever to do with size or gender.

On the other hand, if people keep mistaking your big girl baby for a boy, this is no reflection on you or your child. If you become hypersensitive and decide to "typecast" her as a frilly, pink-clad infant just to be confrontational when others make a natural mistake, you may give her a complex about her natural physical endowments. Looks are very important to us, no matter how much we claim to ignore them. Why not accentuate the attributes we're born with instead of trying to change them? Think of the six-foot fashion models or female basketball players who would never have succeeded without their height. Think of how short many of the world's male political leaders are. Maybe they became "big shots" just because they came in at the low end of the height scale.

Jeff is one father who is clearly anxious about his daughter's size and sex and development in general. He's desperate for Abby to measure up to the norm, but he doesn't see her clearly. In order to feel better about his parenting, he's going to have to think about the sources of his anxiety and examine the ways in which they can help him establish some new patterns and attitudes.

Your Program for Change

The Program for Change will help you to see whether you're intervening too much or too little in your child's inevitable progress toward his personal milestones. For a complete description of how to use this program effectively, see Chapter 4, page 61.

STEP I. IDENTIFY WHAT'S REALLY BOTHERING YOU

STEP II. CONNECT WITH YOUR PAST

STEP III. GET THE FACTS

STEP IV. UNDERSTAND YOUR CHILD'S POINT OF VIEW

STEP V. GROUND YOURSELF

STEP VI. STEP BACK AND SEE THE SCENE WITH DIFFERENT EYES

STEP VII. ESTABLISH NEW PATTERNS

STEP I. IDENTIFY WHAT'S REALLY BOTHERING YOU

When you think about it, you may not see any specific elements that actually trouble you about your child's rate of development. You may just feel a general sense of unease that something's not right. But think further now about the underlying feelings that may provoke your anxiety and decipher what's really going on for you in this situation.

Let's think about Jeff whose daughter isn't walking at seventeen months. *What is it about this experience that's really bothering Jeff?*

He seems to feel that Abby's lack of progress is some reflection on him. This might mean that he's begun to think of his child as an extension of himself and to take any lack of progress as a personal insult. It's true that he was a quick learner when he was little, and he is determined that Abby be just as fast and clever—a "chip off the old block." He feels she should be able to master the basics and then breeze through the tough parts so that he can claim he has the absolute best. Of course, if he has the best child, this means he's the best parent and doesn't ever have to feel anxious about the quality of his parenting.

He's also worried about her physical attributes; he's overly critical of the way his toddler looks and sounds. Since Jeff is the type of person who has to hand out trophies all the time, he needs Abby to be the kind of little girl he'd always imagined so that he can reward her for doing and being what he thinks she's supposed to do and be. He can't seem to give Abby any leeway to do things on her own, in her own good time.

What's Really Bothering You

Some of the major parental concerns about a child's development include the following:

- having a defective child who will always need their care
- not having a "dream" child
- feeling competitive
- feeling their child's inadequacy reflects their own inadequacies

If you are having any anxiety over your own expectations for your child's progress, you might want to look at the following questions that relate to some of the above concerns.

1. Do you ever think with embarrassment that your child doesn't measure up?
2. Do you worry about your child's size?
3. Did you want a boy and get a girl, or vice versa? How does that make you feel now?
4. Do you ever worry if another child is more capable or advanced than yours?

5. Do you tend to read every new child development book and magazine article on the subject that comes out? Or do you try to avoid them?
6. Are you ever concerned about your child's willingness or reluctance to try new things?
7. Do you tend to buy "educational" toys for your child, or do you allow him to pick what he likes?
8. Do you worry about the kind or amount of television your child watches and how it influences her development?
9. Are you concerned if you see that your child is regressing in some area?

It's also useful to compare notes with your spouse. If you're a person who demands a great deal from others and your spouse is more relaxed, you may be giving your child unclear messages about what's expected in the household. Your anxiety about your child's development could be broadcasting the message that you don't think she's good enough or that you don't care how she's doing. By identifying your core issue now, you'll be better able to see whether you have some unrealistic expectations for her progress or whether you both simply have to take a different tactic to work in a nonpressuring way on whatever problem she might be having.

STEP II. CONNECT WITH YOUR PAST

If you're particularly concerned about where your child fits in the normalcy curve, it may be due partly to the way your own parents fussed over or ignored your achievements when you were small. By connecting with your past you may discover some vital memories that will help you handle your current feelings about your child's development.

> *Jeff:* He can recall shooting hoops in the neighborhood playground when he was seven or eight. Always an agile, physical child, he had no trouble scoring against kids who were much taller than he. At some point during the afternoon he was aware that

his father was watching from the other side of the fence. Another alley-oop, and then a fabulous hook shot. He *knew* he was doing okay. Better than okay.

At the end of the game he went to join his father, who ruffled his hair and said, "If you weren't such a little shrimp, you'd really be able to play this game. Too bad, kid." Jeff vowed that he would excel at basketball after that; he'd be better and faster than everyone else, including his father.

How You Can Connect with Your Past

Think back to your own childhood and try to reconstruct your parents' attitudes toward your progress. It may be helpful here to compare notes with your siblings, who may give a different perspective to painful or embarrassing moments that had something to do with your achievements or lack of them. The questions below, while not pertinent to everyone's situation, will help you find your own path back toward the area of developmental milestones.

SETTING THE SCENE

1. What was your place in the household? Only child, oldest, youngest, or somewhere in the middle?
2. Did you have a particularly outstanding sibling?
3. Did you have a particularly slow sibling?
4. Were you ever in the position of having to take care of a sibling?
5. Do you recall your parents treating you like a baby—or did they give you a great deal of responsibility?

Now that you can see clearly, how did you experience your developmental milestones?

Some typical memories that many parents recall had to do with the following:

• getting the message that how well they performed was equated with how good they were in general

- feeling that their parents valued their achievements more than they did themselves
- feeling that their parents didn't understand their abilities and limitations

The following questions that relate to some of the above concerns may evoke certain useful feelings about your past:

6. Did you get a lot of praise from your parents whenever you accomplished something?
7. Were you belittled for your efforts, no matter how good they were? Were you told you could do better?
8. Were you considered "slow" or "fast" when you were growing up?
9. Did your parents ignore you when you told them about some event or achievement you were particularly proud of?
10. Did you put a lot of pressure on yourself to perform?

Regardless of the sometimes unrealistic expectations your parents might have had for you, you don't need to impose them on your own child. You don't have to push him or compare him with others. It may lessen your anxiety if you can recall all the milestones *you* accomplished in life without even trying. All children develop at different rates, and if you can sort out the unpleasant memories connected with your own past accomplishments, you may be able to see your child's natural development more clearly.

STEP III. GET THE FACTS

You want to collect all your facts and figures about development, not just the statistical information about normalcy curves but information about your own child's capacities for progress. The studies and research can be useful to you if you don't take it as gospel, carved in stone. If you can look at the facts logically, they may help you think practically about your child's true path of development.

Jeff: He takes Abby to the pediatrician for a thorough checkup. The doctor examines Abby's legs and feet and tests her reflexes. He assures Jeff that there's absolutely nothing wrong with his child, but he does ask if Abby has been using a walker. Jeff confirms that she has been shuttling around the house in one for the past six months.

The doctor explains that some children tend to use the walker on tiptoe with legs bent instead of in the normal walking position. When they're out of the protective circle of this device, they may have more trouble adjusting to walking unassisted. Abby shows the doctor and her father that she can walk while holding on to a few fingers, so the doctor isn't at all concerned about her progress. He also points out that she is also developmentally ahead of her peers in fine motor and verbal skills.

Consider All Your Facts

Use the following sample questions to guide your investigation in the area of developmental milestones. By understanding the facts and the range of normalcy in the area of child development, you'll be able to sort out your anxieties about your situation and start thinking clearly about the issues.

1. How can you know what's right for your own child, who is unique and special and unlike anyone else in the universe? *Know what can be expected of your child's age group; also know what is practical for your own child. If you have read the books, you will know whether your child is within shooting distance of reaching a certain milestone.*

2. What will your infant be doing in the first days after he comes home from the hospital? *Infants begin life craning their heads toward the source of nourishment, reaching their tiny fists to their mouths, and sucking for all they are worth. Within a few days' time their eyes begin to focus, and their body movements become more organized.*

3. What are some of the first developmental milestones you can expect? *During the first months, infants begin to adapt to a feeding and sleeping timetable; they learn to reach for a toy, to hold and*

*shake a rattle, to recognize their parents' faces and tones of voice,
and to turn over.*

4. When should you wean your baby? *One indicator that an infant
   is moving ahead is when he is able to take a bottle as well as suck
   from the breast and then, at about seven or eight months, when
   he begins learning to drink from a cup. Some mothers choose to
   make a milestone out of weaning around the time when the first
   tooth cuts through; they will stop breastfeeding when their child
   starts biting.*

5. What will your pediatrician do to ensure that your child is
   developing properly? *From the first well-baby visit six weeks
   after birth, he'll begin testing the infant's vision, hearing, reflexes,
   and physical flexibility. He'll ask your toddler to walk across the
   floor and ask your three-year-old to balance on his heels and then
   his toes. He'll ask your four-year-old to hop on one foot. He'll talk
   to your infant by using eye contact and with your preschooler by
   using words and gestures. He'll give you ample time for questions
   about eating and sleeping habits, appropriate toys, toilet training,
   and so forth.*

6. If you don't trust your own opinion about your child's development because you don't think you see your child objec-
   tively, who else can you ask? *Ask your child's sitters or day-care
   providers what they have noticed about your son's or daughter's
   development. Does your baby really try to walk when you're not
   around? Is your toddler chatty and socially well integrated out of
   your presence but not in it? Perhaps you should think about the
   approach you're taking to your child's achievements.*

7. Is it any real drawback if your child is particularly large or
   small for his peer group? *No, it doesn't have to be. Some children
   will have to learn to adapt to their size socially. A large child may
   knock others over because he doesn't know his own strength; a
   small one may be excluded because he's considered too babyish.
   It's your job to make your child aware of his specialness and give
   him a little more help adjusting.*

8. Should you be concerned if you have difficulty understanding
   your toddler's speech? *Probably not. Two- and even three-year-*

olds are still experimenting with the way words sound. They may make up combinations of their own that seem right to them. If your child is three, almost four and RARELY speaks, however, it may be wise to take him to a professional who specializes in late speech development.

9. Should you be concerned if your four-year-old boy likes to dress up and playact, maybe occasionally trying on your high heels? Should you be worried if your four-year-old daughter only wants to play with trucks and guns? No. Children of this age are just beginning to assert their sexual identity, which will progress normally if you don't panic about their play preferences.

STEP IV. UNDERSTAND YOUR CHILD'S POINT OF VIEW

Your child has no idea that he is developing along certain lines; he does know, however, what his peers are doing. He may explain to you that babies cannot eat sweets or climb stairs, but he can. This is his own method of comparison and a way for him to feel proud of his own accomplishments. If you're empathic and can see his development from his point of view, you'll be better able to understand what his place is on the normalcy curve.

Jeff: He noticed that Abby would stagger from one piece of furniture to another, letting go of one and throwing her hands up in the air with a laugh or grunt just before grabbing the next piece. She'd babble happily, a kind of rambling monologue that went something like, "Go, go! Fast we go. Yes, do. Go down, up." But when he held her hand to assist her in walking, she clutched it and frowned, saying, "No, Daddy," or sometimes, "Help me." It became evident when he paid attention to her body that she was more fearful holding on to him than she was when she tried to walk by herself.

Bringing Out Your Child's Feelings

Remember that you cannot conduct a conversation about development with your child. What you can do is get certain clues from her about why she's not progressing in a certain way and

what she feels about doing a particular new thing. Some parents
have used statements similar to those below to elicit their child's
response.

1. "I don't think I ever saw you suck your thumb before. Does
   your friend Susie at the day-care center suck hers? Does it
   make you feel happier if you do?"
2. "John said he'd be scared to go trick-or-treating at night all
   alone with his daddy, but he'd go if you'd show him how
   because you're such a big girl."
3. "Dinner somehow always tastes better to me when you set the
   table. Could you get out the spoons and forks? I'll carry the
   knives if you want."
4. "Are you really going to button up your jacket today? It makes
   me so proud to see that you can get dressed all by yourself."

Remember that trying something new is difficult at any age.
Think about your own reluctance to challenge yourself—for fear
of failing or being made fun of or just because what's old is familiar
to you and therefore easier and safer.

Acting on Your Child's Feelings

1. If you'd like to shape your child's initiative to try something
   new, you might suggest that he teach that very thing to a
   younger or less developed friend. This will give him a position
   of superiority and wisdom he can never have when he compares himself to you or to his older siblings.
2. If your child is getting enormously frustrated because he can't
   master something, let it alone for a while. You may be amazed
   at how quickly he gets it when he goes back to it later.
3. You can encourage your child to try new things by showing
   him what other children his age are doing. There's a good
   series of books entitled *Now I Am Two* (. . . *Three* . . . *Four*), and
   so forth, that will show the child which activities are appropriate at this age.

STEP V. GROUND YOURSELF

It can be very helpful to repeat aloud that your child is fine and doing as well as she should be doing. The amazing thing about child development is that although the progression of events happens in tiny increments, a little each day, the grand result can show itself quickly and completely overnight. What you were so concerned about at one stage vanishes completely as the next stage begins.

> *Jeff:* He can tell himself that Abby isn't just sitting, she's pulling herself around in the walker, she's flailing around from one piece of furniture to the next, she's actively involved in exploring her environment whether she's on her hands and knees or her bottom. And she's talking a blue streak.

The anxiety about watching your child developing too quickly or not quickly enough tends to grow over time—as you watch the same progress or lack of progress in a certain area. The diffusers offered below have helped some parents realize that everything has a beginning and an end, and things do change.

> *Anxious thought:* My child is afraid of clowns and dogs, and the books say she was supposed to have outgrown those fears a year ago. What's wrong with her?
> *Grounding thought:* Clowns do look rather menacing, and a fear of strange dogs isn't bad when you consider how many children get bitten each year.

> *Anxious thought:* My son really is more powerful than other kids his age. He barrels into a group and doesn't know his own strength, so he pushes them over. They'll all think he's a bully.
> *Grounding thought:* He's a sensitive child, too. All I have to do is remind him that the other children get hurt if he pushes too hard. He'll be able to adjust.

Remember that you have a happy, healthy child who is learning as fast as he can. And remind yourself that the minute your child lives up to your expectations, he'll probably turn right around and astound you with something you never expected. Life would be awfully boring if we always got what we hoped for.

STEP VI. STEP BACK AND SEE THE SCENE WITH DIFFERENT EYES

You can let your imagination help you now. By trying out different possibilities in your mind, you may find it easier to be more flexible with your child's real milestones.

> *Jeff:* He would like to worry less about the fact that Abby isn't walking, unlike all the other children he knows in her age group.
>
> He steps back and listens to Abby singing in the bathtub. He imagines one pure sound from her voice lifting her up out of the tub and propelling her across the room. She looks delighted, surprised because she's doing it herself, and all he has to do is stand back and watch. He imagines the rest of her growth emanating from her—eventually at her own pace—in the same way.

Imagine What You'd Like to Happen

If you could suspend reality and stop yourself from taking out the measuring tape each time an issue of development comes up, you might be better able to imagine your child interested in the world and participating in it gradually, taking each new step when he's ready. See yourself at first doing new activities with your child, then standing back and allowing him the freedom to do it himself. Imagine yourself in a group of mothers and fathers talking calmly about your child's accomplishments and really listening to the others without trying to make any comparisons, remembering that their children will have their own timetables and interests that may not coincide with yours.

STEP VII. ESTABLISH NEW PATTERNS

This Program for Change is all about new patterns, of course, but it's also about understanding how the new cannot possibly arrive and take hold until the old is mastered. There are many ways of growing up, and not all of them are recorded in child development books. Try to see your child's growth and progress as a slow, steady journey.

Jeff: Jeff realized that he had a rigid expectation that Abby should measure up to the norm—be the "right" kind of little girl, act feminine, walk when the books said she should. But instead of watching his child progress at her own rate, he was setting himself up for disappointment and frustration. He'd also started battling with Abby over natural accomplishments that should come, and he had to realize that they *would* come, all in their own good time.

Jeff decided to stop making an issue out of his child's development; he also decided to take her walker away so that she would explore on her own, using the furniture. He still had trouble watching other, younger children walking, but he also started enjoying having conversations with his verbal daughter.

PARENTS' SUGGESTIONS

Here are a few suggestions offered by other parents that will probably give you some ideas of your own about how to handle your child's developmental milestones.

1. Encourage your child's milestones by praising what he's done so far, never by making fun of him.
2. Don't protect your child from everything new and different. By first doing for him, then doing with him, you will prepare him for the ultimate break where he can do it for himself. Before he can walk alone he must hold your hand. Then he must let go and come toward you as you encourage him. Finally, you can stand to one side and cheer him on as he makes it across the room, falling and picking himself up again.
3. Allow your child to make mistakes. Only by doing it wrong do we ever get it right.
4. Find out what's stopping your child from progressing. Children's fears are not necessarily based on any real event but, rather, may have a great deal to do with the particular mix of their physical and psychological development. The child who

realizes that he's suddenly able to do something new will also be able to think and feel various emotions about that skill. Those emotions may at first be too confusing to handle, and the child may cease practicing the skill.

5. Play dumb as much as you can. When your child asks you to help him put his shoes on for the fiftieth time, and you've seen that he's already mastered this skill himself, tell him you can't find your glasses or say you've forgotten which way is left and which is right. Allow the child to struggle through the task, offering help only when the frustration level seems too high.

6. Give your child the toys he likes, within reason. A four-year-old doesn't need a motorized, customized car to scuttle around the yard; he can just as well imagine that his tricycle is a Datsun ZX. He doesn't need a gun, either. War toys today look very real and very frightening. If he's desperate for a gun so that he can get the "bad guys," let him create his own weapons with Legos or blocks.

ALLOWING YOURSELF AND YOUR CHILD TIME TO DEVELOP

The fact that you are feeling concern says that you care a great deal about your child's progress and well-being. You want him to be capable of managing on his own in a world that has certain conventions and expectations, so naturally you're eager for him to develop along lines that will help him to adapt.

But seeing that your anxiety only forestalls or hampers your child's progress should encourage you to stand back and wait for future milestones, which will come of their own accord. Keep reminding yourself that your child needs *time* more than anything else: time to be able to master a new skill, time to make connections that will let the skill flourish, time for the thought and feeling that go into the activity to ripen. Development is not linear but cyclical, and that skill your son started to master last year will take a little more shape this year, and even more the year after. You can learn by watching and encouraging as your child grows.

11
Anxieties about Elimination and Toilet Training

Which of the following statements is true for you?

1. If my baby doesn't have at least three dirty diapers a day, I call the pediatrician.
2. I can't stand the way my husband reacts to our son's dirty diapers. He makes such a fuss about changing the baby, I end up wanting to throw the diaper in his face.
3. I get worried about my toddler getting toilet trained. He sits and sits on the potty and can't do anything, so then I end up putting a diaper on him so he can finally have a bowel movement.
4. I'm concerned that my child will only go in our bathroom in our house. It's impossible to plan trips anywhere, and I can't keep him in day care any longer than three hours at a time.

There probably isn't a parent alive who doesn't relate to some of the above qualms about elimination and toilet training. If you find yourself nodding in agreement, it may be comforting to know that most people find the elimination process unpleasant and toilet training confusing and frustrating.

The reason these elements of your child's life cause you anxiety is that society considers urine and feces disgusting. This is the only time in your life that you ever have to deal with the messy by-products of someone else's body. At the beginning it's ten to fifteen diapers a day: cleanup, smell, rashes, leaks, and all. And then when your child is developmentally ready to handle the task himself, you still have to be involved as monitor and bottom wiper. But you may feel guilty about your reluctance to handle this if you think you're supposed to believe, as your grandmother probably said, "everything that came out of my baby was roses."

Our child's urine and feces aren't roses, but they're not something out of a sci-fi movie, either. As you can later explain to the child just beginning toilet training, they're simply things that the body doesn't need anymore and must get rid of. By keeping that fact in mind you'll be better able to handle your anxieties in this area.

AN INFANT'S ELIMINATION

In our society elimination is a good way to judge whether a child is processing his food. It's also a hallmark for many parents as to what's wrong with the child. One way you know you're feeding your child properly is seeing what comes out the other end. For centuries, in various cultures, wise men examined a patient's feces to tell them what was going on in that person's body and soul and how they might best offer a cure for an ailment. Though we're a bit more sophisticated about this today, it's easy to see how elimination anxieties can easily spiral into health-related anxieties.

It's very natural to become anxious if your infant hasn't had a dirty diaper in over forty-eight hours when all the books say that the "normal" baby will eliminate approximately two or three times a day. And it's perfectly understandable to fret over a toddler who has eaten only crackers for five days straight and is straining at his stool.

Lois remembered that her son Tom, now four, was a physically unpredictable baby. "No matter how much breast milk or, later, formula he'd have, I couldn't figure out when he was going to take a dump. I'd be all set to go out for the day, he'd be changed and ready, and then just before I got to the door, he'd have another blowout. Sometimes three a day—sometimes none. I'd get this awful tension in the back of my head, waiting for those grunts, that smell. And then I thought, What's wrong with me? Every mother has to deal with poop and mess.

"When he didn't go for a week, my mother suggested I give him a suppository, and dumb me, I tried it. There was this explosion like you wouldn't believe. Tom got hysterical, and I had poop on my hands, clothes—everywhere. I felt unclean for the rest of the day, as though everyone were sniffing me. And I felt so awful about what I'd done to Tom, as if I'd invaded his privacy."

Anxiety over your child's elimination habits may often be a mask for something else that's going on. An adult's fears of being soiled can go back to childhood and contain many remnants of past experience that may be very hard to alleviate. Many parents deal with their aversion to the elimination process by trying to control it. They attempt to set up a rigid schedule that will produce end products at will. At *their* will. The truth of the matter is that eliminating is involuntary in an infant. The point is that whatever goes in *will* come out eventually, and worrying about when or how or how much doesn't speed up the process.

TODDLERS AND ELIMINATION: A BATTLE FOR CONTROL

As the child grows he develops a certain awareness of his physical functions. He has more muscular control, and generally by the age of two he can tell when he is about to urinate or defecate. Bladder control may be slower than bowel control because it's harder for the urinary sphincter to contain liquid than it is for the anal sphincter to hold on to solids. A toddler who is actively engaged in a battle for independence from his parents may retain his stool as yet another way of exerting control over them. He may also, in his growing curiosity about how his body works, become very proud and protective of anything that comes out of him.

TOILET TRAINING: A CRUCIAL MILESTONE OF EARLY CHILDHOOD

Elimination is a purely physical act; toilet training is learned behavior, and therefore it's something that your child is developmentally ready to master only when all his skills are more subtle and diversified. He'll probably start becoming interested in using a potty at around the time when he can feed himself, start to dress himself, use different creative materials such as crayons and Play Doh, and, perhaps most important of all, socialize with other children and adults outside your loving, protective parental presence.

But there's a big hitch to this dawning sense of worldly accomplishment: because your child's skills are new and untried, they're also vulnerable and fragile; they can fall apart in the face of a critical, demanding parent. Your child's psychological reaction to the world has a lot to do with the way he sees his accomplishments reflected back at him from the people who matter most: his mother and father. If you expect too much or too little of him, he may feel that he's on very shaky terrain much of the time.

Toilet training, one of the most significant developmental milestones of childhood, is an area in which your child needs a lot of support from you. Sometime during the third or fourth year of your child's life you will both reach the end of the long procession of wet and soiled diapers (six thousand to ten thousand for an average baby!) that led from each sunrise to each sunset.

This milestone means far more to you than it does to your child, however. He learned that by getting up on two feet he could reach his toys faster; by feeding himself he could regulate the pace at which he wanted to eat; by talking he could communicate his needs and wishes. But what reward does he get—other than your praise—by going in the potty?

You have to take the lead from your child here and see the toilet-training process from his perspective. You may want your child to learn to put feces in the potty so that you can flush them away, but the child sees his bowels as a part of himself, not as waste. If he lets go of them, he may feel that something of himself is missing. The more you insist on *training* the child according to your schedule, the less control he has over the process and the more difficult it will probably be for him to "give up" these precious personal gifts.

Some parents feel more anxiety about the kind of separation toileting implies. When your child is able to ask to be excused so that he can go to the bathroom *by himself,* it's clear that he has graduated from those tender days when you were everything to him and he needed you to hold him, feed him, and wipe his bottom.

This isn't to say, though, that your nostalgia for the dependent infant you used to know should stop you from encouraging a child who isn't making any attempt to get toilet trained. It's one of the first socializing experiences in life. Once you can go to the bathroom by yourself, it means it's possible for you to coexist with other people who aren't family and have no wish to take care of your physical needs. The child who refuses to be toilet trained is not adapting socially, and if his parents are compliant, they don't help him learn.

Possibly because of her earlier concerns about her son's elimination, Lois really didn't push Tom toward getting toilet trained. But by the time he was four and a quarter, Lois seemed to be having more rather than less anxiety about his toileting.

"Tom marched to a different drummer," Lois said. "He wasn't a clone; he was always his own person. I never wanted his leisurely attitude toward life to hamper him or let him be frustrated. He wasn't *slow* or anything, he just took his own sweet time about things. If he wanted to take two hours to eat his lunch, that was fine with me.

"Tom was funny about the toilet. He liked peeing in it because he could really see what his penis was capable of and that was a lot of fun for him. But he seemed to have this thing about defecating, so I didn't pressure him. The only thing was, he started making a real issue of it. Every time he had to have a bowel movement, no matter where he was, he'd start screaming for a diaper and take off all his clothes. It was difficult when we were in a public place or at my mother's house because she really disapproved of the way I'd handled him. She was always urging me to *do* something about this behavior, and I told her I most certainly would not! Every child does it at his own pace. She pointed out that he'd never get into any decent kindergarten if he wasn't toilet trained. I told her that I didn't care; I wasn't going to try to remake him in her image of a perfect child just because it would be more convenient for me to have him out of diapers."

Lois is at the opposite end of the parenting spectrum from Jeff, whom we met in the previous chapter. She doesn't care at all what other parents or children are doing developmentally; she only cares about her own child. This would be fine if it didn't create some unusual problems for her son. His need for control concerning the issue of having a bowel movement has gone so far that she has trouble dealing with it in public. Because she hasn't indicated her preference in the matter, she's letting her four-year-old decide, and this is not something he's capable of doing. By denying that there's anything wrong with her child's nonconforming behavior, she may be putting Tom at a disadvantage with his peers and other adults.

Your Program for Change

Your own aversion to the elimination process need not come between you and your child. By realizing that your child's toileting patterns bother you and by localizing your particular area of concern, you'll be better able to handle this emotionally tinged issue with some degree of ease. (For a complete description of how to use this program effectively, see Chapter 4, page 61.)

STEP I. IDENTIFY WHAT'S REALLY BOTHERING YOU
STEP II. CONNECT WITH YOUR PAST
STEP III. GET THE FACTS
STEP IV. UNDERSTAND YOUR CHILD'S POINT OF VIEW
STEP V. GROUND YOURSELF

STEP VI. STEP BACK AND SEE THE SCENE WITH DIFFERENT EYES
STEP VII. ESTABLISH NEW PATTERNS

STEP I. IDENTIFY WHAT'S REALLY BOTHERING YOU

By identifying the central issues that bring you close to a loss of control over elimination or toilet training, you will be taking your first step toward making change happen. If you can look beyond the obvious, as Lois did, you'll develop a good sense of what's really troubling you in the situation.

What's really bothering Lois about her son's reluctance to get toilet trained? She remembers that when Tom was an infant, his elimination made her feel unclean. She couldn't predict when it would come, but waiting for it tainted her whole day. It was as if she felt ruled by her child's physical functions. The fact that the smell turned her off made it harder for her to get near her child.

She was also baffled by the unpredictability of Tom's elimination process. She couldn't bear to wait for the child to produce something, so she tried making it happen. When it did, and Tom got hysterical, Lois was horrified at the way she'd tried to force her child's body to do something it wasn't ready to do.

Now that her son is over four, she still feels guilty about meddling with Mother Nature. She doesn't want Tom to be pressured into something just because other children are doing it, but she's certainly aware that no kindergarten will want her child if he can't take care of his own personal needs. Other children will make fun of him for wearing a diaper. He'll be ostracized, and she won't have done anything to prevent that. Does this mean that by trying to allow her child his freedom she's really doing him harm? Does it mean she's a bad parent?

She is also influenced by what her mother thinks. Though Lois believes that bathroom habits are a matter of personal conviction, she is now coming into conflict with people who disagree and who are making things difficult for her and Tom because their outlook is radically different.

What's Really Bothering You

Some of the major parental concerns over elimination and toilet training are as follows:

- dealing with the mess
- getting your child clean
- your child's health
- getting your spouse to share the responsibility
- getting control over your child
- being socially accepted by others

If you're having any anxieties over your own expectations in these areas, you might want to look at the following questions that relate to some of the above concerns:

1. Do you ever feel negatively toward your child when he has a dirty diaper?
2. Do you ever feel soiled yourself when you see your child is soiled?
3. Does the quantity, color, or consistency of your child's urine or feces disturb or concern you?
4. Are you worried that you haven't cleaned in all the various places (behind the testicles, in the folds of the vagina)?
5. Are you worried about your child's regularity?
6. Do you ever get annoyed when your child urinates or defecates while you're in the middle of changing his diaper or giving him a bath?
7. How do you feel if your spouse refuses to change diapers?
8. Do you spend a lot of time trying to persuade your child to sit on the potty? Do you ever bribe him?
9. How do you feel when your newly toilet-trained child has an accident?
10. Are you bothered by your preschooler's constant use of toilet language?
11. Does it upset you if your toddler never allows you privacy in the bathroom?

If the act of changing a diaper or accompanying your preschooler to the potty or toilet is always fraught with tension, you might consider other things that are going on at the same time.

Does your spouse revert to bathroom humor when you're in the middle of a diaper change? Does your best friend always leave the bathroom door open with her child when you prefer it closed? Whether you are more troubled by privacy or control, or whether you simply have a lot of trouble with mess and odor, you'll find it helpful to separate the purely physical aspect of elimination from the feelings of upset you may have about it. It will also be useful to separate the gradual developmental process of toilet training from your need to have it happen quickly and efficiently.

STEP II. CONNECT WITH YOUR PAST

Your anxieties about elimination and toilet training probably go back very far in your own past, as the remnants of difficult moments you had as a child come to bear on feelings you have now about your own child. In a less enlightened time, thirty or so years ago, toilet matters were never discussed, and many of us who are parents today can only remember secrecy and distaste surrounding issues of toileting in our own childhood.

Lois: When Lois was eight her mother gave birth to her sister, Jeanne, and after a few weeks in a bassinette, the baby was moved into Lois's room. Jeanne had chronic diarrhea as a child, and Lois always woke up when the baby had a loose movement, called her mother, and got her to change her sister's diaper. The next morning when she went to school she was always sure that her own clothes must smell just like her baby sister's poop.

Probably because there was such an age difference between her and Jeanne, Lois's mother always expected more of her. No matter how much homework she had, she was expected to learn three new vocabulary words a week, memorize a poem, and be the best in ballet class. Lois was determined never to make a child of hers work for her love. Could this be one reason why she isn't helping Tom to get rid of his diapers?

How You Can Connect with Your Past

Think back to your own childhood and try to reconstruct your parents' attitudes about your progress. It may actually be helpful to ask your parents what they remember about toilet training you. Take note of their reactions to the way you're training their grandchild. Are they matter-of-fact about bodily functions, or do they pretend that feces and urine don't exist? Do they regard your child's accidents as heinous crimes or treat them as normal, everyday occurrences? You're probably influenced, as you work with your child, by the way your own parents dealt with your progress in this area.

Do any images come back to you from your childhood relating to elimination or toilet training? Begin with a general picture and work your way deeper into specific instances. By using the questions below to stimulate your memories you'll be better able to come up with your underlying feelings, fears, and anxieties about elimination.

SETTING THE SCENE

1. How many bathrooms did you have in your house? Which one did you usually use?
2. Did your parents ask that you go to the bathroom at a certain time of day? Was it easy or difficult for you to comply with this?
3. Did you have privacy in the bathroom?
4. Was your bathroom clean and lacking in odor?
5. Was your bathroom unkempt and smelly?
6. Did you ever have trouble going to the bathroom in other people's homes or in public places?
7. Did your parents and siblings indulge in bathroom humor? Or was the subject taboo, never discussed?

Now that you can see clearly, how did you experience elimination and toilet training?

Some typical memories that many parents recall have to do with the following:

- embarrassment about being unable to control bodily functions
- feeling unclean
- feeling pressured
- feeling that elimination was associated with being bad
- feeling that they had to be secretive

The next set of questions, which relate to one or more of the above concerns, may evoke useful feelings about your past.

8. How did your mother and father deal with your eliminations? Your siblings' eliminations? Did they make an issue of them or leave them to you?
9. Did you have frequent diarrhea or constipation? How did your parents handle it? Were you ever given enemas?
10. Were you expected to eliminate quickly?
11. Do you remember feeling humiliated or embarrassed by elimination—yours, your siblings', or your parents'?
12. Were you ever punished for withholding or for having accidents? How were you punished?

By understanding the roots of your present-day feelings you will be better able to deal with your distress and with what you feel are your child's present problems.

STEP III. GET THE FACTS

What can you do to verify your feelings about this issue? Your next step is to make a comprehensive search for facts.

Lois: She realizes that she's concerned enough about Tom's difficulty in adjusting to a play group or school setting to find out what Tom's problem is. She gets several books out of the library and discovers that most children show some interest in toilet training within the third year, though there are exceptions—such as her son.

The pediatrician checks Tom and agrees that the child has no physical problems, that his lack of interest is certainly emotional and may have something to do with Lois's own attitude. She does admit that her manner with Tom when changing his diapers is rather rough and impatient and always has been since he was an infant.

The doctor reminds Lois that it will become harder as Tom gets older to convince him that the behavior he has held on to this long ought to be changed because it's inhibiting his progress in the world.

Lois discusses the issue with her husband Paul to get his fix on this because he really hasn't said anything about it up to this point. Paul notes that Tom is curious—at least with him. He's always showing up at the bathroom whenever Paul goes in and closes the door. One fact he offers Lois is that the diapers don't fit Tom anymore. This is telling him that they won't have any alternative soon: Tom is going to have to learn to defecate in the toilet.

Consider All Your Facts

Use the following questions as a guideline to direct your fact search on elimination and toileting:

1. How often is an infant supposed to eliminate, either urine or feces? *A child care book will explain that an infant's intestinal system is still developing, and some infants process milk or formula better than others.*

2. How often is a preschooler supposed to eliminate either urine or feces? *This will depend on what and how much he's eaten or drunk. It takes about two days to process a particular meal unless it's very spicy or creates a good deal of flatulence.*

3. Are preschoolers supposed to have a daily bowel movement? *Every body is different. Some may go several times a day, some every other day.*

4. What does the color and consistency of the bowel mean? *Your pediatrician will remind you that an unexpected color or consistency of stool may come from something the child ate; beets*

will turn them reddish, carrots will come out as undigested orange flecks. If your child has not eaten any colored foods and you think you see blood in the stool, by all means have him examined. The blood could be from copious diarrhea or a fissure in the anus that can be very painful.

5. How do you know that your infant is constipated? *The movement will come out in small, dry pellets, almost like rabbit droppings.*

6. Do infants ever have other physical problems that might keep them from eliminating easily? *Some infants' sphincters may be underdeveloped and be unable to function normally at first. A pediatrician can do a gentle examination and manipulate the muscles around the anus in order to assist the baby.*

7. Does illness affect the elimination process? *Emphatically yes. The amount, color, and consistency of urine and stool will change radically during any illness and may take a while to get back to normal after the child has recovered.*

8. Is there a difference in cloth and paper diapers in helping your baby's elimination process? *It's been said that cloth diapers are kinder to the baby's delicate skin, and yet they soak through faster, leaving opportunities for diaper rash. They also leak more if your infant is subject to frequent diarrhea. The new superabsorbent paper diapers have been known to create allergic reactions in some children with sensitive skin.*

9. Why does your toddler act secretive about his elimination habits? *He may have watched you flush his bowel movement and feels very possessive about something he himself has produced. It may be better not to flush in front of him for a while.*

10. How can you get an objective view on how slowly or quickly your toddler is getting toilet trained? *Ask your sitter or daycare provider to keep a chart of his progress. Toddlers love to get rewards for accomplishments, and a star on a school chart where everyone can see it might make your child want to progress faster in this area.*

11. Will emotional upset affect your child's toileting patterns? *Emotional reactions to difficult situations, such as death, divorce, or the birth of a sibling, will often have consequences. When*

you've dealt with your child on the particular issue that's bothering him—rather than nagging him about going to the bathroom—his patterns will eventually readjust.

12. How are you and your spouse behaving in connection with your child's elimination and toilet training? *By reviewing incidents that have taken place together, you'll get a better perspective on where each of your anxieties lies and how you can work together to help your child.*

STEP IV. UNDERSTAND YOUR CHILD'S POINT OF VIEW

It's essential to be empathic and understand the way your child views the elimination process if you're going to make it seem natural and easy for him to cope with it on his own. Remember that your own adult view is not your child's view, and his interest in and curiosity about his body may show itself in different ways.

> *Lois:* When she was in the bathroom washing out some underwear, Tom came in and sat down on a closed toilet seat to keep her company. She noticed that he was squirming around, his mouth puckering when he talked.
>
> "Hi, honey. Whatcha doing?" she asked.
>
> "I want a diaper, Mommy," he said.
>
> "You have to do poops?" she asked.
>
> "Yup."
>
> "Well, you're right here in the bathroom. That's where I do them," she offered, keeping all pressure out of her tone.
>
> "I don't. I do them in the diaper."
>
> "You have been. Did you ever try the potty? Remember the one Grandma gave us? I could take it out of the closet for you."
>
> "No! *No!*" Tom begins to run out of the bathroom.
>
> "Hey, don't get all bent out of shape," Lois said. "You don't have to. What's wrong with the potty?"
>
> "It lives in the closet where it's dark and horrible. I won't go in there."
>
> "Well, I can bring it out here."
>
> "No! It's Grandma's," he told her sharply. "It's for her when she comes to visit."

"Sweetheart, Grandma's a grown-up. She uses the toilet."

"I'm a grown-up, too! I'm *not* a baby."

"Did somebody say you were?" Lois asked gently.

"Sammy did. Because I wear a diaper and I smell, and it's too small so junk leaks out of it."

"That was pretty mean of Sammy, but I've noticed that the diapers really are too small for you because you're a big boy now."

"Well, I won't go in a potty."

Lois restrained herself. The conversation was going nowhere, and it would be easier just to forget it. But she decided to try once more. "If your diapers are too small and you don't like the potty, how else do you think you could do your poops?"

"I might fall into the toilet if I sat up there."

"I'd hold you."

"No, I need to be alone."

"Could you try it in the bathtub?" Lois asked, grasping for straws.

Tom suddenly smiled. Then he laughed. "Bathtub? Yes! I could look at my poops right there in the tub."

Lois suddenly understood that Tom was afraid of having his feces go where he couldn't see them, and the potty from Grandma had had very negative connotations—which Lois had probably helped to put there. But using a dry bathtub as an intermediate stage was a great suggestion. After a suitable period of time doing it in the tub, he might feel ready to use the toilet.

Bringing Out Your Child's Feelings

When you see your baby having difficulty with a bowel movement, you will undoubtedly feel empathic, but there will be little you can do to relieve him other than rub his belly and talk softly to him. You can help your toddler or preschooler to express his thoughts and feelings about what is going on inside his body by talking to him calmly and logically.

The statements below may seem laughable out of context, but they can work for you if you put them in your own words and try them out with your child:

1. "You go to the bathroom to get rid of the stuff your body doesn't need anymore. Where do you think it goes from there?"

2. "Does your bottom hurt when you go potty? Maybe we could try sitting in some warm water first, to make it feel better."
3. "Tell Mommy why you're crying. Is it because you had an accident? It happens to all kids, especially when they drink too much juice or milk."
4. "If you feel that you have to pee in the store, let me know and we'll find a bathroom quickly. Do you think you could hold on to what's inside you while we shop?"

Acting on Your Child's Feelings

1. Try making the elimination process comprehensible, so that your child can understand it. Talk to him calmly and logically. Explain that elimination is the end process of eating and that eating certain things make pee and poops harder or softer.
2. Be sure to let your child take as much time as he or she needs to eliminate. This goes for babies as well as preschoolers.
3. Give your child a lot of reinforcement for being such a "big boy" or "big girl." There is something exceptionally wonderful to any small child about their parents dubbing them "more grown-up than baby Timmy on the corner." Children want to progress, they want to move ahead, and when they are praised and rewarded for doing so in any area, they usually welcome change.
4. Start training by encouraging an interest. Buy a book on the subject: *Once Upon a Potty* by Alona Frankel is published in two editions, one for a boy and one for a girl, and is also sold as a package with anatomically correct dolls. Fred Rogers's *Going to the Potty* is reassuring and comforting. You might also have the potty ready, sitting somewhere conspicuously in the bathroom.
5. Make an expedition to a store to buy some "big boy" or "big girl" underpants, and let your child choose the style. When he's reached the stage of being physically ready to control his bowels and urine, you'll be able to encourage him to attempt the feat by stressing all the grown-up "goodies" that he'll get by giving up his babyish ways.

6. Don't ask a lot of questions if your child tends to be secretive about elimination. Remember that children's stages evolve rapidly, and if you don't appear to be prying, your child will eventually let you in on his feelings.
7. Try not to appear upset by your preschooler's constant use of bathroom language. You may find that every other word out of your three- or four-year-old is "pee," "wee-wee," "doody," or "poop." Although you will probably try to restrict this language to the privacy of your home, it may be impossible to do so. A three- or four-year-old is justly proud of his body's creations and wants to crow about it. The more upset you get about your child's use of toileting words, the more you'll hear of them. Teaching your child the correct adult words for these functions may assuage some of your anxiety.

STEP V. GROUND YOURSELF

Talk about what's going on before you begin to spiral. Reassure yourself verbally that you and your child are going to work out your problems with elimination and toilet training together.

> *Lois:* She can tell herself that one reason she never pushed Tom was that she thought she was helping him by letting him do things his own way. Because she has such respect for her son, she's going to be the kind of mother her mother never was—she accepts her child for who he is, not what he does. She can tell herself that because they've now all begun to talk about the toilet situation, she, Tom, and Paul are going to find their own solutions, which will probably be different from anyone else's.

Remember that the human body is engineered to get rid of waste, and eventually development catches up to physical potential. If your baby isn't producing now but is eating and healthy, he'll have a movement tomorrow or the next day. If your toddler is balking at the idea of getting trained, ease up. His peers will convince him it's a good idea to get rid of those diapers and be a "big boy."

Some of the suggestions below are those offered by parents who themselves had difficulties concerning their child's elimination habits. Using these thoughts to guide you, you'll be able to come up with something appropriate to your particular situation.

> *Anxious thought:* My baby's got diarrhea again! There must be something terribly wrong with my breast milk.
> *Grounding thought:* All breast milk is the same, and it's equally good. Maybe my child's just been prone to stomach bugs for the past few weeks. I'll get the doctor to check her out.

> *Anxious thought:* All I have to do is start putting on a clean diaper and he pees in it. Every single time I try to change him, he beats me to it.
> *Grounding thought:* He really has a good, strong system for an infant. I can really see that whatever goes into him comes out. If I waste a few more diapers a day, so what?

> *Anxious thought:* My child's not toilet trained, and every other kid in his class is! I'm tearing my hair out trying to get this across to him!
> *Grounding thought:* Nobody ever went to college wearing a diaper. Eventually, with peer pressure and natural curiosity about trying something new, he'll give up the diapers.

STEP VI. STEP BACK AND SEE THE SCENE WITH DIFFERENT EYES

In order to think about what you'd like to happen in real life, you can create an imaginary scene that offers you a look at the possibilities that really do exist.

> *Lois:* She would like Tom to have good relationships with his peers. Without making him do anything he doesn't want to, she'd like to feel capable of encouraging him to give up his diapers.
> She steps back and sees Tom trying to do something he's never done before: dressing himself. Without her intervention, Tom struggles with zippers, buttons, laces, backs and fronts of shirts

and pants. She imagines that he really wants to put on all his clothes just because it gives him pleasure to learn something new. There's no reward for him other than the accomplishment of knowing he's done something new. She sees him complete the task, then come into her room, where she hugs, kisses, and congratulates him. She thinks about how he figured all this out by himself and how, without pushing him, she was able to let him know he'd done a fabulous job. Maybe if Tom can participate a little more in other areas of being "grown-up," the toileting will seem more important to him.

Imagine What You'd Like to Happen

If you suspend reality and picture yourself and your child outside the tension-filled moment you're going through, you'll be better able to imagine what might be possible. Be as flexible and realistic as you can be, whether you're imagining a more regular elimination pattern for your infant or a toddler who will proceed at a steady pace toward wanting to be toilet trained. Give yourself and your child time to work your way into these new, realistic expectations.

STEP VII. ESTABLISH NEW PATTERNS

When you put together your research from the various steps of this program, you may have some concrete ideas about the problems you have with elimination and toilet training. On the other hand, your feelings may still be vague and unformed. Regardless of how close or far away you are from solving the problem, you will find that your anxiety can come into play in a constructive manner when you attempt to establish new patterns with your child.

Lois: She saw that she'd imposed a huge responsibility on Tom, expecting him to decide to toilet train himself, and he wasn't up to it. She was going to have to help him make the big change from diapers to toilet. She felt somewhat easier about doing this when she realized that she wasn't pushing him or doing it the way her mother would have. She was taking the lead from Tom.

First they used the bathtub, then they put newspapers on the floor so that he could do it "like the doggie." One day she was folding laundry in the bedroom when she heard Tom call, "It's in there!" She wandered into the bathroom and found him sitting on the toilet. He looked so incredibly pleased with himself. She hugged him and asked how it felt to be such a grown-up boy. His response: "Can we take my bike to the playground now?"

PARENTS' SUGGESTIONS

The following ideas will probably stimulate your own creative efforts in thinking up new approaches to dealing with your child's elimination.

1. Regardless of what your personal bathroom habits or fears may be, treat the changing of diapers and going to the potty in a matter-of-fact manner and explain to your child that although there is nothing marvelous or wonderful about what comes out of the body, there is certainly nothing wrong with it.

2. Work with your child's diet. Any good child care book will suggest foods that will add or subtract liquid from the bowel. Ask the babysitter, day-care professional, or preschool teacher what your child eats on a regular basis and what his pattern of elimination is away from home.

3. Forget about books that promise you can toilet train your child in a day. You may think it's a great idea to hurry the event along as quickly as possible, but your child needs time. Toileting is a complex, developmental process that may take some children as much as a year to master.

4. Carry diapers, wipes, training pants, and a change of clothes with you at all times. Be prepared and no accident will faze you.

5. If you have pets, it might be a good idea to allow your child to help with their elimination—in other words, walking the dog or watching you change the catbox. This can open up avenues of discussion between you about the way people and

animals are different when it comes to going to the bathroom.

6. Never reward your child *before* the fact. If you give him a lollipop and tell him to stay on the potty until he's eaten it, you have taught him the value of sitting still but have taught him nothing about eliminating on the potty. By confusing your message, the toilet training will probably take longer to accomplish.

7. If you decide to use a reward system, make it a very concrete one. You might offer a couple of M&Ms after urinating or defecating in the potty, or if you are reluctant to associate food with toileting, put a gold star on a bathroom chart.

8. Make sure your child can see other, older children using the toilet. It doesn't make any difference if he sees you doing it; parents are magical, superhuman creatures while other children are more like him.

9. Don't panic when your child reaches an intermediary stage that seems odd to you. A toddler who gets interested in the potty will initially want to use it just so he can see what's coming out of him. This means that the child may jump up to look, and the end product will often go on the floor rather than in the potty. Let him watch while you put the feces or urine back in the potty and go to flush it down the toilet. Always explain what you are doing and why. You may find that you graduate from diaper to floor to bathtub to potty to toilet—not necessarily in that order. The important thing for the child is to be able to see the end product before it's disposed of.

10. Always ask your child if he has to use the toilet before you leave the house, but don't be surprised if he refuses and then has to go the instant you get to the store, library, or playground.

11. Encourage your child to use different toilets. Many children get stuck and are fearful of any but the one in their own home. If it doesn't bother you, you might want to encourage your son or daughter to urinate outdoors, weather permitting.

12. A newly toilet-trained child must be trusted outside in the world without diapers at some point. When he has acci-

dents—and he will—you simply have to reassure him that his new skill will come slowly and he can't get it perfect overnight. Prepare for the inevitable by reminding him to go to the bathroom often. Carry a change of clothes, and as soon as you arrive at a new location, find out where the toilet is.

13. Never make fun of your child or punish him for having an accident. This is a new skill, and it takes time to learn. It's particularly hard for him to remember to go to the bathroom when he's in the middle of playing—even if you've reminded him. If your child eliminates on the floor, don't panic. You might suggest that your child help take part in the cleanup while you discuss why it might have happened.

14. Remember that night training often comes a year or two after day training, and girls usually master it first. Double padding and sheeting the bed make nighttime changes easier.

15. Some children seem to have difficulty learning to wipe themselves after bowel movements. At the beginning, certainly, you should do it for them so they'll learn the right method. It's particularly important that girls be taught to wipe front to back so as not to get fecal matter into the vagina. If your child is reluctant to learn to wipe herself, tell her you'll check her afterward. Have her practice first, with her pants on, then with pants off when she hasn't had a movement. Finally, ask her to wipe the real thing. Always offer to check the toilet paper rather than the anus so as not to be taking too much physical control. You can make it a challenge for her to keep taking new pieces of paper until there's no more brown stain.

It's very common for a child who has been perfectly toilet trained for a year to lose his training when an upsetting or difficult event takes place in his life. The most common, of course, is the birth of a sibling or a divorce or death, but there may be dozens of other reasons, some of which are not immediately identifiable.

Remember that your child isn't "doing this" to you on purpose. It's perfectly natural to be annoyed that you once again have to pay attention to something you thought your child knew by heart, but it's not so much a matter of forgetting as feeling that he's lost control of a situation and is desperate to regain it. When a toilet-trained child has frequent accidents or wants a diaper again, he's asking for some attention he hasn't been given. Never be punitive, no matter how badly these episodes make you feel. Your child needs your love and consideration now more than ever. The more encouragement you give him, the sooner he'll get his training back.

Going to the bathroom is a fact of life; a psychologically healthy person won't worry about it unless he's ill and his system isn't functioning properly. Though toileting is something that must be done in private, the healthiest approach is to bring the fact of it out into the open so as not to make it a covert, hidden activity. The sooner you and your family are able to look at the process as a natural one, the sooner you will be able to use your anxieties over elimination and toilet training to help effect change.

12
Anxiety about Separation

Which of the following statements are true for you?

1. Even after my child was born I felt she was a part of me, so whenever I left her with my mother or a sitter, it felt as if I was leaving part of myself. I'd wait outside the door for half an hour listening to her cry.
2. I knew that my baby wasn't ready to separate from me, so I didn't consider looking for a sitter. But when he was eight months old, my husband began asking who was having the problem separating—him or me?
3. All the other fathers seemed to have easy good-byes with their kids at day care, but I couldn't do a thing to calm my three-year-old. I eventually got him involved with another child and quickly escaped before he could notice.
4. I feel so hurt when I look through the window and see my child at play group, perfectly happy without me.

Who among us hasn't said something like this? Probably one of the worst moments in your life as a parent was the first time you had to leave your child with someone else. How could you trust a grandparent or a sitter to care as much as you do, to know what your child wants and needs? You probably felt cruel and heartless, going out to work or dinner or a movie. You might even have had the fleeting, guilty thought that you were abandoning your child.

The moment a woman delivers her baby and their physical connection is broken, she has to face up to the fact that this small, wonderful being is no longer a part of her. She's his nurturer and primary caregiver, but she's no longer his sole support system of blood, oxygen, and nourishment. Her baby is going to have to face life without her constantly by his side.

The act of birth separates you from your child; it also makes room for plenty of natural anxieties. When you or your husband leave(s) your baby with someone else, you may feel a sense of vague discomfort about how he'll react without you around, or you may imagine all kinds of disasters that might happen. At the same time, your child may feel lost and abandoned, partly because he's responding to your fears and partly because it's so strange for him to be without you. These anxieties, whether mild or extreme, are completely natural and understandable. Figuring out where they're coming from and how you're going to handle them can be enormously helpful to you and your child.

If you never let him try anything on his own, he'll always be sheltered, ruled, and influenced by your opinions. If you never allow him to get close to an emotionally difficult situation, you'll stunt him developmentally and emotionally. How will your son or daughter learn to cope out in the world if you are always holding him, standing behind him, *doing* for him the things that he must learn to do for himself?

If you're "kind" enough to remove all obstacles and strife, your child will never discover the magic of his own potential. Only by giving him the freedom to explore—within appropriate boundaries and limitations—will he be able to develop the emotional skills he needs to check and test and modulate his own feelings.

THE TWO FACES OF SEPARATION ANXIETY

For the first eight or nine months of a child's life his parent does and is everything to him. An infant assumes that his parents' abilities are synonymous with his own. But as he grows, his sensory-motor world expands, and he begins to recognize more and more his separateness from his parents. It becomes clear to him that when his mother or father is present, he's taken care of; when they vanish, he misses their special warmth and comfort. He starts to wonder what will happen to him when they're not around. And so, when they leave him, he experiences *separation anxiety,* which only fades when one of them returns to take care of his needs again.

Anxiety over separation, on the other hand, is experienced by the parents who have a lot of trouble leaving their child with anyone else. They may have real, conscious concerns about their infant's or child's ability to function without them; in addition, they probably have a lot of unconscious fears that involve their own past and present experiences with being left.

The older child whose parents have great difficulty leaving him will also experience anxiety over separation because his parents' guilt and upset will undoubtedly make him feel that something is wrong.

Lucy was a prime example of a mother torn by anxiety over separation from her daughter Emily when she decided to go back to work after eighteen wonderful months as a full-time parent.

"I did everything imaginable to prepare for this giant life change," she said. "I took a position with flexible hours, and Lowell and I reapportioned our responsibilities around the house so that Emily would see us as much as possible. Then I screened two day-care centers and three preschools, and finally settled on a sitter who would come to our house at eight and leave at six. I gave her a trial run for three days so I could be there and see how she and Emily got along. The third day Emily even ran to the door and greeted Pam with a big hug! I thought, Wonderful, fine, it's going to work.

"But then came the first day of my new job. Pam walked in, I put on my coat, gave Emily a big good-bye hug and kiss, and my stomach fell on the floor. Somewhere inside me was a small voice saying, 'This isn't right. My daughter needs me. I'm being selfish by wanting to go back to my career. I can't leave.' And suddenly, as if she could read my mind, Emily burst into tears and grabbed my skirt, sobbing, 'Want Mommy!'

"I read her a book and she calmed down, but I was a basket case. My ride was due to come for me, and I was thinking, How am I going to get out of here? I could hear my voice getting shrill and completely un-Dr. Seuss-y. So at the end of the book I said good-bye, and the whole tantrum started again. I thought, Why doesn't Pam step in and *do* something? Why did Lowell have to leave for work early this morning? Why am I always the one stuck with Emily when she's in the middle of a tantrum? I left her screaming when I heard my neighbor outside in her car, honking for me."

TRYING TO STAY WHILE YOU'RE TRYING TO LEAVE

What happened to Lucy? Realistically she knows that she's doing what's best for herself and her child. She takes her career seriously; she'll be a better mother when she can be a person in her own right at her job and give her full attention to her daughter when she's home. But she's still anxious about her decision because she can see that it clearly affects her child. And it obviously affects her.

But why? If there is nothing dangerous about the situation in which she's about to leave her child, if she knows from prior experience that Emily is happy with the sitter, why can't she get out the door?

Lucy starts with the guilt-ridden premise that when Emily needs her, she's not there. To make matters worse, her husband left early and the sitter isn't jumping in. As Lucy starts spiraling, Emily starts crying and Lucy stays because she feels needed. When she stays, her anxiety builds and Emily, sensing this, becomes increasingly upset, taking on her mother's fears as well as her

own. This means she has to deal not only with her own anticipation of what will happen but also with Lucy's reaction.

When you're this anxious, you tend to become trapped in a
cycle of frustrating behavior, such as yelling or cajoling or turning
yourself off when your child needs you most. Unless you change
your behavior around the moments of parting, you're loading
your child with your own anxieties as well as hers. If, on the
other hand, you can become more in touch with your feelings
by using the cues your anxiety offers, you'll be able to see the
problem with new eyes and figure out new ways to respond and
react. Your goal is to create an atmosphere where the two of you
can separate without too much pain and strife.

LEARNING TO PART FROM AN OLDER CHILD

Every new situation offers us the possibility to grow and change.
Every new situation is unknown, however, and therefore frightening. To a child, for whom all things tend to be black or white,
the first day of school can be a descent into hell or an open door
that reveals hundreds of terrific sights, sounds, and feelings. A
lot of your child's reaction depends on your lack of conflict in a
new situation.

Let's take the case of Seth, his mother Sheila, and his father
Ken. Ken's a very nurturing man, very protective of Seth, a sensitive, shy three-year-old. Sheila, a housewife, has stayed home
with Seth since he was born; Ken would get his mother to babysit
on the rare occasions when the couple wanted an evening out.
Except for a weekly play group where Sheila always stayed with
him, Seth has had very little exposure to social situations.

Ken and Sheila took Seth to his school for an orientation meeting with his teacher and bought him a book about the first day
of school. They felt very prepared, and Seth seemed genuinely
excited about the prospect of this new adventure—until the actual
day arrived. When they walked in, Ken's eye immediately went
to two boys who were fighting in one corner. The teacher, busy
giving out art supplies, did nothing to break up the melee.

Ken felt panic growing inside him as he glanced down at his

son. "Seth started crying and grabbed my leg. I could feel his little body shaking, and he was moaning, 'Don't leave me!' God, I remembered my own first day of school. I was terrified! When I saw those boys fighting, I just wanted to be there for Seth. I'm on the road, traveling a lot for work. It was Sheila who picked this place, and she seemed completely oblivious to the problem. What she should have done was comfort Seth or get the teacher to break up the fight. Suppose those boys started in on Seth as soon as I left? What kind of a teacher was she, anyway, if she ignored this behavior?

"So I stayed. I told Sheila to do some errands and pick me up in an hour. Seth stuck next to me like glue until finally the teacher started a music period. The instant I saw him involved, I escaped out the door before he ever knew I was going. I felt rotten about abandoning him, but what could I do?"

THE POSITIVE SIDE OF SEPARATION

We might call Ken an overprotective father because before taking his son to preschool he didn't think any sitter or caregiver was suitable for his son except his own mother. Could it possibly be true that no one else was good enough? Ken's anxiety about the school experience seems directly related to his conviction that he's the only one who understands Seth and can take care of his needs.

Ken isn't thinking rationally. It's almost as though he himself were in the midst of his son's dilemma. And his only alternative, having hung around and waited for his son to adapt to school, was to "escape" the minute Seth's back was turned. He didn't resolve the situation because he was afraid to say good-bye.

Anxiety gives you the cue to act. Reactions that come from fear can hurt everyone involved; reactions that stem from clearheaded thinking coupled with self-awareness can allow you to use separation as an opportunity to build confidence and strength in both your child and yourself. This is what Ken is going to have to learn to do.

Remember that the way you make the break will teach your

child how to accept it. Children with ambivalent parents who can't seem to take the reins often end up pushing every emotional button in order to get their mother or father to act. They're simply not ready to handle the responsibility of decision-making on their own, and it confuses them terribly when their parents abdicate power and put them in charge.

It's very important for you to assess how anxious your child really is about separating, whether he's just manipulating you, and how readily he will adjust after you've made the separation. You must also learn to deal with your own feelings of distress about leaving your child in someone else's hands.

It's time to establish new separating patterns if . . .

- you blame your child for your own inability to let go, claiming he's too young, weak, badly behaved, or hypersensitive to be left with a sitter.
- you can *never* seem to find a surrogate (grandparent, sibling, sitter, day-care facility, or preschool) you feel is adequate.
- you find that you are constantly canceling evenings out because you're "too tired" or feel that you're "coming down with something"; likewise, if you have started mounting up too many sick days or personal days at the office.
- you always fight with your spouse before an evening out.
- you find that you shower your child with special treats before leaving him with a surrogate.
- you find that you are extracritical and overly harsh with your child before leaving him with a surrogate.

Each of these patterns indicates that separation causes so much anxiety that you have to invent an excuse, which will make parting from your child extremely unpleasant if not impossible. Denying yourself the freedom of an evening alone with a spouse or an unconflicted day at work is going to disrupt family dynamics, your social life, and your child's development. Your child will begin to expect trouble the minute he sees you dressed for some non-domestic activity and may start to act out his own fears or begin to develop new ones. If these scenarios are at all typical in your household, it's definitely time for a change.

Your Program for Change

For a complete description of how to use this program effectively, see Chapter 4, page 61.

STEP I. IDENTIFY WHAT'S REALLY BOTHERING YOU
STEP II. CONNECT WITH YOUR PAST
STEP III. GET THE FACTS
STEP IV. UNDERSTAND YOUR CHILD'S POINT OF VIEW
STEP V. GROUND YOURSELF
STEP VI. STEP BACK AND SEE THE SCENE WITH DIFFERENT EYES
STEP VII. ESTABLISH NEW PATTERNS

STEP I. IDENTIFY WHAT'S REALLY BOTHERING YOU

The experience of separating has many different facets, and any one of them can give you problems. It's crucial to pinpoint your central issues, which underlie the specific qualms you have, so that you can deal with separating in a useful way.

Let's think about Lucy, who is extremely conflicted about leaving her child with a sitter when she goes to work. *What is it about this experience that's really bothering Lucy?*

Up to this point Lucy has been the most important person in Emily's world. Could it be she's worried that Emily might get more attached to the sitter if she spends a lot of time with her? But the sitter hasn't proven herself yet, and Emily's starting to wonder if she should have hired a person more like herself, more assertive, who can take charge.

Another possibility is that Lucy feels unsure about her own worth as a fully functioning professional. She's been a good mother for the past year and a half, but how does she know she can fit back into the working world and still maintain her moth-

ering role? She's also annoyed that her husband couldn't be
around on her first day on the job to ease the transition. She
might blame him a little for leaving her alone with this unpleasant
task. Maybe, and this is probably the most important assumption,
Lucy is a woman who truly loves being with her daughter. She's
feeling a loss because the time they spend together is something
they'll never be able to recapture.

What about Ken, who is overly worried about Seth managing
on his own, without his father. *What is it about this experience
that's really bothering Ken?*

Ken is worried that, since his son has never been in this type
of setting before, he won't be able to adapt to it. He seems to feel
that he has to pave the way for his son's every attempt and believes
that Seth will fall apart if his father isn't around to glue him back
together.

He's upset about the fact that the teacher isn't breaking up the
fight in the classroom. This school doesn't seem to have a policy
on discipline, so maybe they're too laissez-faire about a lot of
other things. Ken feels that he should have helped Sheila select
their son's school. If Seth hates it, Ken will feel as though it's all
his fault.

He's also clearly worried that Sheila doesn't see the situation
the way he does. He feels as if he needs an ally so that he'll be
justified in saying, "School's not for a three-year-old. He should
be home with his mother." He evidently feels guilty for not spending more time at home with his child.

What's Really Bothering You

Now that you've had a chance to look at Lucy and Ken's particular issues, it's time to look at your own. Some of the major
parental concerns about separation are as follows:

- a feeling that you are physically being torn apart
- upset that your child can do without you
- anger at your child for not allowing you to live your own life
- embarrassment about what others think of your attachment to
  your child

If you're having any anxieties over your own expectations about parting, you might want to look at the following questions that relate to some of the above concerns:

1. Do you find that you feel impatient, wanting to escape when your child is being difficult about parting?
2. Are you ever embarrassed that your child is putting you in an uncomfortable situation when there are others present?
3. Are you ever sad that your child misses you when you're away?
4. Are you ever delighted that you're the only one she wants?
5. Does it worry you when the sitter tells you that your child stops crying for you the moment you are out of sight?
6. Are you ever jealous of the sitter or teacher you select? Are you mistrustful of all caregivers? Do you find yourself saying you can never find one you feel is suitable?
7. Does it bother you to smell the sitter's perfume on your child? Or when your child calls her by an affectionate name?
8. Do you ever find that you feel physically ill just before or after you leave your child with another caregiver?

Share with your spouse the anxieties you feel about leaving your child and try to get an honest assessment of the balance between you in this situation. Is it much easier for your spouse to leave your child than for you to do it? Do you sometimes feel he doesn't love your child as much as you do because it's easier for him to separate? Or do you feel that he loves your child more because he can see him as an intact person, functioning on his own. These feelings and others like them can be brought out into the open and explored.

STEP II. CONNECT WITH YOUR PAST

Thinking back to a time in your past when you were forced to separate from the two people you saw as all-powerful, all-protecting, may be frightening and unsettling. But it's essential to find the cues in your unconscious that trigger your panicked reaction when you separate from your child.

Lucy: Lucy's mother was a piano teacher, but instead of explaining that she was going out to work, she lied to Lucy and said that she was going shopping and that Lucy's aunt Susan would watch her until she returned. Lucy can vividly remember standing at the window and crying, afraid that she'd never see her mother again. When she came home she would invariably let some comment drop about Johnny or Rachel whom she'd "met at the store that day"—and what funny or talented or infuriating kids they were. Not only was her mother choosing to leave her alone, but in Lucy's mind she was going out to spend time with other, perhaps "better" children.

Until that moment in her adult life when Lucy saw her own child's tear-streaked face at the window, she didn't remember how angry she'd been at her own mother all those years for all the lies, which Lucy felt she had to go along with.

Ken: It occurs to him that his and Sheila's family backgrounds were completely different. Sheila came from a big family and had always elbowed her way into her brothers' scuffles, even if it meant getting a few bumps and bruises. Ken, on the other hand, had been an only child, like Seth, not used to rough-and-tumble play. Could Ken have been protecting his son because he himself remembered feeling threatened around rougher children? His father always told him to act like a man and never defended him. Ken had to fight his own battles and hated doing it. When he foresees this as a possibility for his son, he thinks he must be a terrible father, the same way he felt about his own father. And it occurs to him that maybe if he was home more, he could keep Seth away from kids who could hurt him. It also occurs to him that up to this point his own mother has been the only caregiver he's felt comfortable with. Is this another way of reliving his own past?

How Can You Connect with Your Past?

Prepare a picture of yourself with your parents. Now erase the parents from this scene. What does it feel like to remember the way your partings happened and what circumstances surrounded them?

SETTING THE SCENE

1. What's your first memory of your parents leaving you?
2. Were you and the caregiver entirely alone, or were you with a sibling?
3. Did you routinely spend time with another caregiver, such as a grandparent?
4. Can you recall what kinds of situations gave rise to your parents leaving you with someone else? Their work, their trips, a night out, and so forth?
5. Do you remember times when you left them instead of them leaving you? To go to a party, on an overnight, to school, to camp?

Now that you can see clearly, how did you experience separation?

Some typical memories that many parents recall had to do with the following:

· feeling abandoned
· feeling unloved and unwanted
· feeling that you should protect your parents even though you couldn't
· feeling that they loved your sibling better than you

The following questions, which relate to one or several of the above concerns, may evoke certain useful feelings about your past:

6. Did your parents spend a lot of time parting, or did they just walk away?
7. Did they ever trick you or lie to you instead of coming right out and saying good-bye? Did they take your siblings places and not you?
8. Do you recall being left alone too often as a child?

9. Did you ever feel as though your parents didn't want you and were trying to get rid of you?
10. Were you ever left in the care of someone whose behavior made you uncomfortable?

If feelings of having been abandoned are very painful, you may find that you relive the same emotion when you go through a parting with your child now, from your perspective as parent. But just because you're the one doing the leaving doesn't mean that you have to separate from your child as your parents did from you.

STEP III. GET THE FACTS

Try to ascertain exactly what's going on in the situation by getting some factual information. This will allow you to view the separation in a more clinical, detached way.

> *Lucy:* Lucy's first source of information is Pam. She calls the sitter from the office and finds out that Emily stopped crying about three or four minutes after Lucy left.
>
> Then, because Lucy still feels unsure of herself, she calls Amanda, her next-door neighbor, and asks her to stop by and check on Emily sometime during the day. Because Amanda knows Emily and her moods, it will be easier for her to judge than a parent (too close to the situation) or an outside observer (the sitter). And Lucy confesses that she's still a little paranoid about leaving her child with a stranger, and she'd appreciate Amanda's opinion on what's going on.
>
> She asks Lowell if he'll stay home an extra half hour the following day so that he can do the parting. When she calls her husband at his office later, he reports that Lucy did cling to him a bit but didn't cry at all.
>
> *Ken:* Ken calls Seth's teacher that night. She reports that it's very common for children to have difficulty separating in a school setting regardless of how many sitters they've had in the past. Some three-year-olds cry for the whole school year when they separate

from their parents, but this is no indication of severe emotional distress, nor does it forecast problems with school. It generally indicates that they find adjusting to new settings difficult, and this should get easier as the child matures and has more practice at it. She suggests that for a while Seth might want to bring a special toy or blanket that reminds him of home.

She also mentions that Ken could see just how Seth is doing when he leaves by watching for a few minutes through the one-way glass on the window of the classroom.

Consider All Your Facts

Any new situation holds its share of hidden surprises, and the unknown is a breeding ground for anxiety. Although you can't prepare for every contingency, you can certainly alleviate a great many fears by checking the truth of the situation. The following questions will give you guidelines to begin your own factual investigation.

1. How do you find an appropriate babysitter? *Check any and all references a babysitter provides. Spend some time with her and your child to see that they get along well. Quiz her on what she might do in case of various emergencies. Be sure she has all phone numbers for where you'll be and the number of a neighbor you trust as well.*

2. How do you find an appropriate play group? *Decide whether to chose a drop-off group or one where all the parents participate together. Talk to the current members about the rules, the mix of the various kids and parents, and whether the children stay inside or go outside to a fenced-in yard or playground. The first time you leave your child alone in the group, you might want to stay a while until he's comfortable.*

3. How do you find an appropriate preschool or day-care facility? *Ask your pediatrician which preschools he recommends and why. Talk at length to several parents whose children are at the day-care center of your choice. Go in unannounced and watch several classes and teachers in progress. You might want to take a month-to-month contract rather than commit yourself—and your*

money—for a whole year. It's a good idea to make periodic un-announced visits to see how the place runs and how your child is doing.

4. Is it easier for fathers to leave their children than mothers? *Depending on his own past experiences, a father may be more or less anxious. If he subscribes to the misguided belief that men are supposed to tough out any emotional experience, he may deny his own and his child's anxiety. Or he may displace the anxieties he feels by blaming the whole incident on his wife, claiming she's made a sissy out of their child. Another possibility is that he may panic because he has never had the opportunity to see his child bounce back from a serious upset. Watching his son or daughter break down in tears may be simply unbearable to him, and he may feel that he has to "fix it" immediately.*

5. Is it better to be a parent who can't let go or a no-nonsense parent who separates easily? *It's far better to be clinging than distant. The anxiety that comes out during the separation process is one way to show care, love, trust, and emotional support.*

6. Do you think the caretaker you've hired is really mistreating your child? *Your child may be making up stories about all ba-bysitters because he senses how anxious you are about leaving him. One way to get the facts would be to have a friend stop by while you are out and give you an objective view.*

7. Do you ever feel unpleasant physical symptoms when you're about to leave your child? *Anxiety may bring on physical symp-toms, as though you were facing real danger with your child. As your adrenaline starts pumping, your heart may beat faster and your stomach may feel tied in knots.*

If you can see that the surrogate you've selected behaves in a warm and conscientious manner, if you can acknowledge that the day-care situation holds the potential for fun and learning, if your child has previously come home happy from the sitter or the preschool, if the sitter has your phone number so that she can contact you immediately, there is no reason to believe the worst. Your examination of the real situation will help you put your anxieties in perspective.

STEP IV. UNDERSTAND YOUR CHILD'S POINT OF VIEW

It's enormously helpful to elicit your child's perspective on parting. He may not be aware of his troubled reaction or may be very aware. He may say terrible things that may or may not be true. But as the two of you have a dialogue together, you're going to be laying groundwork for the two interrelated halves of your parting: the way you say good-bye to your child and the way your child says good-bye to you.

Lucy: That evening Lucy reviewed the day with Emily, who told her happily that she and Pam had read books and played horsey.

The next morning when Pam came, Lucy hugged her daughter and then allowed Pam to move between them. "When I'm at the office," Lucy said, watching Pam start to take Emily's hand, "I'm going to think about your reading books and playing horsey."

As she started toward the door, she suddenly felt a hand gripping her skirt. "Mommy, stay!"

Lucy decided that Emily was fine and nodded to Pam, who swooped the child up in her arms and carried her to the window. The face Lucy saw as she drove away was not exactly happy, but it wasn't distressed, either.

Ken: On the second day of nursery school, two of the bigger boys were scuffling over a toy when Ken and Sheila came in with Seth. The child's face froze, and he grabbed his father's hand tightly.

"Those kids are really having fun," his mother said cheerily.

"It doesn't look like fun," said Seth. "Looks like it hurts. Maybe we should go home now."

"Naw," Sheila said. "It'll be fine. See you later, sweetie," she said, kissing her son and walking to the door.

But Ken wasn't ready to leave. "Look," he said to Seth, "there are plenty of other kids to play with. Look at that little boy—he seems lonely. Maybe you should go over and help him with that puzzle."

Seth reluctantly allowed Ken to walk him over to the other child. "What's your name?" Ken asked.

"David."

"This is Seth," he said, at which point, Seth sat down across from David and reached for a puzzle piece. "This one goes here," he said. "I'll put it in."

"Okay," the other boy agreed.

"Have a great day, kid," Ken said softly to his son. "Good-bye."

"Daddy?" Seth's face was immediately distraught. "You stay till we finish the puzzle."

Seth hung around his father's neck for a moment and started sniffling, but just when Ken started feeling he had to escape, the teacher came over to help.

"Oh, look, Seth, this is the piece you wanted," she said, nodding at Ken. He could see that Seth was only a little weepy, so he took his cue and left.

Bringing Out Your Child's Feelings

Talk to your child with words and body language to find out what his needs are when you separate. Listen to the quality of what he's saying, not so much the content. Children rarely state precisely what they mean. Watching you about to leave, he may insist, "The toilet here is dirty and you have to clean it!" or "You can leave when the sun comes out and not before. I'll tell you when." He may be acting more distressed than he actually is, for your benefit. You can counter with statements such as the following:

1. "Will you try to remember all the things you did at the sitter's today? Then tonight you can tell me everything."
2. "What do you like best about school? What kinds of toys and puzzles do you have in the classroom that we don't have at home? What are the kids like?"
3. "Wasn't that a nice teacher—the one who showed you how to draw this great-looking bunny?"

Acting on Your Child's Feelings

1. When you're about to leave, make everything concrete for your child, no matter how old she is. Tell her how long you'll be gone, where you're going, and what she will be doing and seeing until you return.

2. Never try to trick your child. If you lie about how long you'll be gone, your child will stop trusting you, and separating will become infinitely more difficult.
3. Try not to read your child's mind or give her the opening for more fears than she may already have. A statement such as "I know you always get upset with me when I go to the city early and we can't have breakfast together" only makes it possible for her to agree with you. Maybe she just doesn't like your harried tone of voice when you're rushing for the train.
4. Some days your child may feel confident and strong without you; on others he may need a little extra help. You can't expect stability and consistent emotional reactions in a developing child whose sense of independence is still fragile and untested. Also, remember that everyone has moods.
5. Do enlist the aid of other caregivers in your parting. If your child is more secure being held when you leave, ask the sitter or teacher to help. If your child is better able to help himself by helping another child, involve him in play before you leave.
6. There are a variety of excellent books for different age groups, including Fred Rogers's *Going to Day-Care,* Mercer Mayer's *Just Me and My Babysitter,* Stan and Jan Berenstain's *The Berenstain Bears and the Sitter,* and Patricia Relf's *The First Day of School.* By reading a story about a character going through the same experience, a young child can identify and understand each step of the process. A companion piece for parents is *Learning to Say Goodbye* by Nancy Balaban.

STEP V. GROUND YOURSELF

Always try to verbalize your worst fear; you'll find that you may be able to come up with a counter to it that will help, particularly at the moment when you *have* to walk out the door and see that bruised look on your child's face.

Lucy: She can tell herself that she's going to have a better relationship with her child when she pays some attention to her own needs as a person. By observing how well Emily is adapting to

Pam, Lucy can see that she's very flexible and does well with the stimulation of other adults. As Lucy becomes more at ease with walking out the door in the morning, her child will accept this as the new daily pattern.

Ken: He has seen that the teacher is responsive to Seth's needs and that there are other children in the classroom who are receptive to playing. He remembers when he and Seth were in the playground two weeks ago; Ken felt he had to help his son on all the equipment. Seth finally turned to him and said impatiently, "I can do it myself, Daddy!" It's clear now that there are many things Ken doesn't need to protect Seth from, and maybe being on his own at school is going to be comfortable for Seth, even though it wasn't for Ken.

When your child appears to be very troubled about your departure, it's easy to feel you're doing the wrong thing by leaving. Some parents have found that the suggestions below help them use the natural anxiety they're feeling to make the separation happen more easily.

Anxious thought: My child is small and could be hurt by the other kids. If he's miserable in this school, it must be an awful place. Maybe I should get him into another school.
Grounding thought: There are teachers here who are trained to see trouble before it begins. Once he gets over his fear of being away from me, he'll be as happy here with these kids and teachers as he would be anywhere else.

Anxious thought: Look at her face. She's going to hate me forever for being selfish and going off to work every day.
Grounding thought: She'll be delighted to see me when I get back, and the sitter's already told me she calms down the minute I'm actually out of the driveway.

Anxious thought: How do I know this sitter isn't an ax murderer? How do I know she'll be all right with my child?
Grounding thought: I know five people who have used her and been really pleased. I have to trust someone my first time out, and she has fabulous references—from parents and kids.

STEP VI. STEP BACK AND SEE THE SCENE WITH DIFFERENT EYES

Imagination can really help you when you're too focused on the actual painful situation of parting. If you can imagine yourself and your child in a mental picture that approximates the real scene, you'll be better able to get a handle on what to do the next time you separate.

Lucy: Lucy would like to leave her child in Pam's care without feeling guilty about going to the office. What does she imagine?

She steps back and sees herself involved with work at the office. Occasionally she glances up at the sight of her daughter and husband in the photo frame on her desk. At lunch break she calls the house and uses a happy, upbeat tone of voice when saying hello to Emily. She imagines that Emily gets teary and asks her to come home right away, and she responds with a heartfelt "I love you, and I'm coming home right after work." She has a mental picture of her daughter suddenly changing the subject—as kids do—and telling Lucy she's going to make a project for her that afternoon.

Ken: He would like to leave Seth at school and feel that his son is in charge, able to manage without him. What does he imagine?

He steps back and sees himself and Sheila leaving Seth at his mother's house. He then imagines his mother dropping Seth at the preschool the following morning. He is delighted to show her around his new school and introduce her to his new friend David. When Ken imagines himself picking Seth up in the afternoon, he can hear his son saying, "Daddy, I'm busy playing right now. You come back later." Ken can then stand in the back of the room and watch his son, apart from him, enjoy the experience of school.

Imagine What You'd Like to Happen

If you could suspend reality, you'd probably conjure up a scene where your happy child waves to you from the window and you both go off to have your separate days without any tears, any trauma. In truth it's the rare child and parent who can part this way *all* the time. Maybe you can imagine a scenario where both of you get a little more relaxed about the prospect of spending time apart, and you're able to admit that there are other competent adults in your child's life. You know that only by his seeing a contrast between his relationships with you and others will he get any real perspective.

STEP VII. ESTABLISH NEW PATTERNS

It may never be easy for you to part with your child. Inside you may always have a lingering doubt about whether you're doing the right thing. But by following the program you will at least see that your child is more capable than you thought and that your physical presence is less essential on a moment-to-moment basis.

> *Lucy:* She was able to see that letting go really wasn't that bad; it was certainly nothing like that frantic feeling she had when her own mother lied and left her every day. As each day passed (some partings were easy, some were still hard) she found that she was very proud and pleased to see Emily functioning on her own, learning new words and skills and doing art projects with Pam that she wouldn't have dreamed of tackling. The pleasure Emily took in showing her mother all her new accomplishments more than compensated for those few moments of guilt she still had.

> *Ken:* Ken and Sheila talked out their differences for the first time. Ken wanted to know why she was so removed from Seth's problems with separation, and she countered by saying that he seemed to be solving things on his own—and did better when Ken wasn't so smothering. She'd been watching Seth play with his puppet theater, acting out his fears with the animals. In the puppet show he played the "father" and took care of all the other characters. Sheila wondered if by making himself the "daddy," he didn't miss his own father so much.
>
> In the playground the next weekend, Ken saw Seth being hassled by two bullies. Though he wanted to intervene, he decided it would be better to keep a watchful distance. He saw Seth get pushed over, and he felt pain grip his own stomach. But Seth got right up

and walked over to another group of children who were getting together for a treasure hunt. The bullies, excluded, walked away. Ken understood that his son was very different from the kind of child he had been himself, and he was delighted to see that and let him be.

PARENTS' SUGGESTIONS

1. Introduce your child and the sitter before you're under the pressure of getting out of the house to get to a job or appointment. If your child will be leaving the home territory, make a preliminary trip to the sitter's house or the day-care facility. That way your child can get the lay of the land with you by his side, examine the toys that are available, see the kitchen where snacks are prepared, and try out the cots where naps will be taken.

2. Wean your child away from you. The first day in a new situation you might stay with your child for a while, then leave her with the surrogate for a few minutes, then return to play with them both. The second day you might disappear for an hour, and so on, until the child is convinced that you will always return after you've been away.

3. Rehearse what will happen when you leave. You might role-play using your child's dolls or animals and pretend that one of them is the sitter or teacher and the others are the children in the class. If your child is an imaginative three- or four-year-old, let him play the mommy or daddy leaving you, and you take the part of the child.

4. Use transitions. Your child must feel mentally prepared to let you go, and one way to do this is to assure him that what happens immediately after your departure will be pleasurable. You can ask your child to walk to the window and wave at you in the parking lot. You can request that the surrogate begin an activity the child usually enjoys, or you can involve him in play yourself, bring in the surrogate, and then suggest that it's time for you to go.

5. Make up a pattern for parting. Children love rituals; they take

comfort in repeating the same activities over and over. A good daily routine might consist of walking into the nursery school holding hands, putting his jacket on the coatrack, and kissing him before saying, "I love you. See you later, alligator."

6. Don't allow your child to panic. If he's sobbing and frantic over your departure, he has no room within his whirlwind of feelings to learn anything from the separation. Stay and comfort a really distraught child, talking to him firmly but lovingly. Only when he's calmer should you attempt to leave again.

7. Talk about what happened with your child the day after the separation experience with the sitter, play group, or day-care center. Don't criticize him for his negative opinions or try to make light of them. It's going to take him and you a while to get used to separating.

How to Separate at Different Childhood Stages: Parents' Suggestions

· At six months, an age when most infants will happily go to anyone, you might speak in soothing tones and retain body contact until the surrogate can hold your child.

· At nine months, when most infants first experience "separation anxiety," you might stay and introduce your child formally to the surrogate, indicating that you like the stranger a lot. Again, body contact should be used, as well as involving your child with a toy.

· From twelve to eighteen months babies are busy exploring their world, crawling, walking, and putting everything into their mouths. They may not be terribly concerned about your departure if you leave lovingly and cheerfully.

· Eighteen- to twenty-four-month-olds will probably be able to engage in parallel play with other children, which may assuage some of their anxiety over separation. However, this is the age of the emphatic "no!" when your toddler must challenge and object to everything. This means that you must have clear goals in mind and act on them.

· Two- to three-year-olds may be ready to take off on their own, but this is a very clinging age when your child really needs and wants you. Try not to fuel your child's fears by acting upset. Being firm but loving and trying to involve him with the surrogate or another child is the key to getting out the door.

· Three- to four-year-olds can be enormously independent and eager to please, yet they can also be whiny and difficult. This is the bossy age, when your child wants to tell everybody else what to do. Separating on some days may be a cinch, while on others it may be impossible to get away until the little king or queen is ready to dismiss his loyal parent subject.

Trusting Yourself and Your Child

At some point, whether you like it or not, you're going to have to walk to the end of the diving board and take the plunge. There is no other way to find out how cold it is or how refreshing and delicious. You have to trust that you've already given your young child the confidence and ability to carry on without you. One way you show someone you really care for him is to help him develop the skills he needs to become independent and manage under the supervision of another responsible adult. If you can look at each new experience as a chance for growth, it may be easier for you to make the break with your child.

A parent who believes that her child isn't happy without her is doing him a great disservice. All children need their parents, but they don't need them hovering over them twenty-four hours a day. The ironic joy of parenting is that we can keep them close only until we can teach them to walk away. If we do our job right, they'll want to leave us.

You unlearn anxious behavior by finding new consequences to old fears, by realizing that this time the story can have a happy ending. You'll always be connected to your child by some invisible bond, too strong to ever be broken; you don't have to be together to enjoy that special alliance. When the two of you have learned to separate amicably and easily, your reunions can only become more exciting and fulfilling.

13

Discipline and the Loss of Love

If any or all of the following statements make you feel guilty, upset, ashamed, or frantic, you're in good company.

1. After a day of my child having temper tantrums, running away from me in the mall, and throwing toys all over the living room, I don't know what to do but scream.
2. When my child bites another child in the playground, I'm so worried that the other mother will think I'm an awful parent.
3. My child hates me when I spank her, but I'm doing it for her own good so she'll learn right from wrong.
4. I get nervous about telling my wife when our son misbehaves because she's incredibly strict and I know she'd punish him.
5. Whenever I yell at my child about something, he screams back, "I hate you! You're a horrible mother!" And you know, I think he's right.

Everyone gets angry at their child, everyone has had their child furious with them. Feeling that you've lost your child's love is one of the most devastating emotional experiences a parent can go through.

We all want to be loved, and we all imagine that someone will stop loving us if we say or do the wrong thing to them. But what is the wrong thing? It can sometimes be more difficult for you to set boundaries than for your child to stay within them because you can see both sides of the issue. You love your child and want her not to be disappointed; yet you know that your child will learn to set her own limits only by watching the way you do it for her.

One of the most common anxieties a parent can have is that he's not providing enough direction, not intervening at exactly the right moment. Ideally we should all be wise, caring, empathic people who can see the root of a temper tantrum and stop it before it accelerates. Ideally we should be able to make important rules and enforce them, particularly when it comes to our children's development into well-socialized individuals. We should be able to look past our own sensitivity and say, "Well, he says he hates me for sending him to his room, but he doesn't really mean it."

Of course he *does* mean it at the time. And it hurts, probably worse than any other rejection you've ever had. When you discipline your child, you might fear that your child will hate you forever and that if you lose your child's adoration, you're not a good parent. You might even believe that your spouse will look down on you because you've turned your child against you. You might actually bend over backward *not* to discipline because you want to make sure your child continues to love you.

WHAT ARE LIMITS FOR?

A child is basically an egocentric being who takes the world as he receives it. He feels safe and secure in unsafe territory because he doesn't have the experience to understand what danger is all about. A child on his own will not limit himself: before he understands that too much of a good thing can cause a stomachache, he'll drink four bottles of milk or eat all the Halloween candy in one sitting; before he understands the value of rest and sleep, he'll stay up all night watching TV.

As a parent, then, you must act as the realistic judge of the situation and impose your direction based on your decisions about what's good and what's bad for him. Your awareness of the consequences of a situation will help you to gently shape your child's behavior. You've got to see that he takes that injection at the doctor's office so he'll get well. He may be furious when you tell him, "This is for your own good"—even after you've explained *why*. You just have to live with that temporary loss of love.

Setting limits is a parental tool for creating the optimal learning situation. What you're doing when you say no and explain why is curbing your child's egocentrism in favor of adjustment to reality.

Setting limits also teaches a child to get along with others in the world. It's the major tool of socialization. Limits are a way to help a child gain control over his moods and begin to understand why hitting, punching, kicking, or saying hurtful things to someone else is an antisocial thing to do. By helping him to distinguish between himself and another (whether this other is you, your spouse, or another child) you're helping him develop the ability to think about two different points of view at the same time. If you say to your child, "It hurts Daddy's feelings when you say you don't want him to put you to bed tonight," you allow the child to think about not just what he wants but what that desire does to another person he cares about.

SAYING NO; SAYING YES

Rules are information messages, and different families have different rules. It's useful to say, "In our house, we never hit," because it gives your child a sense of his own family's expectations. It may be all right for Jimmy to eat popsicles before lunch, a practice that's strictly forbidden at Joey's house, but Jimmy may be forbidden to ride his bike up and down the driveway, which is something Joey is allowed to do all the time.

When you have rules you can start to put some order on reality, and organize experience. If you have no rules, you have no way of expressing your limitations. A parent who is reluctant to put his foot down for fear of stunting his child's emotional growth or for fear that he'll lose out in his child's estimation is doing his child a real disservice. A child's natural inclination is to test all the limits; if he doesn't bounce up against a wall every once in a while, he begins to think that he's the center of his world and everyone else is out of step but him. Setting limits is a way of protecting your child by putting up an internal and external barricade against things that might injure him and others.

It's perfectly natural to say yes for the wrong reasons. Maybe you have a rule that your four-year-old must clean up her room before dinner, but on a particular day she refuses. You're tired and can't deal with the inevitable battle, so you give in. On another day you might be feeling anxious because you haven't been sticking to your household rules, so you might say no yet wish you could say yes when your daughter asks if a friend can come over to play. It would really be easier to have the two children entertain each other.

All members of your family will feel less conflicted when limits are set and consistently adhered to, but they don't have to be carved in stone. It's more important to pick your battles. Your child has a limited capacity to hear and absorb "no," so it's not a good idea to use it indiscriminately. If every encounter is a testing ground and if you feel you have to be on top all the time, you end up forbidding everything, and your child winds up fighting you every step of the way. Her reaction may make you feel that she doesn't love you anymore and that you don't love her, either.

Loss of love comes from two directions, and it's devastating in either form. If you discipline your child and he breaks down in tears or seems frightened of you, you may be torn apart by his reaction. You can tell he feels he's lost your love. You want to make it up to him and reassure him that you can be angry and still love him at the same time, but you worry about undoing the good effects of your discipline.

And what of the second form—your own feelings of the loss of your child's love? None of us likes to change the perception our child usually has of us—that Mommy and Daddy are wonderful, all-knowing, all-powerful people who deal out fun and games and goodies in a way that's tender and caring and strong. We all want to be the "good parent" all the time and may resort to every tactic we can think of before disciplining, which will turn us into the "bad parent" in our child's eyes.

After you've pleaded, cajoled, asked nicely, and formally stated your point of view, you may resort to threats ("if you don't join the family for dinner right now, there will be no TV for the rest of the night") or humiliation ("Margie always comes to the table when called—why can't you?"). And at last, meeting with complete resistance, you may decide you have to punish.

By delaying this long to enforce a rule you've done three things that will make it impossible for you and your child to come to any agreement: you've made her feel that the rule is meaningless because it's arbitrary, dependent on your mood; you've made doing or not doing something into a contest of wills; and, finally, you've made her feel awful by comparing her to another, "better" child who always obeys.

DISCIPLINE AND PUNISHMENT

Your child learns what not to do by making mistakes. When he goes outside the boundaries of what's acceptable, you will need to enforce your decisions, to impose your particular philosophy of household rules. This is *discipline*. In order to show your child exactly what you want and shape his behavior, you have to use certain concrete mechanisms—the maintenance program of your philosophy—to get your message across. These are *punishments*.

Like love, respect, and appreciation, discipline and punishment should be used not to manipulate a child but to open him up to experience. He has to get the notion that if Mommy and Daddy get mad when he does something, maybe it's not the right thing to do. Maybe it hurts someone else; maybe it hurts me.

If he repeats his mistake and you consistently show him how strongly you feel about it, he'll start to get a very clear notion of where the boundaries are, and maybe the next time he'll impose them on his own. If you pick your battles and you treat the child's errors with respect and understanding, you won't have to ram your message home in a cruel, heartless way.

Physical punishment is abuse not only because it's taking advantage of another human being but because it makes the child feel smaller and weaker than he really is. When you punish too harshly, your child doesn't have the leeway to think on his own about what he's done; he's just overcome with pain and fear.

Physical punishment does one thing only: it gets the child's attention. He's learned nothing about what he did wrong, only that you've lost control. All he can think about is you—not what he's done. He takes your message the wrong way and believes that *he* is bad, not that what he has done is bad. On the other hand, when you delay in punishing or punish in too lax a manner, you obscure the importance of learning about the mistake. The optimal method of punishment gets his attention and also makes him aware of what he has done wrong.

With a very young child you have to set limits to protect him from danger. This means forcibly pulling him away from a hot stove or yanking him out of the middle of the street, saying "No!" very loudly. He can't understand or rationalize about his activities, so you have to do it for him. With an older child who is experimenting with autonomy, you have to judge why the child is behaving a certain way and discipline him appropriately *so that ultimately you don't have to punish again.*

The punishment you select should fit the crime. A parent who overreacts to something that's wrong but not terrible is probably working off some anger or frustration, perhaps about some past wrong of his own. But your child doesn't understand why you're screaming at him that he can't go to the Smurf Show just because he forgot to clean up his room. He can be very confused by your enraged message and learn nothing from the experience. But if you have good reason for disciplining, you must do it. It's not so bad to turn into the "punishing parent." You do want your child to see a difference between the gratifying mother and the one who has been injured in some way by the child's behavior. Regardless of the bad press discipline and punishment generally get, they are just as much part of the nurturing experience of parenting as helping your child fall asleep at night or encouraging him to climb to the top of the slide. Remember that you're still helping your child when you discipline him because you're showing him another part of life and another part of your own emotional self. As we can see, though, this is hard for a father like Gary, who had a real stake in maintaining his two-year-old's unquestioning love. It took the perspective of Jill, his wife, to make him see what he was doing by not punishing Michael.

TURNING AGGRESSION INTO ASSERTIVENESS

Gary was gung-ho about boys. As a matter of fact he went out and bought a bat, balls, and a fireman's hat long before Jill gave birth. Michael was an active, curious baby who grew into a strong, playful toddler. Because Gary worked at home he was able to take Michael to his weekly play group.

"Michael was smaller than some of the boys, but he kept up. The only thing was that he couldn't stand it when another child took a toy away from him, and his immediate reaction was to bite. The first time it happened, some other mother pointed it out to me, but I said, Hey, that's how two-year-olds deal with frustration, isn't it? But then Michael started getting really aggressive. I knew it wasn't good, but I figured he'd grow out of it.

"Anyhow, one week I was sick and Jill took him to the play group. She came home fuming. Michael had really laced into a real wimpy boy, and he went crying to his mother. The woman told Jill the other parents were fed up with Michael's behavior and wanted him out of the group. They implied that I never paid attention to this because I was a man and thought aggressive behavior was okay.

"Jill was furious at me. She wanted to know why I let it go on so long. I was angry at these ladies and at her for kowtowing to them. I said you have to put yourself out front in life. Whether Michael was a boy or a girl, I'd want him to stand up for himself.

"The next day I saw him punch the three-year-old next door and take his tricycle away. I told him to stop and give it back, but he was out of control. I gave him another warning, but he kept going after the kid, who at this point was hitting, too. I didn't do anything because I thought kids should resolve these things on their own, and I didn't want Michael to think I wasn't on his side. Then the kid's mother came out of her house screaming and calling me a bully. Me! I guess that's the first time I thought that maybe something was wrong with the way I was handling discipline, that maybe it was time to do something. Only I couldn't figure out what."

Gary is having problems with his son's behavior, but he's also having problems with his own reaction. He feels his son's behavior is "natural," but his wife has pointed out to him that his approval of Michael's aggressiveness was making problems for all of them. How can he make such a personal turn-around in his expectations? He's going to have to deal with his own anxieties about setting limits because it has become evident that what Michael has been doing with other children is antisocial.

HATING THE ONE YOU LOVE

A three- or four-year-old knows better than the two-year-old how to press her parents' buttons to get control of her world. Rather than just acting on impulse, like the toddler who bites and hits because he desperately wants that toy, the preschooler will try to strengthen her position in relation to her parents and others by consciously doing power-oriented things: protesting, ignoring, or making a scene and yelling. The thrust of this behavior is that Mommy and Daddy always seem to be making rules, so why can't I? This is a time of real testing, where many of the boundaries of early childhood seem to change. You expect one thing from your child based on past experience, but she's in the process of developing and gives you another reaction.

Some parents seem to have hair-trigger reactions to their preschooler's behavior. They jump from being the "good parent" to the "bad parent" without affording their child an opportunity to anticipate an angry reaction. The child can't tell when she's gone too far until she's already there and it's too late—she's going to be punished.

It's enormously difficult to spend a day with your funny, in-
telligent, compassionate, endearing four-year-old and then to have
her suddenly turn into a crazed, whiny baby. You probably know,
as did Joanne, the mother of four-year-old Karen, that this kind
of behavior pattern is absolutely typical, but Joanne still found it
hard to deal with Karen's new autonomy. She had been a very
compliant, easy toddler, but her newfound independence and
skills were causing Joanne a lot of conflict.

"It'll sound horrible, I guess, but I found that after a day alone
with Karen, I disliked so many of the things she did that it was
hard for me to love her the way I used to. With a baby, the love
between you is just there. I never had to yell and then have Karen
look at me as though I were the creature from the Black Lagoon.

"There was one Saturday when my husband Ted, who is a
professor, was at a conference and Karen was in my hair from
the moment she woke up. First she got mad because I gave her
a new cereal, and she threw the bowl on the floor accidentally on
purpose. Then she had a royal tantrum at the shoe store when
the salesman got her sock twisted. She pretended to hit me when
I offered to fix it for her. I warned and threatened her. I finally
told her I would tell her father when he came home, and he'd
punish her if she pulled any more of this stuff.

"That quieted her down a little until after lunch when we went
next door to the neighbor's to play. She was awful, making fun
of the other child and calling her a crybaby. I could feel a tide
of anger rising in me, and all I could think of was 'What's she
going to do next?' I expected her to get worse, and she did.

"She whined all through dinner preparations for a cookie.
When I didn't give it to her, she refused to eat dinner. Ted kept
asking me what the hell was the matter, as though it was all my
fault, and I jumped down his throat, saying he hadn't been subjected to her all day and should just keep his opinions to himself.

"It went on through her bath, where she splashed water all
over the floor and then jumped out of the tub and ran around
naked, refusing to put her pajamas on. Well, I'd had it! I yanked
her toward me and smacked her bare bottom twice, really hard.
I could hear the sound my hand made: it was awful. I was stunned,

terrified by my own violence. And she stood there in the middle of the hallway, tears streaming down her face. Very quietly she said, 'I hate you, Mommy.' It was the worst moment of my life."

Setting limits has its own limitations. As Joanne tried to be a disciplinarian without punishing, she began to anticipate further bad behavior from Karen. She let her frustration and anxiety build up, spill over onto her husband, and spiral out of control. When she couldn't tolerate any more, she lashed out in an inappropriate way—by hitting.

How can Gary and Joanne use the anxiety they feel about Michael's and Karen's behavior? How can they work with their spouses to get some helpful messages across to their children? This is a time when identifying the source of the anxiety and breaking it down into its component parts is of critical importance.

Your Program for Change

For a complete description of how to use the program, see Chapter 4, page 61.

STEP I. IDENTIFY WHAT'S REALLY BOTHERING YOU
STEP II. CONNECT WITH YOUR PAST
STEP III. GET THE FACTS
STEP IV. UNDERSTAND YOUR CHILD'S POINT OF VIEW
STEP V. GROUND YOURSELF
STEP VI. STEP BACK AND SEE THE SCENE WITH DIFFERENT EYES
STEP VII. ESTABLISH NEW PATTERNS

STEP I. IDENTIFY WHAT'S REALLY BOTHERING YOU

The incident or series of incidents between you and your child that trigger your fury may be hard to sort out, but by examining the way Gary and Joanne identified their central issues you may get some clues that will be helpful with your own struggle with loss of love.

Let's consider Gary, who is not intervening in his son's antisocial biting and bullying behavior. *What is it about this experience that's really bothering Gary?*

Michael, at two, has no way of knowing that he has gone too far; he is only trying to gratify his needs. Gary's tacit approval of Michael's bullying has only succeeded in antagonizing his wife and in their being asked to leave the play group. Now he realizes it's his responsibility to help Michael understand that what he's doing with other children is unacceptable. He has to show him how to assert his personality and desires in the group without hurting anyone.

On the other hand, he's afraid to criticize his child's behavior and help him to change it because he knows how angry Michael is when he's disciplined. And he can't bear the thought of taking away his son's freedom, which is the way he imagines Michael will view any restrictions. He's also worried about not having Jill on his side. He feels an enormous responsibility, as though it is all up to him to make amends with the play group; otherwise, his wife is going to keep him out in the cold, punish him by rejecting him.

What about Joanne, who is so frustrated with Karen's uncooperative behavior that she ends up hitting her? *What is it that's really bothering Joanne?*

She never questioned her love for her child before, and now she finds herself capable of physical violence, which frightens her. She thinks that as an adult she should have control of her emotions, and as a parent she should accept her child no matter what kind of behavior she is exhibiting. But she's also worried about Karen who was never a "problem child" before. Is there something wrong with her? Is there something wrong with Joanne's parenting abilities that is making her child suddenly do so many obnoxious things, as though she was asking for punishment? And she's taking some of it out on Ted who is upset by Karen's actions but steps in only to discipline when Joanne has set it up for him in advance.

What's Really Bothering You

Gary's and Joanne's problems will undoubtedly sound familiar to many. And there are other issues that you personally may be going through right now with your child that you may find useful to explore. Some of the major parental concerns over loss of love are the following:

- your delivery of the type and degree of punishment
- lack of support from your spouse
- feeling you have to make up for your overreactive spouse
- feeling hated by your child—as though you're always the bad guy

If you are having any anxieties over your own expectations, you might want to look at the following questions that relate to some of the above concerns:

1. Do you tend to blame your child or excuse your child when she does something you didn't expect?
2. Do you warn your child when she's done something worthy of discipline, or do you discipline immediately?
3. Are you ever concerned that you feel incapable of disciplining? Do you always put the responsibility on your spouse?
4. Are you ever concerned that you may go too far in disciplining?
5. Do you think your child will hate you if you restrict him from doing something?
6. Does it worry you if your child breaks the same rule over and over? Does it make you question the rule you've made?
7. Are you ever jealous of your spouse because he or she never gets to the point of having to punish?

Try to think about a particular instance when you realized that your child had gone beyond the limits. Did you get angry quickly, or did you do a slow burn? Did you warn or punish immediately? Was it a series of infractions or just one big one that made you realize your child was out of control and you would have to step in? Take the incident apart and try to recall each facet of it and the emotion that went with it. This will help you figure out what really presses your buttons. It's helpful for your child to learn to anticipate what his behavior will make you do. When he knows that you're going to punish him if he goes beyond your breaking point, he'll learn to modify his behavior before you explode.

STEP II. CONNECT WITH YOUR PAST

We can all probably recall humiliating, painful, terrible memories about punishment that summon up incredible emotion. When you think back, it may feel almost as though you're a child going through it all over again with your parents.

Gary: Gary's father expected all his children to toe the line and gave out spankings—or sometimes strikes with his belt—for any misdeed, serious or trivial. Gary thinks of discipline as the chief cause of his fury against his critical father, who never gave him praise when he deserved it. Gary decided that he would never, under any circumstances, hit a child of his own.

Once, when his brother Sam didn't make it onto the varsity wrestling team, their father grounded him for a month for not being "tough enough." Gary stood up to his father, saying this was unfair; his father, furious that Gary would dare to challenge him, handed him the same punishment as his brother.

It occurs to him now that his lax attitude about Michael's behavior seems like a very strong reaction against his feelings for his father. He couldn't bear for Michael to feel about him the way he does about his own father, and any punishment—not just corporal—is difficult for him. At the same time he realizes he's carrying around a lot of old baggage about the worth of aggressive behavior. The two are in conflict.

Joanne: Joanne's twin sister was the "good" child, always doing what she was told, making Joanne look bad by comparison. When her sister discovered that she was rewarded for being a "goody-goody," she set out to make it look as though Joanne was always causing trouble. Their older brother Tom used to take great delight in pointing up their differences to their parents, which meant that Joanne felt punished from all sides. Misbehaving became the only way she got attention from her family. Could she be identifying too strongly with Karen's need to be someone in her own right?

How You Can Connect with Your Past

Try to think back to a scene from your childhood when you did something that occasioned discipline or punishment. Start by making a mental picture of yourself misbehaving. Did it give you pleasure? Did you realize it would disturb your parents? Were you doing it on purpose to get back at them for something? Did you have no idea that it was wrong? Now add your parents' reactions and see what kind of feelings emerge.

SETTING THE SCENE

1. Were your parents strict or liberal? How do you perceive those terms? Or was one strict and one lax?
2. Did your parents always make their limits clear? How?
3. Did you know when you were overstepping the boundaries? Why would you have chosen to do that?
4. Did you ever allow a sibling or another child to egg you on toward behavior that was not permitted?
5. Did you feel you had to sneak around your parents? Challenge your parents?
6. Was there one thing that you were strictly forbidden to do that you used to try to get away with anyway?

Now that you can see clearly, how did you experience discipline and punishment?

Some typical memories that many parents recall had to do with the following:

- feeling that their parents hated them
- being frightened by the impulses that made them misbehave
- being frightened of the consequences of their behavior
- feeling like a "bad" person for doing a bad thing

The following questions that relate to some of the above concerns may evoke certain useful feelings about your past:

7. Were you frightened when your parents punished you? Or were you defiant?
8. Did you hate your parents or admire them for punishing you?
9. Did they ever talk about how "bad" you were in front of other relatives or friends?
10. Did you feel your parents hated you when you misbehaved?
11. Did they hold a grudge? Did you? Or did you make up afterward?
12. Were you as a child and are you now very hard on yourself when you feel you've done something wrong?

These are not easy questions, and they may provoke some anxiety as you think about them. But by trying to get at the meaning behind them you may find that you understand more about your own reactions toward limit-setting today.

STEP III. GET THE FACTS

It's vital to know exactly what is going on for yourself and your child in the particular setting that occasions a loss of love.

> *Gary:* He notices that Michael's first impulse is to make his presence known in a group. If he doesn't get what he wants from another child immediately, he becomes physical and grabs. If he meets resistance, he bites.
>
> A call to the pediatrician reassures Gary that biting is a very natural thing for a young child to do. After all, children first learn about the world by putting things into their mouths. But Michael has to be made to understand that biting another person will not be tolerated. Either he is going to be taken away from the situation to cool off or be convinced that he can solve his problem another way, such as taking another toy that's not in use.
>
> Gary mentions to Jill that Michael never pays any attention to his warnings; she tells him she thinks it's because he knows that his father's threats are empty. The same as when they argue, she says. Gary rants and raves and then gives up. She suggests that Gary doesn't discipline Michael because he's afraid of being over-whelmed with fury. When he was a child, he was powerless to

protect himself against his own father's rage, and he remembers how awful that felt. How could he inflict the same terror on his own son?

Joanne: Joanne realizes that Karen's "bad" periods are cumulative; that is, she starts by testing in one realm and then goes on to another. Joanne consults a child care book and sees that many four-year-olds keep asking to be punished. The child feels guilty about something she did wrong, but her parents haven't helped her deal with it, so she does something else. She has to keep trying until she has the parental reaction, no matter how bad it may be. Maybe Joanne thinks she has been ignoring Karen because lately she hasn't been as "in love" with her as she was when the child was younger and more compliant.

She and Ted finally talk about Karen's behavior patterns, and Ted says that he feels he has been really left out lately. Karen refuses to let him do things with her, and Joanne includes him only when it's time to punish. Ted says that he resents this "wait till your father gets home" position he has been in. They realize that they've never actually hashed out their opinions and differences about their rules, their breaking points, their expectations, and their method of enforcing discipline. They both tend to blame the parent in charge for Karen's infractions.

Consider All Your Facts

1. How do you know when it's time to discipline? *When your child's actions make you feel bad, they're probably making him feel bad, too. He may be asking to have a limit set simply by doing something he knows is a turnoff to you.*
2. Why doesn't your child stop misbehaving when you yell at him? *When you raise your voice, your child can only respond to the shrill sound and the anger it embodies, not the reasonable content of your request.*
3. What's a good way to discipline your child? *Discipline should be a learning experience, which means that the best treatment is to have the child undo what he did wrong. If he wrote on the wall on purpose, he should help clean up. If he took a toy away from a child, he should be encouraged to give it back and apologize.*

4. Why won't your child apologize after doing something wrong? *An apology is tantamount to canceling out one's efforts as a person, which can be very difficult for some children to do even when they understand how much they've hurt someone else. It may be necessary to ask your child to say she's sorry when she's ready.*

5. Is it beneficial for your child to see a friend disciplined? *Yes. One way that a child feels mastery over a situation is to be able to compare her parent and her type of discipline to another child's. This gives her perspective on her own feelings and actions and allows her the important experience of empathy for another child. If the punishment she witnesses is harsh, she may also be able to start judging what kinds of limit-settings are appropriate and which are inappropriate.*

6. What constitutes punishing for the wrong reasons? *You should not punish from your own frustration. If you've had a bad day and punish the first time your child ignores your request, you aren't tuning into his experience. This doesn't allow your child to separate himself from your feelings. He may stop doing what you dislike because he wants your love back, but he'll never understand why it's wrong to do what he did.*

7. Are there any effective physical ways to punish a child? *If you hold his hands and look into his eyes as you tell him what he's done that you don't sanction, he will get your intent. A tap on the back of the hand can go a long way, particularly with a younger, preverbal child. If he's used to being stroked, a tap is as effective as a slap.*

8. What can you do when your child excludes one parent to the point of being hurtful about it? *You can protect your spouse by telling the child firmly that he is hurting someone you love and you can't allow that. Then you can step back and let the rejected parent express his own hurt.*

The facts about the reasons for punishment, about doing the punishing, and about the way you and your child interact after punishment should help you to sort out the enormous range of feelings that both of you are experiencing. The limits you set and the way you set them will become more evident over time, as you learn to separate fact from fantasy.

STEP IV. UNDERSTAND YOUR CHILD'S POINT OF VIEW

Can your child talk openly to you when you ask how she feels about what she's done? How does she react when you threaten and then don't punish? Or tell her that her daddy will punish her when he gets home? Or tell her that you're sick and tired of her *always* acting awful? Or if you simply don't comment on what she's done but give her the cold shoulder without explaining why. The main point of punishing is to increase your child's conscious awareness of what's going on—*never* to make her feel that she's a bad person. Let's see how the two parents handle this.

> *Gary:* He calls one of the mothers in the play group to tell her that Michael is ready to come back and that from now on Gary intends to make sure Michael doesn't hurt any other children.
>
> As soon as they arrive, Michael is all over another child, Sandy, and roughly takes her toy away. She resists him. With a war whoop Michael lunges for her and bites her arm. The girl howls, and Michael clutches the toy.
>
> Gary immediately goes to the girl, picks her up in his arms, and cradles her. "Here, Sandy, let's get you an ice cube to put on that. Does it hurt? Yes? Here, we'll make it better."
>
> Michael starts yanking at Gary's leg and holding on to him protectively. "My daddy!" he yells. "Mine!"
>
> "I'm your daddy," Gary acknowledges, unhooking his hand and walking away from him with the other child, "but right now I have to take care of Sandy because she's hurt. You see how much you hurt her?" He is hoping that a little guilt will go a long way.
>
> Later in the morning Michael starts throwing sand from the sandbox into another boy's eyes. Gary stalks over and says, "You can't do that to him because it will hurt. Remember when you bit Sandy? That hurt, too. Do you want to be somebody who hurts or somebody who makes things better?"
>
> Michael slowly sits down in the sandbox and, mimicking his father taking care of the little girl, wipes the sand out of the eyes

of the boy he was persecuting. "Like this, Daddy?" he says, demanding his father's approval.

Gary nods, relieved that he was able to make his child step back. It didn't hurt quite as much as he thought to correct his son. And the other mothers, of course, are beaming at him.

Joanne: On their next visit to the mall, Karen starts acting up— running away, having a tantrum when they can't find a nightgown in her size, spitting out the first bite of her sandwich at lunch, pronouncing it "yukky."

Joanne is trembling as she yanks her child out of her seat. "I hate you, don't hit me!" Karen screams in front of the entire restaurant.

Joanne takes a breath, then hustles Karen into the deserted ladies' room. She takes her child by both arms and stares her in the eye.

"Let's talk about this."

Karen avoids her gaze.

"Karen, I have to tell you that when you're uncooperative about so many different things—running away from me, yelling, spitting out your food—it's hard for me to cooperate with you. Why don't you tell me what's bad about today and I'll tell you what's bad, and we'll see if we can make it better for each other."

"Are you going to punish me?" Karen asks in a small voice.

"No. Right now I want to find out what's making you so sad and mad."

Karen, looking relieved, says, "I didn't know I was far away from you when you said I had run away. That was a lie. And you promised me the nightgown, and I didn't get it. And they put mayonnaise on my sandwich, and I hate it."

"I see. Okay, there *were* a lot of things wrong today, but screaming, yelling, or spitting isn't going to fix any of them. Next time you have tantrums in public places—whether you're with me or Daddy—you're going right home for a time-out. Do you understand?"

"Yes, Mommy. I don't really hate you, Mommy. I was just mad."

"I know, sweetie," Joanne said with relief.

Bringing Out Your Child's Feelings

When your child is most unlovable to you, you're most likely to be most out of sync with him. What you want to do in setting limits is tune in to his frustration instead of yours so that you can see where to help him step back.

You might try some statements other parents have used that deflect the moment of punishment by trying to find out what the child is feeling that's causing the behavior. And you might come up with some warnings that fit the behavior and will make the child think twice. Here are some examples:

1. "I know you were mad at the dog, but you can't pull his tail because that hurts him. The next time you do that, you won't be allowed to have him sleep in your room."
2. "Why did you run in the living room when you knew you weren't supposed to? I know you didn't break that bowl on purpose, but I'm mad because I told you that you had to be careful in here. If you do it again and something breaks, you'll be punished."
3. "You are not allowed to hit me when you're mad at me; nobody hits in this house. It's perfectly all right to get mad at me, but punch the pillow to get rid of that anger."

Acting on Your Child's Feelings

1. Find out what your child feels about what he's doing by asking pointed questions. If you encourage him to speak strongly about himself, he'll learn that his point of view counts.
2. When your child is making a scene, use the experience to teach something. If she routinely has a tantrum about having her hair combed after a bath, insist that she learn to comb her hair herself.
3. Take the responsibility of the punishment if you're the one who witnessed the "crime." If you as the mother tell your child that Daddy will take care of it when he comes home, you're conveying the message that you can't shoulder your own responsibilities and that Daddy, who was previously uninvolved and might have been an ally, is against her, too. By the time your spouse does punish, the "crime" is long past, and it's nearly impossible for your child to remember what she did

that is causing Daddy to hate her now just the way Mommy did then. Also, it's unfair to make your spouse deal with something he didn't even witness.

4. If you are always the "good parent," overly lavish in your praise, overly concerned with keeping your child happy and desperate not to lose her love, it's going to be very confusing when you turn into the "bad mother." The optimal situation is that you stay in a mid-range most of the time, accommodating her needs while maintaining consistent standards.

5. The way your child feels about himself comes from the way he sees himself reflected in your eyes. If you're always critical, telling him he's bad, he will begin to believe you and act accordingly.

6. Guilt is useful with an older child when used in moderation because it lets him see your point of view. Since he clearly wants to win back your love, he may comply with your wishes. Eventually the guilt will be internalized, and he can monitor himself. This is the beginning of the development of his conscience.

7. One of the best books on the subject of loss of love is Maurice Sendak's *Where the Wild Things Are* because it shows acceptance of both the "bad" and the "good" mother.

STEP V. GROUND YOURSELF

It's crucial to give yourself some emotional leeway when you're very anxious about losing your child's love or see that he's fearful about losing yours. Diffusing the overwhelming feelings with a grounding statement can give you a new perspective.

Gary: Gary could start by assuring himself that Michael doesn't feel about him the way he felt about his father. By helping his child to cool off in a social situation, by showing him compassion for others, he is making a statement to his child about how nurturing parental authority really can be.

Joanne: She can say that even though Karen isn't a compliant toddler anymore and even though she has some very strong opinions that annoy Joanne, she is a far more interesting person to be with now that she's growing up. Joanne can also tell herself that kids, who don't monitor their feelings as well as adults, often say hateful things. "I hate you" doesn't have the same meaning from Karen as it would from Ted because it's a momentary outburst rather than a considered statement.

You might try some of the grounding thoughts below that other parents have used successfully:

Anxious thought: I can't stand another minute of his whining and crying. All I want to do is whack him. What kind of an abusive parent am I?
Grounding thought: I haven't struck my child. All I did was yell, which got his attention. Now I can sit down with him and talk to him in a level tone to find out what's going on.

Anxious thought: He's in the middle of destroying my vegetable garden, but I'll just ignore it. If he doesn't get the attention, he'll stop.
Grounding thought: The reason he's acting so bratty is that I've been ignoring everything he does. If I have him help me garden and put back what he's torn up, it'll help both of us.

Anxious thought: My husband gets furious at me when my son acts like this! Why are they always both against me?
Grounding thought: His feelings toward me have nothing to do with our child's behavior. Maybe we should talk.

STEP VI. STEP BACK AND SEE THE SCENE WITH DIFFERENT EYES

If you can break away from the moment and use your imagination to define the scene a different way, you may get some insights into your own behavior and your child's.

Gary: Gary would like Michael to stop being the aggressor in social situations, but he'd like to be able to correct his child without feeling that he was the "bad guy."

He imagines asking Michael to wash the car with him and thinks about how he might react if Michael turned the hose on him. Sure, he'd be angry, but he wouldn't blow up. He'd calmly take the hose away or walk to the faucet and turn it off, telling Michael he won't be allowed to do this again until he learned that he shouldn't get his father soaking wet. By withdrawing a privilege from Michael, he'd get his point across. If he can do that when Michael is bullying another child, he knows he will have accomplished something good for both of them.

Joanne: She would like to feel in control when Karen is out of control. She'd like to get rid of the feeling that she can't love Karen when she's misbehaving.

She steps back and thinks of times when she and Karen are in sync, when she can be empathic enough to understand what her child is going through but firm enough (not harsh) to make her position clear. She imagines a day when they'll be all dressed up to go to Ted's mother's house for her birthday. In her mind she pictures Karen running upstairs and changing into a bathing suit. Joanne tells her to put her party dress back on and it triggers a tantrum. But before it can escalate, Joanne imagines sitting down with Karen and assuring her that she can go dressed as she is, but everyone else there will be in party clothes and Karen may feel out of place. Karen would probably think about it, decide how she wants to look, and go to change. Maybe if Joanne can give Karen the time and chance to make her own decisions she'll be able to make her feel important.

Imagine What You'd Like to Happen

Naturally you'd like a friction-free relationship with your child, but those don't exist. (People who *never* fight or fear a loss of love have severe problems with reality.) What you can do is imagine yourself outside the stressful scene, maybe viewing it with humor, maybe seeing it as your spouse sees it. What you'd like is to be able to resolve conflicts effectively so that everyone feels they've won a little something. What you may get, with practice, is an understanding that you don't necessarily have to be an ogre in a situation where you set a limit and stick to it.

STEP VII. ESTABLISH NEW PATTERNS

Your child may be surprised and delighted to find that you are curbing former tendencies to scream, threaten, cajole, or spank in favor of more helpful forms of discipline. This doesn't mean that you won't dampen your child's affection for you from time to time; in restraining his natural impulses and shaping his behavior you will have to insist on certain things that won't be accepted easily. But as we look at Gary's and Joanne's new patterns, we can see that change is possible, even around the volatile issue of setting limits.

> *Gary:* Gary consistently reminded Michael that he didn't have to bite, hit, or grab when he played with other children in order to have a good time. Whenever Michael was having trouble controlling himself, Gary would give him until a count of five and then, if the behavior hadn't stopped, he'd remove him from the scene. He had Joanne take Michael to the play group a few times so it would be clear to him that both of his parents expected him to act the same way. Michael seemed much happier because the kids really wanted to play with him, and Gary felt better because he saw that his actions had a positive effect.

> *Joanne:* She and Karen both tried to tell the other when they were reaching their breaking point. On days when Karen was particularly independent and clearheaded, this worked. On days when she was still feeling babyish and insecure, it didn't work. But Joanne found that talking out what they were doing to each other and giving Karen certain parameters within which she wanted her to function made her less likely to explode.

PARENTS' SUGGESTIONS

The following ideas have worked for many parents, but you, your spouse, and your child will come up with many other workable solutions for setting limits.

1. With a younger child, point out in a consistent way, verbally and with gestures, the things he's not supposed to do. When discipline is necessary to protect him from harming himself, it should be immediate and pointed—a light slap on the hand with a "NO!" for running into the street or reaching for a hot stove.

2. Counting is very helpful with an older child. By telling him he has until a count of three to do a certain thing allows him to remember what happened the last time, anticipate what might happen this time, and regain control on his own.

3. Removing your child from the scene can help him cool down. This takes him physically away from what has just happened, which allows him to also break away mentally from his anger.

4. Whenever you think you're going to yell or hit because you've reached your limit, step back and give yourself a second to cool off. This will allow you to connect your impulses with your judgment.

5. Withholding a privilege is a useful punishment, but think before you speak. Perhaps it's more suitable to restrict TV tonight than not allow her to go to her best friend's birthday party on Saturday.

6. Don't talk to other people about your child's misbehavior. Talking *about* your child instead of *to* your child makes him feel like an outsider.

7. Don't belittle him or ridicule him. Irony and sarcasm are completely lost on a child under the age of four, but the scathing tone of voice is not and transmits the message that you are displeased with your child, not his actions.

8. Don't compare him to anyone else. Whatever he's done, his actions and feelings are his own. Whether his best friend has or does not have temper tantrums is beside the point, and by comparing them you only serve to make him resentful of the "better" child.

9. If he is passive around other children and is always being picked on, you can help him become more assertive. A passive child feels insecure, not well enough connected to what he's doing to be direct about it with others. He may not react

when bullied by another child because he's afraid that you'll be mad if he fights back. It's important to coach a passive child in ways to assert himself, such as walking away from the bully, laughing at him, or saying loudly, "Don't do that!"

10. Don't expect him to conform to your standards if he doesn't understand them. If he refuses to kiss Grandma good-bye at the end of a visit but you force him to do it, the scene that should have encouraged tenderness and good family feeling may end in resentment. If you've explained how important it is to you to have him kiss Grandma, he may wish to do it to please you, which in turn will probably make him feel appreciated.

11. Look at the effect your punishments are having and be sure you and your spouse agree on the method and reasons for the discipline. If your method isn't working, try something else. Don't undermine each other's efforts to set limits, or your child will learn to play you off against each other.

KEEPING LOSS OF LOVE IN PERSPECTIVE FOR THE WHOLE FAMILY

Sometimes you may feel angry at your child and take it out on your spouse. This is particularly harmful when you can't reach a decision about what limits you feel are appropriate for your child and from each other. If you don't figure it out, you may be laying the groundwork for some real family hassles. The problem between you and your child may turn into a problem between you and your spouse. But if you have a good gauge of where you both stand and you come up with a general game plan of what you expect and how much you'll tolerate, you're sending a message that your child can really learn from. When you can give him this kind of direction, eventually he'll get to the point where he can be independent and separate from you and will be able to impose the rules—not too harshly or too leniently—on himself.

14
The Superbaby Syndrome

Which of the following statements is true for you?

1. I'm going to be out there on the playing field with my son every weekend to help him learn to throw and catch. My father never did that for me.
2. My daughter is brighter than all the preschoolers in her class, and I'm afraid I won't know enough to help her advance her education later on.
3. My fifteen-month-old is phenomenally beautiful, so I'm going to start her on modeling because she's really cut out for it.
4. My mother thinks I'm pressuring my four-year-old to write, but he really didn't mind staying in for several afternoons to copy the Christmas cards.

We all tend to think our children are the most brilliant, most beautiful, most extraordinary on the planet. And we all worry that we may miss some facet of their specialness, that through oversight we may neglect to bring out the best in them. But if any of the above statements sound familiar to you, you may be putting too much stake in your child's abilities. You may, as a matter of fact, be projecting your own feelings about *your* inadequacies or achievements. If your needs for your child's success are too great, you may be thwarting the process of his natural development.

The Superbaby Syndrome, as it has become known, is the imposition of the adult world on the developing child. Because of your own insecurity over your parental judgment, you may unknowingly push your baby or child to proceed too fast, urging him on toward some elusive kind of perfection. You may be anxious to help him reach ahead in every realm, from his Apgar scores through his entry into the best kindergarten to his fast-track career path.

On its good side, wanting your child to be a superbaby is a testimony to how much you admire him and envision for him in the future. But there may be other complicating, anxiety-laden issues underlying this desire that your child get ahead in the world. Maybe you feel that your own parents stunted you; maybe you have a need to compete—with yourself, your spouse, or other parents. Wanting to develop a superbaby can also stem from a lack of true understanding of your child and his natural timetable.

How can you really know your child's true potential? And why is it so easy to become anxious about it? The pace at which he has reached his various developmental milestones tells a little bit but not everything. Your child has a certain biological potential that you can encourage with environmental opportunity. But as a child grows, his abilities go beyond the biological; his psychological acuity and developing interests come into play. It's at this point that a parent can become anxious about whether he's paying proper attention to the special skills of his child.

The problem is that you just don't know if your two-year-old who counts to twenty forwards and backwards is going to be a brilliant mathematician. And you can't tell whether your exceptionally physical four-year-old is going to be an Olympic gold medalist. The agony of this confusion may make you feel that if you don't give her all the opportunities, you may be stunting a potential world leader, athlete, artist, or nuclear physicist.

It's not just the confusion about how your child is doing on his own that makes you anxious but also the comparisons you inevitably make. What about your own potential? It's easy to feel fresh pain and humiliation about how your parents overlooked your talents, how you might have "been somebody" if only they'd encouraged your special gifts. Certainly you'll also be aware of how other children are functioning in certain areas. With the advent of developmental assessment tests being given to four- and five-year-olds to determine their potential in school, you may already be experiencing sweaty palms on behalf of your preschooler. If you were a poor tester, you certainly don't want him to follow in your footsteps.

Looking at the fervor of other parents around you, you may worry that you're not doing *enough*. If your friend down the block is racing her son to one advanced nursery school interview after another, and you've been content with the play school around the corner, you may start feeling guilty for not pushing your child ahead even though he's perfectly happy where he is.

It's always best to take the lead from your child. You can encourage certain interests, of course, but it's very difficult to know at this stage what level of brilliance or competence you're really dealing with. The two-year-old who can count so quickly and easily may turn out to loathe long division in third grade, and the boy who is a monkey at four may prefer sitting for long hours practicing the piano at ten.

A child's progress is like a flower unfolding. Typically, one or two petals will open first, and others will follow. Some may lag behind, but eventually the flower stands completely open. By six or so, most children catch up to one another developmentally and go on to show their particular talents. They forge ahead based on their own sense of what is interesting and what is right.

If you become too anxious about what your child is able to do, you may unwittingly broadcast the message that your child is valuable *only* for his achievements and activities. His response is either to do more and more to please you, or to find himself so glutted with experience that everything becomes boring and he burns out very quickly. But if you ask yourself, Who am I doing this for, me or him? you may be able to head off the incipient anxiety you feel about your child's achievement.

Our culture puts the emphasis on getting ahead, being first, doing more than you did yesterday. If you feel your child should be first and he comes in second, your disappointment may inflict a lot of unreasonable feelings on him. If, on the other hand, you make it possible for him to experience many facets of life and encourage him to find his own way, he may well succeed beyond even your goals.

WHAT IS INTELLIGENCE?

The ability to *use* the world is the chief means of identifying intelligence. It's more indicative, for example, that your child is thinking and connecting experiences when he looks at the night sky and says, "The stars look like when I got drops of milk all over the black floor," than when he's able to recite three poems that someone else wrote for children about stars.

The more exposure a child has to the world, the more its pieces begin to fit together. But the process of absorbing information, of putting the individual experiences into a continuum, takes time to click into place. Children are more likely to know something because they can make it theirs and do something with it. The two-year-old who is always put to bed before it's dark doesn't know that there's a world without daylight, but by the time he's three and is allowed to stay up later, he'll want to know where the sun goes after dinner or why the moon doesn't make it as bright outside as the sun does. Then finally, by the time he's four, he may tell you that he doesn't like going out to dinner, only to lunch. The reason: his fear of the dark. He can *anticipate* that every day at a certain time the light will go out of the sky. This is a developing intelligence.

A child's intelligence can be judged by how analytical it is. Let's say we're trying to understand a three-year-old's assessment of being small now but growing into a big adult. We ask two girls what they want to be when they grow up.

The first child, who has had exposure to certain professions and has a baby brother, says, "I'm going to be a mother, a teacher, and a ballerina." The second child, with the same exposure but a more analytical mind, says, "I'm going to be a mother, but when my babies are sleeping, I can teach other children. Maybe I'll just have one baby 'cause they take up so much time. When she's big enough we can both be ballerinas together."

You don't have to worry about your child learning a great many specific things. It's better that he be tuned in to what's going on in the world around him than to have facts at his fingertips. When your child has the interest and inclination, he'll take the exposure he's had to so many different elements and integrate it into what he can do.

THE ACTIVITIES CONTEST

There is a sense, these days, that there's no time to waste and you had better start early if you're going to get good at anything. So there are classes offered for very young children in swimming, music, computers, gymnastics, dance, and more. It's fine to offer your child this smorgasbord of activities—*as long as you can look at the pursuit of these interests through his eyes, not yours.*

Children absorb everything, and giving them a lot at an early age is one way to open many new doors for them. But if you're hustling your superbaby from one activity to another so that he will maximize his potential, you might want to consider your reasons. A little girl may adore her ballet lessons for the first three months, then get interested in riding her bicycle; maybe the motor skills that make her able to ride have improved partly due to her ballet lessons. But when she then refuses to go to dance class because she'd rather be riding her bike, and her mother pressures her, how is she going to respond? Probably, like most four-year-olds, she'll sulk, whine, and go only under duress.

When this incident is multiplied by three or five, or however many activities a parent asks the child to perform, it can cause early burnout. A child who is pressured to do everything all the time—and like it, too—is likely to rebel. She may end up claiming that she doesn't want to do anything. She may become overly competitive and have tantrums when she sees another child doing something "better" than she can. Or she may manifest extraneous symptoms—lack of appetite, extreme sleepiness—that will keep her from her classes. These symptoms are the child's way of saying that she can't continue to satisfy her parents' need for achievement.

EXPECTATIONS: SOCIAL CONTACTS AND PHYSICAL APPEARANCE

It's hard not to get caught up in the sweep of comparisons, especially when every other parent you know is doing it. If you were brought up with the belief that the "right people" could help you get ahead, you may feel anxious about encouraging your child to form the "correct" social contacts. You may worry unduly about getting her into the "right" play group when she's a toddler so that she can be accepted into the "right" kindergarten so that she can get into the "right" prep school. But remember that "right" as in "appropriate" means nothing to a four-year-old.

Similarly, looking "right"—as in projecting a proper image— doesn't help a child get a good sense of himself. If you see your son as a future power broker, you might buy him a Winchester coat with a velvet collar and knickers. If you secretly want your little girl to grow up to be a major media star, you might think it was fun to get her a gold lamé sheath. But if your child feels awkward or embarrassed in these clothes, they aren't suitable. A growing, tumbling, dirt-digging, fun-seeking child needs the most comfortable, knock-around outfit—and for special occasions, something that makes him feel special but not so unusual as to stand out.

If you get caught up in the need to have your child look prettier/ handsomer than every other child, you're starting a difficult game of one-upsmanship that can be damaging to your child's sense of worth. He or she may begin to feel that only the way he looks makes him lovable and important in your eyes.

THE INSIDIOUS ROUTE TO SUPERBABYHOOD

When you're aware of the wonder and interest of childhood, why shouldn't you foster it? Naturally you should. If you put your infant in a water-baby class and she does brilliantly, you may go on to give her swimming and gymnastics as soon as she's able to walk and talk. The more she can do, the more you'll want to encourage her to try.

And this can be exciting and challenging for both of you, or it can be a burden that you feel compelled to shoulder. It's the extent to which you take it that will indicate whether you're following your child's inclinations or your own. You have to sit back, as one mother finally did, and ask who you are doing this for: your child or yourself.

It took Lacey a long time to figure that out. She was a talented musician and teacher, someone who had always put a great deal of stock in achievement. When her baby Ryan was born, she was determined that he was going to exceed all expected norms.

"My little man was special," she began. "I was just so bowled over by him. We'd have these talks our first week home from the hospital. I'd say 'Ooh,' and he'd answer, 'Aah,' and I'd come back with 'Ooh,' and we'd keep this going for ten minutes. My mother never took that kind of time with me. Even when I did something wonderful, such as learning the piano at the age of four, she treated it as if it was nothing, like turning on a faucet and expecting the water to come out. Well, I vowed I'd never let anything about Ryan escape me.

"When he was fourteen months, several of his other little friends were talking and he hadn't started. I got him flash cards for vocabulary and started music—pitch and rhythm drills, just like the ones I give to my students. He really seemed to get into it, but then when I had my aunt over, Ryan wouldn't say a thing or sing any of the songs he knew. I was probably expecting too much, but it gave me a stomachache to see him sitting there like a baby, playing with his blocks.

"He became really physical very fast, so I enrolled him in Gymboree, and when he was two we started swimming and tennis. I got a real kick out of taking the lessons with him, but I sort of worried that in a year he was going to outstrip me in everything and then I'd have to find expensive advanced teachers.

"We interviewed extensively to choose a nursery school when

he was about three. My husband Richard wanted a real milk-and-cookies play school, and I wanted the most sophisticated, advanced place—the one where most play group people were sending their kids. I couldn't believe Richard's attitude, that if Ryan was really better than everyone else, he'd shine no matter where he was. Richard, of all people, who turned out to be just an accountant when one of his brothers is a doctor and one's a lawyer!

"In the end I won, and we started Ryan in a very challenging preschool program. If my mother had given me the opportunities we're giving Ryan, I'd be teaching at Juilliard today instead of being stuck in the awful school I'm at.

"He did fine at school and made new friends and kept up all his afternoon classes—tennis, swimming, computer, music—until just before his fourth birthday. He was suddenly cranky all the time, and going anywhere became a huge production number. I couldn't even get him out of bed in the morning; he was picking fights at school, and then he lost his toilet training. I was absolutely panic-stricken, and those awful stomach cramps returned. I felt dreadful, as if it were me instead of him."

Lacey is obviously feeling anxious about everything her child does and doesn't do. When she loads him with expectations and he regresses physically, she thinks this is a reflection on her. She feels bitter about her own parents' lack of interest in her abilities, and therefore she feels inadequate when she talks about keeping up with her son. But her fear for his lack of progress is becoming a psychological combat zone. Ryan's accomplishments have become more important to her than he is himself; she seems to feel that if he doesn't achieve, then she doesn't either.

There's no reason why Lacey can't be deeply involved in her son's burgeoning interests without making herself miserable and making him feel pressured. If she can begin to make some changes in her attitude, she'll be able to consider his needs first so that he'll have the optimal chance of growing and developing according to his own timetable.

Your Program for Change

For a detailed explanation of how to use this program effectively, see Chapter 4, page 61.

STEP I.   IDENTIFY WHAT'S REALLY BOTHERING YOU
STEP II. CONNECT WITH YOUR PAST
STEP III. GET THE FACTS
STEP IV. UNDERSTAND YOUR CHILD'S POINT OF VIEW
STEP V.   GROUND YOURSELF
STEP VI. STEP BACK AND SEE THE SCENE WITH DIFFERENT EYES
STEP VII. ESTABLISH NEW PATTERNS

STEP I. IDENTIFY WHAT'S REALLY BOTHERING YOU

If you're thrilled about your child's potential, as Lacey is, but are also anxious that you're not doing enough, it's particularly difficult to sort out your confusion; it seems to you that you have the best, and you are desperate to keep it or make it even better.

But let's look at the reasons for Lacey's anxiety and see if there aren't any parallels in your own life. *What is it about Ryan's progress that's really bothering Lacey?*

Her child has recently begun regressing physically and socially, which indicates to her that he must feel something is wrong.

She has been comparing his experience with hers as a child, but right now he's not reaping the benefits of his special schooling as she imagined he would. She has also compared him to her husband; clearly she has been disappointed with Richard's place in his family and his own career goals. She wants her son to turn out "better" than she or Richard did. This is putting a lot of stress on her marriage.

Finally, she has physical symptoms of her own—those stomach cramps; she feels almost as if she's going through his experience herself. In a sense, Ryan's newfound autonomy—his *not* doing everything his mother has laid out for him to do and, in fact, doing things that make him appear younger and less capable than his age—is making her sick.

What's Really Bothering You

Some of the major parental concerns over raising a superbaby are as follows:

- chronic disappointment in yourself and your spouse
- the feeling that your child gives you a new chance to "make it all better"
- feelings of inadequacy, that you're not up to helping your child become the greatest
- a sense of bitterness about what your parents never did for you
- associating lack of success with an inability to be loved

If you are having any anxiety over your own expectations, you might want to look at the following questions that relate to some of the above concerns:

1. Do you always compare yourself and your spouse to others?
2. Do you ever feel inadequate about your parenting? Do you fear that you aren't providing your child with enough activities to stimulate him?
3. Do you find yourself constantly comparing your child to others, even if they're older and more developed?
4. Do you feel that you don't understand his real abilities and interests?
5. Do you fear that time is running out? That he'll never get ahead if he isn't on a fast track now?
6. Are you worried that no school will ever appreciate your child the way you do or take note of his exceptional abilities?

To try to figure out whether you are pushing your child or simply allowing him to follow his natural inclinations, think back to some situation where he didn't do particularly well or couldn't keep up. Could you accept it? Were you embarrassed that he was showing you up in some way? Were you feeling that he'd never succeed at anything because he couldn't manage this one thing? By coming closer to your central concerns you'll be better able to see whether they're realistic and pertain to your child or whether they are based on some old issues of your own.

STEP II. CONNECT WITH YOUR PAST

Lacey must start to think about the way her own parents treated her in order to understand what's going on with herself, Ryan, and Richard. Recognizing the old feelings will be painful for her— as it will be for you—but this is the only way you're going to see where your expectations fit into your child's development.

Lacey: She remembers her mother sitting across the room during every piano lesson. Even when her teacher said she'd played something well, her mother insisted that she do it over. She once entered Lacey in a state piano competition over the teacher's objections, saying that she knew Lacey could win it. Her schoolwork fell off because of her increased practice hours, and her mother criticized her for the B's on her report card. Lacey began having terrible stomachaches on a regular basis. She didn't place in the competition, either.

After that, her mother seemed to lose interest in her completely. Over the next few months Lacey tried to get closer to her father, but her parents were separating and he was in the process of moving out of the house. Lacey could never get over her nagging feeling that both her parents were disappointed in her, that she had ruined the family and was responsible for the divorce.

Lacey's reaction to her parents' expectations was to take everything onto herself, and she seems to be continuing this with Ryan. She realizes that she's been neglecting her relationship with her husband due to her overinvolvement with her son, but she's starting to wonder if she may be keeping Richard at arm's length in order to prevent the kind of conflict in her marriage that her own parents had in theirs.

How You Can Connect with Your Past

The mental picture you conjure up of yourself and your parents dealing with your accomplishments may fill you full of pride or shame, depending on the circumstances, but it's important to think back. If you're loading your child with expectations you never fulfilled for your own parents, you may be in for a second disappointment.

SETTING THE SCENE

1. How did your parents handle your accomplishments? Did you feel that you'd pleased them?
2. How did they handle what you considered a failure? Was it the same as what they considered a failure?
3. How did they handle your siblings' achievements and short-comings? Did they compare you?
4. How did they handle their own accomplishments and short-comings?

Now that you can see clearly, how did you experience your parents' needs for you to achieve?

Some typical memories that many parents recall had to do with the following:

· feeling unlovable if they hadn't "produced"
· being incredibly pressured to excel in everything
· having to put up with constant comments about how they were expected to "make up" for their parents' failed ambitions

The following questions that relate to some of the above con-cerns may evoke certain useful feelings about your past:

5. Do you recall your parents talking about how bad things used to be when they were kids, combined with unrealistic hopes for your future?
6. Did they compare you to themselves—urging you not to be the "loser" they'd turned out to be? Or telling you that you would become a "loser" if you kept going the way you were?
7. Did your parents ever criticize you for doing well—but not well enough—in an area that was of particular importance to them?
8. How did they deal with your report cards? Were you ever punished for failing?

9. Did you ever have any time to yourself, or did they keep you on the go with classes and activities?
10. Did they urge you to compete, to be better than the rest? Did they make you feel that only being number one would be good enough?

STEP III. GET THE FACTS

It's not easy to get factual information on this topic because, as we've noted in Chapter 10 (page 183), development is different for every child. But it's useful to get an informed opinion of your child's progress if you're anxious about how he's doing.

> *Lacey:* She really wants to know from professionals if Ryan can be judged special. Explaining that he's going to play some games with new friends, she takes him to a child-development center where he's interviewed by a psychologist who specializes in gifted children. The staff then gives him an I.Q. test and some musical aptitude tests. The consensus is that Ryan is above average but not genius level. His musical acuity is no more and no less than any other child in his age group.
>
> Lacey then talks to all the different instructors Ryan sees during the course of a week. They all feel that Ryan isn't performing up to his abilities because of his intense need to be better than the other children. And the tennis teacher is particularly concerned about Ryan's fighting. He says that he doesn't seem to initiate the fights out of any passion but rather a desire to be the center of attention.
>
> Lacey finally talks to Richard about their son. He says that he has felt for some time that Lacey has been pushing him away, making decisions about Ryan on her own. He says that he doesn't feel included in the household anymore and wonders whether Ryan's fighting might be a reaction to his distant relationship with his father. Lacey has to admit that she has been neglecting her husband for the sake of her child. She has kept him apart from Ryan and kept herself apart from him, partly out of a fear that if they brought things out into the open together, he might challenge her point of view.

You, too, can learn a lot from those who care for and instruct your child, but you'll probably gain the most from a frank, open discussion with your spouse. A factual investigation of the way that your superbaby is taking in all the various stimuli he's exposed to will help you assess whether he's comfortable with them or not.

Consider All Your Facts

1. Is your infant or preschooler engaged in an appropriate number of activities each week? *It depends on the individual child how many different skills she can absorb at one time. If she's giving you signs that she can't keep up, she may be overwhelmed, not stimulated. If you're getting more out of her doing all this than she is, you might want to consider cutting back.*
2. Is your child burning out from too much pressure? *Ask the caregivers who spend time with her how she has grown or changed in the past months. How are her moods and her reactions to the other children?*
3. Is there one area in which your child stands out? *It's possible she is indicating a preference for one activity over the many she is involved in.*
4. Does your child have enough alone time? *Every child needs time to dream and play and just plain goof off. If every minute of her week is accounted for, she may feel that she's not trusted to make decisions on her own.*
5. Are you concerned about regressive behavior? *A three- or four-year-old who begins using baby words or takes up new habits such as thumb sucking or wetting is asking to be held back. Too much pressure can be very wearing on a child who will react the only way he knows: to go back, developmentally, to a time when he was completely dependent and cared for by his parents.*
6. Is your child losing friends? *A child who is expected to perform well in every activity is naturally going to feel threatened by peers who are also trying hard. But it's more important for a very young child to be able to tolerate frustration and play in a cooperative manner with his peers than to be the best and please his parents.*

7. Is your need for your child's overall excellence affecting your marriage? *A few conversations with your spouse about your involvements with your child are certainly in order. It's very common that when your child's development becomes of foremost importance to one or both of you, you tend to neglect other areas of your life.*

STEP IV. UNDERSTAND YOUR CHILD'S POINT OF VIEW

In order for learning to take place, it must happen at the child's rate, when it means something to him. Only by getting out from under the urgent feeling that your child must do better than you did will you be able to talk to him empathically and elicit his real feelings.

> *Lacey:* When Lacey comes to pick Ryan up from tennis, she finds him fighting with another boy who has just called him a "dumb baby" because he wet his pants again. She asks what happened.
>
> "Oh, that kid, I hate him. I'd like to cut his head off."
>
> "Ryan! We don't say that about people. That's awful."
>
> "I do! I hate him, and I hate this stupid game." He throws the tennis racket as far as he can, then starts to cry.
>
> Lacey takes a deep breath and asks, "Would you rather not take tennis lessons?"
>
> Ryan looks at her nervously. "No, that's okay. I know you want me and Dad to play, and I have to get good so we can."
>
> "I'd like you to . . . but you don't have to. I tell you what, why don't we try having an afternoon off next week and see how it goes?"
>
> Ryan nods. "Yeah. What could I do instead?"
>
> "You could practice piano or do some word drills. Whatever you like."
>
> "Could I watch Looney Tunes?" A deep breath.
>
> "No! Absolutely not!" Lacey is horrified, but then she sees the look on her son's face. "We could rent a good video, though. Or maybe if it was a nice day we'd just go to the playground and play. Maybe Daddy could come with us. What about it?"

It's obviously going to take Lacey a while to loosen some of her control and let up on some of her expectations. But in giving

Ryan back some free time, she is letting go of one part of him she's been at odds with for a long time.

Bringing Out Your Child's Feelings

It's not possible to ask a three- or four-year-old if he feels pressured because he simply doesn't have the life experience to understand what that means. Children are natural sponges who absorb everything, and if you've been urging your child toward a variety of fascinating, challenging activities, he's probably been throwing himself into them, as much to prove something to himself as to please you. But when you understand that your motives in involving him may have little to do with his natural inclinations, you can make a difference by asking some direct questions, such as the ones below:

1. "What's your favorite after-school sport?"
2. "Do you think you and Melanie would rather play dolls this afternoon and skip your ballet class?"
3. "Mrs. Oakley told me you fell asleep during school today. Do you think you'd like to go back with the nappers?"

Acting on Your Child's Feelings

1. Experiment with the schedule your child has now. You might try concentrating on his favorite activity and skipping those he seems less enthusiastic about.
2. Spend some time as a family doing what you might consider nothing special: go on a picnic, a nature walk, an evening drive.
3. If your child has been regressing or acting differently around you, you might want to give him some choices about where he's going to go and what he's going to do. This will help to make him feel more in control.
4. See what your child has to say about your interest in his activities. You may be surprised to learn that he's doing them more for you than for himself.

STEP V. GROUND YOURSELF

Talking out your confusion can help when anxiety threatens to overwhelm you. The kind of reassurance these grounding statements give allows you time to bring your concerns back to manageable size.

> *Lacey:* She could tell herself that her child is exceptional just for having attempted the various things he's been involved with. She can also remind herself that it's possible he might want to pick up an activity he drops now when he's older. After all, a four-year-old can't really play tennis with his father because he lacks the size and skill to compete, but he can play ball with his friends and learn the same skills of hitting, catching, and running. She can assure herself that her own stomachaches will probably vanish when she sees her child having fun.

If you're feeling insecure about your part in your child's progress, you might try using some of the suggestions below as quick diffusers of the anxiety you're feeling.

> *Anxious thought:* He'll never learn this! He'll be just like me!
> *Grounding thought:* He has plenty of time to learn, and anyway, it's okay if he doesn't do so well at this. He's great at lots of other activities.

> *Anxious thought:* He's never forgotten his grammar before. What's his teacher going to think of me?
> *Grounding thought:* She probably takes a four-year-old's bad grammar in stride. It's my own craziness because my parents don't use correct English.

> *Anxious thought:* She's so beautiful and popular, but she never lets me comb her hair and she picks her nose in public. I can't stand it!
> *Grounding thought:* She's still a baby, and her bodily functions are part of her, nothing more. She's not old or experienced enough to have social graces yet. Give it time.

STEP VI. STEP BACK AND SEE THE SCENE WITH DIFFERENT EYES

Imagination can do a great deal for the parent of a superbaby because it was imagination that got you here in the first place. If you can imagine your young child climbing Mount Olympus, winning the Moscow piano competition, or discovering a cure for cancer, you can certainly imagine her playing in a sandbox, laughing with her friends, or creating a world from a ball of clay.

> *Lacey:* She steps back and sees Ryan as a baby struggling with his first steps and words. Realizing what a feat it is for every child to overcome these hurdles, she's better able to think about him as a child again—not a small adult expected to perform up to her standards or Richard's. He isn't Richard, after all, and he can't make up for the kind of disappointment she feels in herself and her marriage. She imagines him, instead, coming home from school with a new painting that he's proud of, a new friend he enjoys playing with, a desire to make his own cheese sandwich for lunch. Those goals, for now, may be—for him—larger than all the accomplishments in all the classes he's attending.

Imagine What You'd Like to Happen

Step back and see yourself, your spouse, and your child making joint decisions about activities you can all enjoy. This may mean occasionally doing things that you consider unworthy of your child's abilities; it may mean doing "nothing" once in a while. Imagine taking the lead from your child and discovering a new interest of your own from something he shows you.

STEP VII. ESTABLISH NEW PATTERNS

You may discover, after working through this program, that you feel no closer to the source of your anxiety. You may, in fact, have an exceptional child who is pushing ahead in every realm. But if you've been feeling that you're not up to the task of parenting your child, if you've been getting indications that your son or daughter is unhappy with the scope of his world, or if you and your spouse are in disagreement about your child's aptitudes and inclinations, you may wish to try paring down your expectations.

> *Lacey:* She phased out Ryan's computer and tennis classes and let Ryan make some choices of his own on those two afternoons. She was still uncomfortable with letting him watch TV cartoons, but she no longer insisted that everything he did had to be "educational and worthwhile." Occasionally after work Richard would pick Ryan up, and they'd go out by themselves for a hamburger. Lacey tended to feel very uneasy when they were both out, so she joined a singing group and fostered some of her own thwarted ambitions. One night a week they all went out together to dinner or for a walk.
>
> Ryan had no more accidents and gradually stopped picking fights. He formed a very strong friendship with Paul, a boy that Lacey would have said was Ryan's intellectual inferior. Still, she liked the relationship because it obviously gave both boys a lot of pleasure. When Ryan told her he wanted to go to swimming day camp with Paul during the summer, she agreed to car-pool with Paul's mom. She and Richard started talking more—about everything, not just Ryan.

PARENTS' SUGGESTIONS

Some of the ideas below may help you to work with your child's real potential.

1. Do give your child the chance to try out several different activities. Don't be surprised or disappointed if he drops out halfway through his course or wants to take a week off. Young children's interests are fickle, and their concentration spans are still limited.
2. If your child obviously excels in one particular area and loves doing it, by all means foster it, but not at the expense of the rest of her life.
3. Don't push your child too quickly into the adult version of his casual entertainment. Just because he had fun riding a

pony at the county fair doesn't mean you have to start horse-back-riding lessons, which may seem frightening and difficult, and turn him off completely.

4. Try not to be critical of your child's failures; he's probably trying as hard to please you as he is to come in number one, and that kind of stress may affect his performance.

5. If you're in the habit of showering your baby and child with presents, you should take a step back and ask yourself if you're overcompensating for all those birthdays *your* parents ignored.

6. Some excellent books on the subject are *Don't Push Your Preschooler* by Louise Bates Ames and Joan Ames Chase, *The Unhurried Child* by David Elkind, and *The Superbaby Syndrome* by Jean G. Fitzpatrick.

PLAY: THE MOST IMPORTANT TEACHER

Children learn from play, and the more they are able to make the play their own, the better. Getting a slew of fancy toys may pale in comparison to being shown how to attach a string to a stick and catching a real fish with it.

If you allow your child to go at his own rate, he'll feel connected to where he is and what he's doing. No matter how you felt your parents let you down or how eager you are to help your child along, you can't push any harder than he's emotionally and psychologically ready to go.

It's best to encourage your child to immerse himself in all kinds of experiences, not expecting that he will excel in everything you mastered or fail in everything you flunked. Your world isn't his and can't be—not now because he's a child and you're an adult, and probably never because you're two different individuals. When you see his aptitudes and interests emerging, you can encourage them fully and then step back and watch as he dives right in, ready to pick and choose from all the myriad possibilities you've laid out before him.

15
Sibling Rivalry

Which of the following statements is true for you?

1. The worst thing I ever did to my older child was to bring his new baby brother home.
2. I can't stand all these babyish habits my four-year-old has picked up since the birth of her brother. I keep trying to shame her out of them, but it's not working.
3. It makes me feel guilty to see my kids fight because I believe every battle is for my attention. But the only way they're going to learn to share is for me to stay uninvolved and distant from the whole thing.
4. When my second child was born, I thought, Thank God, at last a boy. Now I can really be a parent.

As the above statements indicate, many parents are very conflicted about their ability to give sufficient love and care to each of their children. As much as you've looked forward to expanding your family, as often as you think about the benefits of siblings learning to care for one another and developing close ties over the years, you may still fear, as many parents do, that something

you say or do will set the children against one another and start
a rivalry that goes on for life.·

Rivalry is the need to best your opponent and get for yourself
what appears to be a limited supply of something precious. *Sibling
rivalry* is the natural, normal competition between brothers and
sisters for their parents' love and affection, and it exists in every
family to some degree or another.

Many parents have an underlying worry that having more than
one child means depriving the others; they bend over backward
to be absolutely fair and then realize that they can't be. They
become overly anxious about regressions they see in their older
child and worry that they've spoiled all the good work they did
in the first formative years just by having another baby. These
fears are completely natural and are fed every time the children
fight over a toy or the older bullies the younger. Regardless of
how perfect a parent you try to be, your children will still occasionally make you feel as though you've displaced the first in
favor of the next—someone they fear is newer and better.

THE ORIGIN OF RIVALRY

At first your one child had you all to herself. Any time she wanted
your attention, all she had to do was gurgle or cry or wink, and
you came running. She learned as she grew that certain things
she did—and, later, said—afforded her quicker access to you
and more immediate comfort. But then along came the New Baby.
Let's imagine a possible scenario.

You probably felt preoccupied from the minute you brought
the baby home from the hospital and your preschooler started
making demands. You might have been unnecessarily brusque
when she asked you to read to her when you were in the middle
of preparing a bottle or changing a diaper. The baby's needs were
simpler and more immediate than your older child's, but they
took time. You couldn't figure out why your previously self-
sufficient preschooler now couldn't seem to dress herself or get
her own snacks.

You tried to be absolutely fair and give exactly the same amount of time to each child, but it was impossible. Your preschooler sulked, screamed, grew uncooperative. And to compound the problem, your spouse wasn't much relief when he came home. Instead of paying attention to the demanding older child, he went right to the playpen to spend time with his gurgling, happy infant. No wonder your preschooler says she hates the baby and you feel overwhelmed and annoyed at your spouse.

Any parent in this situation is going to have a lot of anxiety about divided obligations and the kind of rivalry that seems to be sprouting between the children. You and your spouse are going to have to learn to apportion your roles differently, and this will take time and practice. When you drop your expectations about being fair all the time, you can concentrate more on balance. When you see that it's important to get to know each child separately as well as together, there will be less chance of anyone feeling shortchanged.

COOPERATION VERSUS COMPETITION

You'll have to work out your balancing act with the ages of your children in mind. When you have a four-year-old and a new baby, you may have less rivalry than with a two-year-old and a newborn. The preschooler has already had Mommy and Daddy all to himself for quite a while and is moving on into the world, separating happily to engage himself in play groups, preschool, and other friends' families.

The two-year-old, on the other hand, is only beginning to experiment with autonomy and freedom, and is clinging to babyhood at the same time that he desperately wishes to let go. The parents of two children who are close in age or who are twins have to make sure that there is enough of them to go around. Children of this age sincerely believe that parental love, like a cake, has only so many slices. If they see their parents giving away those precious slices to someone else, they fear that there may not be any left over for them.

This distorted view of the amount of available parental love is compounded by your own motivations for wanting a second child.

Many couples who have drifted apart in a marriage think of a second child as a way to reunite; and some who were disappointed with the way the first child "turned out" see the second as another chance to get it right. Some who longed for a certain sex child and at last got their wish the second or third time view the newcomer as their "dream child," their favorite.

But the rivalry for your affection will exist whether you have an emotional stake in one child or not. How can you feel less anxious about the regressive behavior of your older child or worry less that he may suffer in life because he feels he doesn't have enough of you? How can you encourage cooperation among your children instead of feelings of jealousy? How can you use sibling rivalry to your advantage and your children's?

Jealousy is a natural feeling: someone else appears to have an advantage I don't have, and even if I didn't want it originally, I want it because now he has it. Children are jealous of their parents' love and attention for another sibling and also envious of toys, clothes (if the children are the same sex and close in age), and maybe even a room. You can foster a spirit of cooperation between family members and downplay the rivalries by encouraging their differences and showing them the benefits of being who they are.

A SENSE OF PLACE IN THE FAMILY

When your second child is born, you're typically more easygoing, less anxious about details of daily routine and fluctuating moods because you've been through it all before. You also know what's coming up developmentally because of your firstborn. No matter how different all your children are, they all learn to roll over, walk, talk, and experience the terrible two's on some sort of schedule.

Your anxiety about how to parent a *child* undoubtedly lessens the more children you have, but the anxiety you may feel about how to parent *many children* may grow. Because the more you have to divide your attention, affection, interest, and instincts, you may fear that you're overlooking one or overemphasizing the problems of another. And the more anxiety you have about the amount of influence you hold over your children's rivalry, the harder it can be to sort out your feelings and use them for the family's good.

PREPARATIONS FOR THE NEW BABY

The more your child can feel safe and secure in the understanding that she will retain her own place in your affections and in her home, the more easily she'll adapt to the birth of a sibling. When she can anticipate the event, she'll be much better able to deal with it emotionally and so will you.

Here, as always, it's best to take the lead from your child. You might initiate the conversation with a few probing questions about your child's knowledge of and interest in where babies come from. If, as the months pass, she asks lots of questions about childbirth, mimicking child care with dolls and animals, you can fill her in on a few more details, but it's best not to overload her with more information than she wants. A trial run sleeping over at Grandma's or a friend's can be a treat for her and will allow her to anticipate the time when you have to go to the hospital.

You want to paint the new family situation in a good light, but you don't want to make it so rosy that reality will disappoint. The older child may have a vision of a new playmate and may be disheartened when she sees this helpless, crying infant who needs an incredible amount of attention. You want to let your older child know that you're going to appreciate her help, but you don't want to burden her with responsibilities she feels no connection with. Needless to say, even though second children seem to demand less attention, you can't ignore the newcomer's needs because you're so worried about neglecting your first child.

The homecoming of the new baby is a time when your older child can feel particularly lost and displaced. Everyone comes to the house to make a fuss over his baby brother or sister, and she's often ignored. It's crucial that you and your spouse work out a good balance for the first days of your new routine.

Suppose on the first day home from the hospital your husband takes your older child out for ice cream while you get the baby settled in his room. Suppose you have a brand-new baby doll waiting for your preschooler so that she can take care of her own "child" when you're taking care of the baby. Suppose you make a point of showing your child how helpful she can be by getting the changing table ready or bringing a toy over to the bassinet. The more useful and cherished she can feel, the less clinging and dependent she'll act.

It's a good idea to have several discussions before the birth with your spouse about how you're going to juggle tasks and emotional needs. Then, once your new family is in place, you may want to rethink your decisions. A lot of it will flow naturally, just as your balance grew on a daily basis with one child, but the way you manage siblings together will play a big part in just how rivalrous your children become with one another. The more they feel a lack of mommy or daddy, the more they may feel usurped by one another. In order to forestall this, they all have to be assured that they are people in their own right, with personal needs and times for getting special attention.

DEALING WITH YOUR CHILDREN'S AGGRESSION

Parents naturally tend to become frantic when they watch their previously well-socialized four-year-old beating up his one-year-old brother who happened to knock down his sand castle or shred his latest painting. But it doesn't mean that they're set against each other for life, nor does it mean it's all your fault that they can't get along.

Aggression between children occurs most often when they feel they're being unfairly treated. When sibling rivalry sparks hottest, a child is unable to think out or talk out his frustration. From the very beginning, the day the baby is brought home from the hospital, you can help to downplay the aggressive feelings of your older child by explaining that since he's older and wiser, he'll have certain privileges and also certain new responsibilities. If you can temper your own nervousness about how vulnerable and fragile the baby is, and simply but clearly explain how even hard hugging can hurt or how babies just pull hair because they don't know any better, you'll be helping encourage interest rather than aggression. Your older child will start to understand his favored position.

Rivalry begins with the notion: "I want, and I'm the only one who exists." By having to deal with a new baby every day, this notion is rubbed two ways. It becomes more insistent when your child sees you ministering constantly to the "outsider," but it becomes tempered with understanding when you can also make room for the older child's interests, wants, and needs.

As your children grow together, they'll develop their own methods of arguing and negotiating. Unless they're really being violent, it's best to let them settle things themselves. It's also true that no matter how much we want things to work out perfectly in our favor, life isn't fair; a sibling is the best teacher of this hard lesson. But a parent's input can make sense of the fact that what's "fair" for a four-year-old isn't "fair" for a one-year-old. Just as you and your spouse learn to balance your roles, so you can teach your children how to balance theirs.

PLAYING FAVORITES

But emotional balance may elude you, of course, no matter how grown-up you are. As much as you try to see each of your children as an individual with his or her own attributes and assets, you may find that you simply do prefer one over another.

Regardless of how guilty you feel about playing favorites or how well you think you're hiding your preference, children sense this instinctively, and it certainly adds to the rivalry in the household. It's very easy for a parent to contribute to a child's feeling of not making the grade by comparing siblings. An offhand comment such as "I wish Paul could be good and quiet like his brother John" is as detrimental to the relationship between the siblings as it is contributory to Paul's feeling that you can't stand how wild and noisy he is.

As much as possible, you should try to avoid labeling your children. "Maggie's the smart one; Cheryl's the pretty one" is the kind of statement that will make both girls dissatisfied with what they are. They will forever be striving to attain their sister's role and so gain your acceptance.

The same applies with meting out discipline and punishment. Even when you know from experience that Paul generally starts the battles and John just follows through, it's best to be even-handed. The children should be talked to together and then separately about what they've done. Both children should be disciplined at the same time and in a similar, though age-appropriate manner.

Sometimes it's very evident that one child always starts it. He'll misbehave more to get more of your attention, and you end up punishing him so much that it begins to look as though you don't love him. In this situation he's telling you he needs more of you. Giving him positive attention may help to quell his jealousy of his sibling.

GIVING YOUR FIRST CHILD ROOM TO ADJUST

Lynne, Don, and their three-year-old, Rose, entered what Lynne termed "the era of the tornado" when Anna was born. Lynne felt overwhelmed and had a lot of anxiety about raising two such different girls.

"Rose was this curly-haired, watchful, quiet baby and toddler. She rarely had tantrums, had amazing self-control, and an ability to entertain herself for hours on end. When I got pregnant, she was so excited. She helped us get the new room ready and buy diapers, and she was very motherly around her dolls. She really wanted a baby sister, and I told her we would all love whatever we got—boy or girl.

"But we were expecting the baby right around Rose's birthday, which was where the problems started. She wanted to know whether I'd be there for her party. I kept assuring her that everything would go as planned, but wouldn't you know it, I went into labor just as we were hanging the streamers the night before the party. We had told Rose that if the baby came in the middle of the night, Gran—my mother—would come over and stay with her. Of course we missed the party.

"For the next year I think I was always trying to make it up to her. Rose was very angry at me and wanted nothing to do with Anna, which made Don furious. He kept telling her she was the big girl now; it was time for her to grow up. (I wanted to tell him he ought to grow up a little, too, because he was suddenly too busy for any baby chores. With Rose we had split the diapering and bottle feeding, but this time I was on my own.)

"I wouldn't say Rose regressed, she just withdrew. She and I had been so close, and suddenly she wouldn't kiss me anymore. I felt so powerless to get her to like her sister. Nothing I could do or say made a difference. When she came home from pre-school, she was sullen and cranky about sharing me with the baby, and she wanted Daddy, who was generally at work. Every once in a while she'd say how much she loved her new sister or how she was going to teach her to play dress-up one day. These were all things I'd said; when they came out of her mouth, it sounded as though someone was repeating a foreign language tape she didn't really understand.

"One day when Anna was about ten months old I had to go to the bathroom, and I told Rose not to let the baby get on the dining room table—Anna was very active and physical. Rose was playing with her dollhouse in the corner and didn't seem to be paying any attention to the baby. But when I got back, she was yanking Anna away from the house, and before I could reach them, she smacked her sister hard across the face.

"I screamed at her and picked up the baby, who was hysterical. Then Rose looked me square in the eye and said, 'I won't be four. I'm gonna stay three forever.' And I thought, Oh, Lord, they hate each other and it's my fault."

Lynne and Don are going to have to do some thinking about what Rose and Anna each need. The unfortunate coincidence of their birthday notwithstanding, each girl is going to have to be given room to adjust to the other if the friction that already exists isn't to overwhelm the family. When Lynne and Don can step back and see how they contribute to the girls' rivalry, it will be easier for everyone involved to work toward change.

Your Program for Change

For a complete description of how to use this program effectively, see Chapter 4, page 61.

STEP I.   IDENTIFY WHAT'S REALLY BOTHERING YOU
STEP II. CONNECT WITH YOUR PAST
STEP III. GET THE FACTS
STEP IV. UNDERSTAND YOUR CHILD'S POINT OF VIEW
STEP V.   GROUND YOURSELF
STEP VI. STEP BACK AND SEE THE SCENE WITH DIFFERENT EYES
STEP VII. ESTABLISH NEW PATTERNS

STEP I. IDENTIFY WHAT'S REALLY BOTHERING YOU

When you have more than one child, you can easily have more than one set of anxieties functioning at one time. That's why it's essential to break down the various surface elements of your sibling rivalry problem and get to the central issues that threaten to overwhelm you.

Let's think about Lynne, whose daughter Rose seems to blame her new sister Anna for everything she considers unfair about her life. *What is it about this that's really bothering Lynne?*

Unreasonably, Lynne faults herself for her daughters' coinciding birthdays. Rose's comment that she's never going to turn four indicates to Lynne that she's blaming her mother for robbing her of something that was exclusively her own—her birthday; in other words, her very identity as a person.

Lynne also has problems with Don's attitude toward Rose. While she's being protective of her older daughter, Don seems to feel that she should have left babyhood behind during that one night that Anna was born.

Lynne used to think she and Don had an exemplary balance, but now he acts put upon whenever she asks for help. Although he's willing to take Rose alone for an afternoon, he won't take the baby and won't take both girls together. This means Lynne never gets a break, nor does she get time alone with Rose.

It also seems difficult for her and for Rose to deal with a second child who is active and physical rather than quiet and cerebral. Is she worried that she's always going to care more about Rose because she feels more in sync with her?

What's Really Bothering You

Some of the major issues of sibling rivalry are:

- feeling overwhelmed with children's demands
- feeling cheated—not enough time for self and spouse
- concerned about loving one more than the other
- concerned about causing war between siblings
- guilty about displacing the older child

If you're having any anxiety over parenting more than one child, you might want to look at the following questions that pertain to the above concerns:

1. Do you ever find yourself ignoring the baby so that your older child won't feel you're ignoring her?
2. Do you ever feel like throwing up your hands and caring for neither child?
3. Are you annoyed when the younger child picks up bad habits from the older one?
4. Does it bother you when one child looks or acts very much like you? Or like your spouse?
5. Does it upset you unduly when your children tell you they hate one another?
6. Do you ever feel as though your entire life has been reduced to a power play, where someone is always trying to be the winner?
7. Do you ever feel that your children are ganging up on you?

You and your spouse should decide together where the major difficulties lie. Your siblings may share toys well but argue incessantly over who got the biggest piece of cake or who's allowed to sit up front in the car. You may feel that your spouse has stirred up dissension in a certain area or that you have yourself. Only by examining the pattern of all these incidents together will you be able to see where the rivalry is strongest and where you can both help to ease it.

STEP II. CONNECT WITH YOUR PAST

If you were an only child, you may feel ignorant about dealing with the needs of two or more children. If you came from a large family, you may find yourself constantly comparing one of your own siblings to one of your children. This can be confusing and ultimately detrimental to your current family's functioning. But recognizing those old feelings you had as a child and seeing how they relate to your present-day circumstances is going to help immeasurably in establishing new patterns.

Lynne: Lynne was eight when her mother brought her baby sister home from the hospital, and she remembers resenting having to take time from her own friends and homework to help with the baby. She viewed her little sister as a pest, and even now, living halfway across the country from each other, they still aren't close. When Anna was born she had been determined that Rose wouldn't have the same experience. Maybe she has been bending over backward to make sure that Rose likes her baby sister and doesn't see her as too much of an intrusion.

Don: Don was the second in a family with five children. They never had much money, and since both parents worked, Don and his older brother were responsible for their younger siblings. He decided then that he was going to have only as many children as he could comfortably afford to raise himself. He feels more financially responsible now with two children to send through college and anxious about working harder so he can increase his income. He was furious with Rose when he heard she had hit the baby. His own father would have walloped him if he'd done anything like that, but Lynne just froze; as he sees it, she's overprotective

of Rose. Don feels that kids have to learn to adjust. If you're too
indulgent of their complaining, they just do more of it.

How You Can Connect with Your Past

The mental picture you conjure up of you and your siblings
will be filled with good and bad memories, of course, but by
calling up certain meaningful experiences you'll be better able to
compare and contrast your own children's experiences with yours.

SETTING THE SCENE

1. How many siblings did you have? What was your birth order?
2. If you were an only child, did you ever want to have siblings?
   What were your reasons?
3. How did you feel about your older siblings? Your younger
   ones?
4. How did your parents treat you? Was there a favorite?

Now that you can see clearly, how did you experience sibling
rivalry?

Some memories that many parents recall have to do with the
following:

• feeling intense admiration for their siblings
• feeling intense jealousy
• a desire to have one's parents' exclusive attention
• a need to have an ally against the parents

The following questions that relate to some of the above concerns may evoke certain useful feelings about your past:

5. Did you ever feel shortchanged, as though you were sure
   your siblings were getting better treatment than you?
6. Did you ever feel you'd been given undeserved rewards?
7. Was there a time when a sibling came to your rescue?
8. Was there a time when a sibling got you in trouble?

9. Did you notice that your parents were nicer to you if they were angry at one of your siblings? Or at each other?
10. Did you ever feel you and your brothers and sisters were allied against your parents?

If you were a sibling yourself, you may be able to look back at your childhood and pick up some very telling clues about how your own children strive for your attention and attempt to retain their own place playing, fighting, and living together.

STEP III. GET THE FACTS

When you have some hard information about the circumstances of your children's rivalry, it will be easier for you to work toward change with them.

> *Lynne:* She decides to keep a log of how much time she and Don spend with the children, alone and together. She finds out that Rose's alone-time with her is severely limited now, particularly since she has started preschool. Don is spending practically no time with the baby.
>
> She also looks around at the house to see whether Rose is being made to share too much. She has her own bedroom, but the children share a playroom. Many of Rose's old toys are now Anna's, but it turns out that they both play with all the toys. Seeing Anna interested in her old baby things sparked Rose's interest in them again.
>
> She notes that Anna, who is very physically adept, seems to be in Rose's space a lot. It looks as though Anna gets the best of most situations, even though Rose is older and more coordinated. At their last joint birthday party Anna was the one who got to blow out the candles on the cake, and she received more toys, too. It must look very good to Rose to be the baby (to "stay three forever") because this particular baby gets all the goodies.
>
> Lynne also checks with the preschool teacher and discovers that even though Rose plays well with older children, she bullies the younger ones, who undoubtedly remind her of her sister.

310 THE ANXIOUS PARENT

Consider Your Own Facts

1. How can you and your spouse adjust to the addition to your family? *Be honest and open about the kind of cooperation you expect or feel prepared to give. Some parents who felt they had more than their share of the burden the first time may wish to juggle responsibilities better the second time.*

2. Have you been sufficiently involved in both children's lives since the birth of the younger? Has your spouse? *You may wish to reevaluate the kind of time spent with all your children. You may be overly concerned with protecting the older child and short-changing the baby, or vice versa. Take the lead from your children to see how much of yourself you should be apportioning.*

3. Are you unconsciously playing favorites? *It's a good idea to check out the kinds of physical behavior you show each child. Do you tousle the hair of your older child when you go out but only wave good-bye to the younger? Do you play more intently with one child because you happen to feel more comfortable with his stage of development?*

4. Are you treating them in an age-appropriate manner? *Sometimes parents tend to treat all their children the same—infantilizing the older ones or expecting too much of the younger. Try to allow the older special privileges that are right for his age, and give the younger more help when it's appropriate.*

5. How can you negotiate between them without interfering? *If they're not succeeding in solving their own battles, you may wish to give them some inducement to work together, that is, a reward for joint room clean-up. This will show them that they both get more positive attention from you the more they cooperate with one another.*

6. What can you do about regression? *The older child regresses to babyhood because she can see what kind of attention the new baby commands. It's best not to criticize the thumb-sucking, bed-wetting, and so forth, but instead make extra time to do "grown-up" things with that child alone. Peer pressure will also probably help a great deal to discourage the behaviors.*

7. If one is misbehaving more or getting sick more, how can you tell if this is an attention-getting device? *Step back and see whether you are having trouble juggling your own needs and your children's. You may want to be a bit more lenient about the misbehaving and a bit less concerned over injuries and malingering. Again, more alone-time will make the child feel more secure.*
8. When is aggression between children too much? *When it turns to violence. Children who are hurting each other should be separated and spoken to individually. Their separation and loss of playtime should be sufficient punishment and an indication that learning to cooperate together is their goal.*

STEP IV. UNDERSTANDING YOUR CHILD'S POINT OF VIEW

The process of understanding your child's point of view is complicated when there are more children and more points of view. The best parent plays Solomon, listening to all sides of an issue and then helping the children decide together on the outcome. The more you can encourage the idea that despite their rivalry they must learn to live together, the more you give them a good model for life.

Lynne and Don: They sat down with Rose and Anna after dinner one night to have a family discussion about the girls' upcoming birthdays.

"We were thinking," Lynne began, "that since you're the oldest, Rose, you should pick what kind of party and cake you want to have."

Rose scowled because Anna had just started running her wooden trains over Rose's feet. "Stop that!" she yelled at her sister.

"Why don't you move aside or sit in that chair," suggested Don, but he physically moved Anna away from Rose and said, "Don't hurt Rose's foot, Anna!"

"Anna blew out the candles on the cake last year, stupid baby!" Rose growled.

"Well this year you girls are old enough to have your own cakes," Lynne said. "Rose, your party will be on your birthday. Anna doesn't know what day is what, so she can have her own party the week after, okay?"

Rose's face softened. "You mean she wouldn't be there to mess up my things? She'd go away for my party?"

Lynne and Don looked at each other. "We thought you'd both go to each other's parties."

"No!" Rose stated firmly. "I don't want to share birthdays. Ever."

Lynne nodded. This was obviously the one thing Rose couldn't give up. It ought to be her decision. "Okay, we'll do the parties separately. And Daddy will take Anna out for a while when your friends are over."

Don's head jerked up. "I will? Lynne, wait a second. I'm not so good with babies, and . . ."

"Anna's not going to be a baby much longer, Daddy," Rose pointed out. "She's gonna be two. She'll grow up."

Don smiled and shrugged as Lynne cracked up. "Okay, I guess you're right. I'll do it."

Rose went over to her sister and patted her hair. "We're gonna have two birthdays!" she told her confidentially.

Rose has gotten the one thing she really wanted from her sister: the chance to be her own person on her birthday. She's even been able to help her father see that a reorganization of priorities, just for one day, can be important to family well-being.

Bringing Out Your Child's Feelings

Below are some useful statements that parents have offered. You'll probably wish to adapt these to your own situation, and they may trigger some other ideas, too.

1. "I don't care whose fault it was. Let's see what we can all do to make it work."
2. "I don't care who started it. You both hit each other, which means you both forfeit something." (Each child should have to give up something that is meaningful to him.)
3. "Brian can stay up later tonight because he's older; Katy gets to ride in the stroller right now because she's the little one."

4. "You know how your younger sister looks up to you. You could help her get settled at the play group because you've been there and know all the kids and parents already."
5. Books on the subject are plentiful; for example, *Sisters* by David McPhail, *That New Baby!* by Patricia Relf, and *A Baby Sister for Frances* by Russell Hoban.

Acting on Your Child's Feelings

You may notice patterns in the rivalry in your household. If so, it may be helpful for you to get to the causes behind the symptoms and act on them. Here are some examples:

1. You might prepare your older child for the birth by allowing him to help get the baby's room ready or paint his old crib or put away diapers. If he's going to have to share a room with the newcomer, it's best to do some rearranging with him now.
2. When sharing possessions is a problem, you may wish to designate certain toys or parts of a room as specifically the province of one child.
3. It's a good idea to let the older child have time when he doesn't have to share. Give him free run of the house and toys when the younger child isn't around.
4. Try not to assume things about your children's relationship. Asking the older child, "How can you hit your younger sister when you love her so much?" may make the child question what love is in comparison to his true feelings.
5. Don't force your children to be openly affectionate with one another. Making your older child kiss and hug the new baby when she doesn't want to may simply encourage exaggerated squeezing or hurting the baby.
6. Remember to avoid characterizing or labeling your children according to one thing that strikes you. They deserve to be viewed as individuals.

STEP V. GROUND YOURSELF

When you can talk about some of your worst fears concerning the rivalry that exists, you can stop your feelings from escalating into a spiral.

Lynne: She tells herself that Rose is still very young and has a lot of patience about certain things. She's very good about helping to get her sister's meal ready and tucking her in for the night. Lynne can assure herself that she hasn't neglected Rose and will be able to spend more alone-time with her the following year, as Don becomes more tolerant of Rose's strong feelings and more willing to spend time with Anna.

Other parents have used some of the suggestions below as quick diffusers on a rivalry situation:

Anxious thought: If he bites his brother again, I'm going to hit him!
Grounding thought: If I split them up and spend a little time with each one separately, we'll all calm down.

Anxious thought: I was late putting the baby down for his nap, and now my older daughter is going to miss her ballet class and be furious.
Grounding thought: I can call my next-door neighbor and see if she'll drive my daughter to class. Then I can pick her up after the baby's awake.

Anxious thought: Every time I discipline my younger son, the older one comes to his defense. He hates me!
Grounding thought: It's good that they can look out for each other, and the discipline was necessary. I shouldn't take it personally.

STEP VI. STEP BACK AND SEE THE SCENE WITH DIFFERENT EYES

If you can imagine yourself outside the particular situation that's making you anxious, you'll be better able to be flexible the next time a difficult moment arises between your siblings.

> *Lynne:* She would like Rose to accept Anna and would like Don to take more responsibility for being with both children. What does she imagine?
>
> She steps back and remembers coming home from the hospital with Anna. Although Rose was annoyed with her parents for missing her party, she was still excited to meet her new sister and climbed into bed with Lynne to be close to the baby. Don sat on the edge of the bed and hugged "all his girls." Lynne imagines recreating the feeling of that moment of closeness over and over.

Imagine What You'd Like to Happen

If you can suspend reality briefly and see what you'd like to happen among your family members, you'll gain a better perspective on what is really possible. This is not to say that you won't have days fraught with tension or that your kids will stop squabbling over toys and privileges. That part of rivalry is normal. But if you can imagine that the disagreements are all part of a larger picture, where your children are teaching themselves to negotiate their places in your family, you'll be able to take comfort in their developing relationships.

STEP VII. ESTABLISH NEW PATTERNS

Having a child means living with some degree of chaos—messes, noise, and mischief—and it's more chaotic when you have more than one. If your expectations aren't too high, you can establish new patterns with your family that will help you use the rivalries that exist for mutual growth.

Lynne and Don: They each set aside one half day each week for some alone-time with each child, whether it was an outing for a special treat, just doing errands, or hanging around the house. Lynne encouraged Rose's new facility with letters and began reading to her in the afternoons during the baby's nap. Don enrolled Anna in a weekend baby-swim class so that they would have an activity they could participate in together. They also helped Rose make a chart to mark household chores she'd done for herself, her sister, and her parents.

PARENTS' SUGGESTIONS

Some of the ideas below may work for you. They'll probably trigger some new thoughts as to what might work best for your family.

1. Family conferences can be helpful even when your children are very young. The more they know that you will listen to their point of view, the less they may vie with one another for your attention.
2. Time well spent with each child, participating in something you both enjoy, is more valuable than equal time with each.
3. Caring for a family pet is good practice nurturing for a toddler or preschooler and also can demonstrate how gentle you have to be with a new baby.
4. Mealtime can be an excellent opportunity to downplay rivalries and get kids to cooperate. You can show your oldest how much you trust him by empowering him to help you prepare the meal and help the younger one eat.
5. If there's a particular time of day or set of circumstances—trips to the supermarket, rides in the car—that sets off fights, try to rearrange the event. Revising standard seating arrangements or unconscious preferential treatments can go a long way toward fostering harmony between siblings.
6. A couple of good books on the subject are *Raising Cain and Abel, Too* by John McDermott and *Siblings Without Rivalry* by Adele Faber.

Making Time for Your Marriage

Regardless of the rivalries that exist, nothing can replace the sense of comaraderie and loyalty that exists in a multi-sibling family. When you've seen your older one defend the younger from a bully in the playground or watched as he taught his little brother to brush his teeth, you know you've engendered a nurturing sense in him that comes directly from you. He's mimicking what you've done with him and his brother: caring for another human being less developed and experienced than he is.

Though you may not be able to believe this when you have two or three children under the age of four, siblings *can* and *will* eventually entertain each other. When you take advantage of their mutual interests and encourage their being together, you can get some of your own time back for yourself and your marriage. And this is enormously important.

The daily hassle of juggling, being fair, and taking care of all your children's needs can be very wearing on you and your spouse. It's crucial to give your own needs consideration also, so that your parenting doesn't become a rival for your marriage.

A good backup system of babysitters and grandparents is essential if you're going to make time to spend alone with your spouse. A mini-vacation—a romantic or relaxing night in a nearby country inn or a four-day stint in the Bahamas—can help you renew the intimacy that brought you together in the first place.

Even when you're home, going through the regular motions of your ordinary days, you should try to reserve a little time together to talk about something other than your family responsibilities. The more children you have and the more of your personal time they require, the more vital it is for you and your spouse to relate as people, not just as parents.

16
Social Relations

Which of the following statements is true for you?

1. I get so upset when I see my child shy away from other children in the playground. I think, I used to be just like that, and I still hate going to cocktail parties full of strangers.
2. I always dread having play group at our house. My child is impossible when it comes to sharing on his own turf, and I'm afraid the other kids are growing to dislike him because of it. And the mothers think my child is antisocial and I'm to blame.
3. I'm terrified that my child is turning into a pervert: he masturbates every night in the bathtub.
4. I have to keep my child away from that foul-mouthed fresh kid down the block. He's a terrible influence.

If the above statements sound familiar to you, you may be having some anxiety about your child's burgeoning social relationships. Children are basically egocentric beings, but at the same time they naturally gravitate toward other people—other adults who will satisfy some of their needs, other children with whom they can play and share creatively. Humans instinctively seek other humans for companionship, but at the same time they instinctively fight to hold on to their own space. This can cause much anxiety to a parent who wants to be involved in his child's social relations but knows he has to stand at a distance.

We tend to feel very protective when our toddlers and pre-schoolers start having their own relationships. They have other caregivers, they make new friendships, they learn they'll have to give and take without us intervening all the time. At last they figure out that they can function without us.

But it's not an easy transition for many children from the relative safety of the home environment to the big, wide world. You may feel, while watching your child shy away from other kids at a party or bullying a smaller child in the playground, that somehow you've fallen down on the job of helping him become socially acceptable. You may be concerned that your child deals well with you but not with his friends or that he seems more comfortable with new caregivers than he does with you.

All it takes to throw you back to your own childhood—or perhaps adolescence, where being "accepted" was everything—is seeing your child get the cold shoulder from a bunch of thought-less playmates. How poignant it is to remember how *you* couldn't get into a certain clique or how you were left out of school or neighborhood activities because you weren't popular. It's perfectly natural for you to be concerned that your child might suffer the same awkwardness and embarrassment with others as you did. The way you manage your anxiety about this issue can ultimately make a big difference in how well or badly your child learns to cope on his own.

Your child's first social contact, of course, is with you, his parent. Your newborn opens his eyes for the first time and en-counters two looming objects: a smiling, doting father and mother. He cries for food or attention, and one of these objects satisfies his needs. He senses cold, and the objects make him warm. He depends on them entirely, but not just for food and warmth. Part of what makes him human is that his needs are psychological as well as physiological. He *needs* the smiling and the touch of comforting hands on his skin just as much as he needs the bottle or the blanket.

The way you act toward your child, laughing as you tickle his toes or singing to him as you wipe his bottom, helps to influence his expectations of what social contact is all about. If you rush to his side each time he calls out, he comes to expect that others will satisfy him even before he makes demands. If you're slow to respond or don't respond, he'll get the notion that he isn't worthy of much attention.

Because of the way you've encouraged that first early social relationship, your child will learn what to expect from other adults—with a few variations. His grandmother may coddle him more than you do, his uncle may be rougher, or the man in the hardware store may always growl at him in mock anger. Over time your child will come to understand that these other people are potential "friends," not just objects who satisfy his needs.

If your child has a sibling, he'll begin to see how relationships with other children are different from those with adults. Second and third children in a family tend to socialize better, sooner, because they have an example to follow. But siblings, like parents, will be fairly accommodating to each other's whims and moods. This is not necessarily the case with friends. When your child plays with others his own age, he has to learn to modify his wishes and begin to accept the fact that he can't be the center of his own world all the time. Someone else with whom he wants to spend time has another point of view. And if he wants to keep on playing, he has to make room for someone else's wants and needs. The ultimate lesson of socialization is that it's more important for two people to be moderately happy together than for one to be completely happy alone.

What really makes a child liked and admired by her peers? Generally her tolerance for other children (ability to share), the breadth of her imagination, and her physical abilities and common experiences. It's typical for a four-year-old to say, "I like Jessica because she has long hair with the same barrettes as me, and we like the slide but we both hate the seesaw."

HELPING YOUR CHILD LEARN TO SHARE

At the beginning of your child's life you are the only arbiter of social conduct. You encourage him to play and explore by showing him how a certain toy works. He responds to you and mimics your actions. This sets the scene for his first social contact with another child.

Before the age of one, most children play·alone or will watch an older child play. When your child is about eighteen months old, he'll be ready for parallel play with another child; that is, play beside but not with someone else. You may not think they're interacting at all, but in fact a great deal is going on from this exposure. The two children get to watch each other manipulating a toy, and that gives them input for future play. They may even decide to switch toys so that although they have less time to enjoy one, they have two toys to play with half the time. By exposing your child to other children, you allow him to come up against another set of needs just as strong as his. This way he can see the advantages of social interaction and learn how to make the necessary accommodations.

Just when you're getting anxious that your child will never really engage himself with another child, he crosses the next boundary of time and sophistication and starts to interact. When he's about two and a half he begins to play and, unwillingly, to share. He doesn't need you hovering because he and his friend have created a world unto themselves, with two perspectives, working together in discord and harmony. At about three and a half, children get really interested in cooperating to use the world they imagine as well as the world they see. When two little girls put on their mother's hats and shoes and mimic going shopping, they are involved in a very creative social endeavor.

The way you present yourself to others is naturally going to be a model for your child. Parents can become very anxious about the messages they're delivering. A terribly shy mother may worry that she's going to infect her child with her own terror of other people. A gregarious, fun-loving father may be upset when his son isn't outgoing.

Your child's relationships with other people are a good barometer of how you've gotten your message across, but you can't expect social adeptness to be a constant at this stage because your child is still developing. You may find that there are days when your four-year-old is completely selfish and pigheaded around you, but his babysitter may tell you that he remembered it was her birthday and made her a card. You may despair that your three-year-old pulls her baby brother's hair, but her preschool teacher may tell you that she is never physically aggressive with her friends. Or, on the other hand, just when you're feeling that your baby has turned into a rational, reasonable human being, your neighbor may come over to complain about how her son and your son just dug up her entire garden.

HOW TO FACILITATE INTRODUCTIONS BETWEEN CHILDREN

In the best of all possible worlds you'd be able to take your child to a play date or sitter or new school, give him a kiss, and then watch him forge ahead into the strange setting, introducing himself and engaging himself in play with others. For some children, meeting new people is easy, as it is for many adults. But if your child hangs back and withdraws, clinging to your pant leg or hiding her head, it's easy to feel anxious about her social awkwardness. You may feel you have to intervene, to pave the way and make everything "all right" for her. This might put a temporary end to your own anxiety, but it won't help your child overcome the difficulties she's experiencing. Only when she learns to meet and greet people on her own will her and your anxieties begin to diminish.

If you walk up to a new child in the playground and make introductions for your child, you're not giving her the opportunity to develop her own social competence. If she wants to be shy and just watch for a few minutes, so be it. Allowing her to take her time and do things at her own pace will make her feel more comfortable, and if she sees that your anxiety about her lack of initiative has lessened, she may feel ready to let go.

But suppose you have a child of a different temperament, one who wants to take charge immediately. When you see your four-year-old bossing everyone in the playground, you may be worried that the others will reject her. You may be tempted to pull her back and ask her to be a little more considerate. But this kind of admonition can be very embarrassing and may have the opposite effect. Her best restraint will be the other children themselves. If she's too bossy, they'll let her know by bossing her back or refusing to play, which in turn will teach her to modify her demands.

This isn't to say that you can't have any input, but you should measure your feelings and expectations for her socialization against your own experience. If you overcame shyness yourself or if you tend to monopolize the conversation at parties, you may have an unreasonable desire for your child to either mimic your tempo of meeting and greeting or change it entirely. Parents who expect too much of their children tend to reinforce the shyness or bullying. But you can assist your child by finding out what's making her uncomfortable and pointing out—before and after the social event—what she was doing that might have attracted or alienated others.

MAKING YOUR CHILD AVAILABLE

The casual collection of children gathering spontaneously to play in various neighborhood backyards is almost a thing of the past. Today, particularly with two-career families, opportunities for social interactions between children have to be carefully arranged. It's important for your child to have exposure to other children and adults. Play dates and play groups afford excellent social opportunities.

A one-on-one play date with a neighbor or friend may be the easiest to manage with young children, although play groups where either all the mothers attend or one mother is in charge afford a chance for your child to mingle with many playmates and maybe decide on a few favorites. A preschool or nursery

school is an even more socializing event since your child will
have to be without you for a considerable period of time, adhering
to new rules made by other caregivers and other children.

If you find yourself reluctant to plan social events for your
child, you might ask yourself if this could have something to do
with an anxiety that she won't be able to handle the experience.

As much as you may worry about exposing your child to that
vast new world of people, as much as you know that everyone
isn't always nice and fair and kind, it's these early experiences
that afford your child a wonderful chance to discover new things.
When he can show you that he's functional in a world of his own
that you have no part of, you'll begin to see the real meaning of
separation and independence.

FRIENDS AS INFLUENCES

The first time your child comes home spouting "bad language,"
talking back to you, or perhaps telling you a lie, it's easy to become
concerned that he has met up with some terrible influences. When
you call him on this behavior, he'll undoubtedly say something
like, "Well, Johnny does it." Naturally you're going to worry that
Johnny's influence has become more powerful than your own. (This
is the origin of the momism, "If Johnny jumped off the Empire
State Building, would you do it?")

It's a good idea to speak to the offending child's mother to see
whether the two of you may be able to work something out. It's
possible that she's not aware of her child's social infractions and
will be grateful for your input. If she's not, you can simply point
out to your child that Johnny behaves a certain way because that's
okay in his family but it's not okay in yours. There's no advantage
in telling him he can't play with Johnny because, after all, the
world is filled with people you don't like, and you can't stay away
from them all the time. Your influence is still the strongest presence
in your child's life, and when you're able to help him differentiate
acceptable from unacceptable ways of acting, he'll get the message.

EARLY SEXUALITY IN FRIENDSHIPS

Many parents find that friendships between small children are very physical, and they may worry about contact between play-mates that looks suspiciously sexual. If you've come upon your child playing doctor or running around naked or playing with her own genitals while with a friend, you may feel uncomfortable and confused as to what to do.

But intimacy between children can be physical and not sexual; it's simply a part of exploration. If you're anxious about your child exposing herself or masturbating or even seeing you and your spouse naked, you can simply explain to her that certain ways of being are private and not to be shared.

Another natural concern you may have is your child coming into contact with some disturbed adult who wants to touch or view him naked. It's not unreasonable to talk to your child hon-estly, in a nonthreatening way, about the fact that no grown-up other than Mommy and Daddy and the doctor should touch his body—because it's his. You can caution him, without scaring him, that if anyone ever touches his genitals, he should yell loudly and quickly go and find another grown-up he knows.

A PRESCHOOLER'S ADJUSTMENT

Carole and Ian talked a lot about their daughter Mimi's reluctance to meet new kids. Ian, a gregarious commercial artist, was worried that Mimi played well only with her best friend Boko who came over every afternoon. Carole liked the arrangement, but Ian had a nagging fear that he should do something to expand his daugh-ter's social world.

"I figured preschool would do it for her, but I figured against the nature of my own child. The first few weeks, she was miser-able. The teachers said she played by herself or next to the other kids but not with them.

"Then she came home and told me some boy—Kyle—had thrown a ball accidentally on purpose at her. I told her some children did things like that so she'd pay attention and play with them, but she didn't believe me. And it apparently got worse because the teachers mentioned that a few kids had been picking on her because they saw the cringing way she reacted. To top it all off, she was taking out her frustrations on Boko—bossing her around and being real mean when she came home from school.

"Carole just didn't seem to get this, maybe because she doesn't make friends easily on her own. She has always sort of tagged along and accepted my friends. But she was trying to suggest that I was compounding Mimi's problem by wanting her to be outgoing. She said that was just like me, that I monopolize every group I get into. I was really annoyed with her.

"One night I was putting Mimi to bed and she started crying. She said she wanted me to go to school and beat up Kyle, that her mom had told her girls didn't fight and she should just ignore him and he'd go away. But I told her she'd feel much better if she'd stand up for herself. As soon as the kids figured out that she was tougher, they'd start to respect her.

" 'Let's practice,' I said. 'The next time Kyle bothers you, you put your hands on your hips and say, very loudly so the teachers can hear, "You stop that right this minute!" ' She did it, but in a very scared voice. I told her she'd have to speak up, but she kept saying she wanted me to do it for her.

"The next day she came home from school and said that Kyle had kicked her. The teacher had put the boy in time-out and spoken to his parents, but that didn't make Mimi feel any better. I asked if she had tried yelling at him the way we practiced. She said she hadn't, that she couldn't do it; that she hated school and never wanted to go back. I was so upset for her, but I didn't know what to do."

Ian is having trouble figuring out how to help his daughter over her hurdle and how to explain to his wife that it is a hurdle. He understands it's important for her to have a social life without his interference, but his anxieties about her social relations are making problems in the family as well as for Mimi personally. He's going to have to examine his real feelings before he can do anything to help her.

Your Program for Change

For a complete explanation of how to use the program effectively, see Chapter 4, page 61.

STEP I. IDENTIFY WHAT'S REALLY BOTHERING YOU

STEP II. CONNECT WITH YOUR PAST

STEP III. GET THE FACTS

STEP IV. UNDERSTAND YOUR CHILD'S POINT OF VIEW

STEP V. GROUND YOURSELF

STEP VI. STEP BACK AND SEE THE SCENE WITH DIFFERENT EYES

STEP VII. ESTABLISH NEW PATTERNS

STEP I. IDENTIFY WHAT'S REALLY BOTHERING YOU

There are always a variety of elements involving social interaction that can be problematic, but there's probably one central concern that's causing you to feel upset. Let's take Ian's situation as an example. *What is it about this experience that's really bothering Ian?*

He's upset because Mimi's patterns of interacting with other children don't seem to be working for her. She bosses the one child she has always gotten along with but is terrified of dealing with an aggressive child who comes after her.

In some way this reminds him of Carole's way of dealing with the world. He describes his wife as self-sufficient but says that she "tags along" after him. And Mimi has reported that Carole has cautioned her against getting involved with this boy. Does he fear that Mimi is patterning herself too much on her mother, who doesn't have much facility for social relations?

He also doesn't like the fact that he feels impotent in the scope of Mimi's new world. He wants her at preschool so that she can learn to fend for herself, but she's not doing that, and he's not around to help her. And he worries that in wanting to help, he's crowding her out.

What's Really Bothering You

Some major parental concerns over children's social relations are as follows:

- feeling upset that their child can't function alone because they've kept him too dependent for too long
- having friends and neighbors suspect they are bad parents because they have a difficult or aggressive child
- feeling jealous that their child may be influenced by people other than family
- feeling anxious that their child may endanger himself because he's too friendly with strangers
- having a sense of loss and loneliness that their child doesn't need them anymore

If you are having any anxiety over your own expectations about social issues, you might want to look at the following questions that relate to some of the above concerns:

1. Are you reluctant to make a play date because you fear that your child may act badly and disrupt it?
2. Do you get angry when your child is selfish and won't share?
3. Do you tend to blame the other children—not yours—for a difficult play session? Do you blame their mothers for not raising them right?
4. Do you load your child up with "don'ts" before preschool or a play date or sleepover where you won't be present?
5. Do you feel a need to interrogate your child after a social event he has been to without you? Do you need to interrogate the mother in charge?
6. Do you worry that your child will be confused by having to play by different sets of adult rules when in someone else's care?
7. Do you panic when your child is away without you?

If you can examine your own reactions while watching your child interact with another adult or child, and determine whether they tend to stem from anger or jealousy or fear of the unknown, you'll have taken the first step in your investigation. It's your job to differentiate the realistic concerns you may have from your overly emotional reactions.

STEP II. CONNECT WITH YOUR PAST

The way you dealt with others and the way your parents encouraged or discouraged you from forming friendships is of utmost importance when it comes to handling your feelings about this matter now as a parent.

> *Ian:* Ian was an Army brat, and the family moved around a great deal, making and leaving friends on a regular basis. Ian's mother was a volunteer in numerous organizations, and the women she invited over for meetings invariably brought their children, so that Ian and his sisters learned to flow with the personnel who were around. But his father disliked having his private time disturbed, and Ian could remember some terrible arguments between his parents about having "those yakkity-yak tea ladies" over so often. Ian felt torn between his parents' perspectives; he truly enjoyed being with lots of people, but he was aware of his father's feelings that superficial relationships were worse than no relationships. He always wondered if he disappointed his father, if his father thought his son didn't have good judgment about people. Is he worried that Mimi may also lack judgment about handling herself in a social situation, and does he feel inadequate to help her?

How You Can Connect with Your Past

Prepare a mental picture for yourself as a child dealing with others, and ask yourself questions that will deepen your perception about the way your family handled social relations.

SETTING THE SCENE

1. When you were growing up, do you recall your family being gregarious, entertaining, and visiting? Or were they solitary?

2. Were you allowed to bring kids home from school and go to their houses to play?
3. Were you allowed to ask a friend to stay to dinner? To have sleepovers? At what age?
4. Did your parents have close, intimate friends, a circle of acquaintances, or both?

Now that you can see clearly, how did you experience social relations?

Some typical memories that many parents recall had to do with the following:

• fearing outsiders, a sense that only family was really okay
• a sense that they never had privacy, that their home was always being invaded by outsiders
• a feeling of being stifled, as though they had to escape
• a sense of jealousy, that others had things better than they did

The following questions that relate to some of the above concerns may evoke certain feelings about your past:

5. Was it hard for you to make friends? Did you think nobody liked you?
6. Did your parents trust other children's parents to supervise you?
7. Did your parents gossip about people behind their backs?
8. Did your parents compare you to your friends? Favorably or unfavorably?
9. Were you ever punished for something you did with a friend?
10. Do you remember keeping secrets with friends from your parents? Lying to them about things you'd done without them?

Just because you remember feeling either socially awkward or socially adept doesn't mean your child will necessarily relive your past. When you can examine your own experience, it may be easier for you to separate your old feelings from those you're having now as a parent.

STEP III. GET THE FACTS

Try to collect whatever factual information you can gather about your child's social relations.

> *Ian:* He schedules a conference with Mimi's preschool teacher and asks her how some of the other children in the class handle teasing. She explains that some of the girls have started sticking together and that the more rambunctious boys seem to stay away from them. She says she's been trying to introduce Mimi into this group, but she's been reluctant. There is one very shy new girl, Jessica, who sometimes sits with Mimi on the bench, but they haven't really started relating.
>
> Ian gets the phone number of Jessica's parents and arranges a play date for the girls at a nearby park after school. Mimi makes no attempt to go to Jessica but clings to Ian. He tells her to please play for a while because he wants to do some sketches. He notices that Mimi doesn't involve herself with any of the other children in the park but keeps drifting back to Jessica. After an hour the girls start digging in the sandbox together, making up a story about being on the beach. He can see that they are trading toys and sticks back and forth.
>
> He learns from a child development book that although social skills grow as the child grows, children of less adaptable temperaments will always be slower to warm up to others. He also reads that it's best to allow your child room to deal with others on her own. Only if your child is being a tyrant or is getting hurt should you step in.

Consider All Your Facts

1. Do you really fear your child is asocial or antisocial? *Ask another caregiver who has been with your child over a period of time. Observe your child in a variety of different social settings before making judgments.*
2. Do you think your child's attitude toward others is overly

influenced by your own? *Children sometimes compensate for their parents' way of socializing. The child of a gregarious person might be less outgoing; the child of a terribly shy person might race toward social contact.*

3. How can you modulate your child's behavior in a social setting without interfering? *By setting a good example yourself and by talking to your child in an uncritical way about what you've seen her doing or not doing with friends and other caregivers.*

4. What can you do if you don't like the parent of the child your child wants to play with? *You can send your spouse or another caregiver on the play date or offer to take both children to your house. It's important that the children be able to play without the friction between adults getting in the way.*

5. What do you do if other parents are giving you "bad" reports about your child's behavior? *Think about the differences in your parenting attitudes; the others may be stricter or more liberal than you. Question your child to see if his point of view conflicts. Assuming there's some truth on both sides, it's best to explain to your child what things are and are not permitted at other children's houses.*

6. How should you deal with what appears to be early sexual behavior? *You should emphasize the importance of privacy for masturbation or nudity. These are both very natural and normal in the development of the preschooler, and if you can, try to keep your own discomfort out of it. Give your child only as much information about his body and its functions as he's capable of absorbing at this point.*

STEP IV. UNDERSTAND YOUR CHILD'S POINT OF VIEW

When your child is old enough to have friends of her own, her opinion and her friends' opinions are the ones that count the most. Only by being empathic when you talk to your child about her friends and other caregivers can you really make sense of any situation involving social relations.

Ian: Mimi had Boko over for an afternoon "tea party" one Saturday. The girls were sitting on the porch with their dolls, and

Mimi was pouring tiny cups of tea from her new tea set. Ian told them he was going to bring out the cake and went into the kitchen.

"Now, Boko, you put your doll in time-out because she was rude," Mimi instructed her friend firmly.

"No, she wasn't," Boko argued.

"Was too!" Mimi very huffily took the doll and shoved it toward the end of the porch. "She can't have any cake!" Mimi declared.

"You're the one who can't have cake. You stink!" Boko shrieked.

Mimi burst out wailing and lunged for Boko. Ian, who had heard some of this from the kitchen, burst through the doorway, juggling the cake plate. "Stop that!" he said sharply to his daughter. "What's going on here?"

Mimi, her face streaked with tears, pointed a finger at her friend. "Boko's as mean as a boy. She said I stink."

"She said I had to put my doll in time-out," Boko countered.

"Look, I thought you were having a nice tea party. How are you supposed to entertain each other if you're screaming?"

"I'm gonna cut the cake," Mimi demanded bossily.

"No, me!" Boko countered. Both girls lunged for the cake server.

Mimi was really crying now. "I never get to go first. She's always first. I want Boko to go home!"

Ian felt terrible, and he sympathized with the other child. "Mimi, you hurt Boko's feelings. Apologize!"

"No! You apologize to her. You're always nicer to her than you are to me anyway." She glared up at him with hatred.

Ian realized that he was about to scream or send Mimi for a time-out herself, but he also realized that she felt he'd hurt her just as she'd hurt Boko. Maybe he shouldn't have interfered, and it would all have blown over. But it was too late now. "I tell you what," he said. "One of you gets to cut the cake, and the other gets to choose the first piece. One pours the lemonade, and the other picks the first glass. Who's doing what?"

Mimi nodded. "Boko, you can cut, and then I'll pick."

Boko smiled. "Uh huh. And you pour and then I'll pick."

"Okay."

Ian watched his daughter hand over the cake server as if sharing was as easy as anything. Her friend carefully cut four pieces, two big ones for the girls, two small ones for the dolls. Then Mimi asked, "Boko, can I cut one for my daddy?"

"Sure." Her friend nodded and handed over the knife.

Mimi looked up at her father and looked down again. She cut a gigantic piece for him. "I talked back to Kyle yesterday," she confided. "I told him to stop kicking me, and guess what? He ran away. Okay, Boko, which piece do you want?" she asked genially.

Ian's own anxiety lessened as he started feeling that he had helped equalize relations between them by giving them both "important" choices. But he also felt a huge weight lift off his shoulders when Mimi told him how she'd taken care of Kyle—all by herself.

Bringing Out Your Child's Feelings

Try to put yourself in your child's place and see the world through her eyes. When she says things about social situations that seem strange to you, try to think the way she thinks, seeing the world fresh every day. You might elicit her thoughts with the following:

1. "That boy in the sandbox looks lonely. Would you like to try and make him feel better by asking him to play?"
2. "If you want to play alone today, that's okay. But Emma asked if you could come to her house tomorrow. What did you and Emma do together the last time you played?"

Acting on Your Child's Feelings

1. You can make things easier for your child by doing them at her pace. If she hates roll call because she has to raise her hand and therefore stand out from the group, explain this to the teacher and bring her to school a little late.
2. Don't force her to socialize when she's not ready or if she's had enough. She may prefer spending the afternoon alone if she's been at preschool all day playing with other children.
3. Try not to be critical of her style of playing with other children or being with other caretakers. These relationships tend to work themselves out over time.
4. You don't have to curtail your social life because of your child's preferences. There's no reason to feel guilty about visiting people you like if she doesn't happen to be crazy about their children. You can simply explain that the world is full of lots

of different kinds of people, and she doesn't have to love them all to spend a little time with them.

5. A book can help your child relate to different social situations. Two good ones on the subject are *Best Friends* and *Will I Have a Friend* by Miriam Cohen and Lillian Hoban.

STEP V. GROUND YOURSELF

Talking out your anxiety can help you to get a temporary fix on where you really are and ground you before you spiral out of control.

Ian: He can tell himself that Mimi has come a long way socially since she started preschool. Going from a rather sheltered existence with just family and one best friend, she has expanded her horizons to several different teachers and caregivers and one burgeoning friendship at preschool, as well as the social contact she has by watching the other children at play. He can remind himself that not all children can entertain themselves alone as well as Mimi, and he can reassure himself that she is learning, although slowly, to play with others. He can hope that her creative imagination will eventually click with that of another creative child and that her social skills will blossom as she decides it's fun, even inspiring, to share with someone on her own wavelength.

You may want to try saying aloud something like the statements below. They can act as quick diffusers of your anxious feelings.

Anxious thought: Oh, God, he's kicking and punching, and all that boy did was take his ball! Where's his mother, and what's she going to think?
Grounding thought: I'm going to go over and separate them. Maybe the other kid said something to provoke him. And where *is* his mother? At least I'm there when my child needs me.

Anxious thought: Suddenly my child is a social butterfly. She never wants to be with me anymore. Has she stopped loving me?
Grounding thought: It's great that she likes other people. And I was always complaining that she was too clinging with me.

Anxious thought: She hates every babysitter I pick. Why can't she deal with other authority figures?

Grounding thought: She's always annoyed when we go out at night without her. That doesn't mean that she can't handle adults telling her what to do. Her teachers say she's great in preschool.

STEP VI. STEP BACK AND SEE THE SCENE WITH DIFFERENT EYES

When you can mentally remove yourself from the scene and use your imagination, you can open yourself up to all sorts of new possibilities for social situations.

> *Ian:* He remembers last summer on the beach. He had been out in the surf, and when he came back he was astounded to see Mimi and Carole entertaining two other three-year-olds on their blanket. His usually reticent child was dumping sand into one child's bucket and laughing as the other new acquaintance buried her feet in sand. If Mimi could get involved happily when she was three, he realized, she was going to be able to do it again at another stage of her development.

Imagine What You'd Like to Happen

When you can stop thinking of yourself as the ultimate "overseer" of your child's life, you're going to be a lot more relaxed about the outcome of the social relations he has—both in your presence and out of it. You're not the only determinant of his social acceptability and adeptness, though right now you're certainly the most dominant, persuading, and guiding influence. If you can see yourself in this flexible, helpful role, you may be better able to step back and allow your child the freedom to relate to others.

STEP VII. ESTABLISH NEW PATTERNS

Some parents are surprised to find that what they thought was their most central concern is really peripheral, that perhaps the most difficult thing about their child's burgeoning social life is that it takes their child further away from them. Our children grow up fast these days, and their new friends and caregivers represent the first push out of the warm nest we've created for them. Yet if we can see this push as a necessary and useful one, we'll be more comfortable with the new patterns we establish.

Ian: Ian and Carole started talking more about their own way of sharing and about ways in which they interact with other people. Ian told Carole he was very upset when she accused him of taking over all the time; she said that it was grudging admiration of his style. She admitted being defensive and realized that she could give a little more in social situations.

They began car-pooling with a neighbor down the block when they learned that she had just started sending her child, Rachel, to the same preschool. Mimi was shy with Rachel at first, but when the younger child began asking her questions about preschool and she became the "big kid," it seemed to give her a feeling of power and control.

Ian and Carole also got involved in the neighborhood Sunday softball game and brought Mimi along. Sometimes Boko came, and the girls paired off to the exclusion of other children, but as the weeks passed Ian noticed that Mimi was expanding her social circle to include bigger kids who liked to throw and catch with her. Every once in a while he'd notice that she was sitting by herself, but not unhappily. She seemed to be adjusting—slowly but on her own—to the social world around her.

PARENTS' SUGGESTIONS

1. From the beginning of your child's life, take him to the market, the park, the library—anywhere that will offer him exposure to new people. If you're fortunate in having a wide selection of babysitters, use qualified people of all ages and temperaments.

2. You might think about having two of the same toy handy on early play dates, especially something that lends itself to joint play, such as walkie-talkies. This will mitigate the difficulties of having to share one toy.

3. To encourage sharing on play dates, explain to your child that he can play with a toy for a limited time, after which you expect him to give it to his playmate for that same amount of time, and then he'll get it back.
4. If you're nervous about meeting new people yourself, you can offer your child a social setting where you don't have to get involved with other adults, such as a playground or a drop-off play group where only one parent is in charge at a time.
5. Allow your child the freedom of playing in places that will make him most comfortable. If he's best with quieter groups, you might try the libraries' reading hour for tots; if he likes a lot of action, you might enroll him in a baby gymnastics class.
6. It's useful to share responsibility for play dates with your spouse and the host family. This will allow you both a little freedom and will allow your child the experience of additional caregivers.

EQUALIZING RELATIONS

A child learns a great deal about how to behave with other people by watching her parents. If their relationship is adversarial, built on snide comments or overt hostility, the child will probably treat her friends the same way. If fighting and making up is something the parents manage smoothly, the child will learn that it's okay to be angry with friends if you negotiate a settlement afterward. If the parents share duties, possessions, time, food, and so forth, the child won't feel at a loss when she has to share things that are important to her.

The best thing you can do for your child and yourself is to open up the world and make it as nonthreatening a place as possible. If you can get across the message, through your own relations, that other people add richness and variety to life, your child will grow to believe it, too.

Epilogue

You may feel that it's almost an impossible task to figure out on a day-to-day basis what you're supposed to be doing as a parent. And you may never know exactly how your influence affects your child's life.

The kind of person your child becomes is ultimately up to him, but your presence will always make itself felt. Even now if you eavesdrop on your son or daughter admonishing a doll or toy, you may find yourself saying, "My God, that sounds exactly like me!" Regardless of the friends he makes, the mentors he selects, how well he does in school, or the career path he takes, you have a hand in it—sometimes unconsciously, sometimes with deliberate intervention, but you're always there.

Looking back on the few months or years you've already spent as a parent, you can probably see how the anxieties that have fueled your thoughts and feelings have come to bear on your child's development. How the kind of person he or she becomes is bound up in the kind of nurturing you provide. Whether you are worried about his sleeping, eating, separating, or the way he goes or doesn't go to the bathroom, you will soon be able to see that each of these problems is simply a part of the whole.

Sometimes your effect on your child becomes clear to you only when you're able to examine another vital relationship: the one you had from the time you were a child with your own parents. This was the case with Gloria, the parent of four-year-old Kristin.

Kristin was not a particularly affectionate child but a smart, thoughtful, and stubborn one. She had a passionate temper and by four was determined that she would be the best at everything. Gloria was anxious about her daughter's competitive tendencies because they reminded her so much of her own.

It worried Gloria that Kristin was much closer to her than to her husband Evan, until it occurred to her that, after all, she was around most often, which made her the most trustworthy in Kristin's eyes. And the pediatrician assured her that it would all switch when her daughter turned five or six and reached the jealousy stage. Gloria was unusually anxious about the father-daughter relationship, though; she had had trouble relating to her own father, who remained a distant, detached person.

One summer weekend her father and stepmother came over, and they all spent the afternoon at the town pool. Gloria was delighted to see that Kristin was finally warming to her grandfather. On other occasions she had had to remind the child to kiss her grandparents hello and good-bye, and she practically had to hog-tie her to get her to write her name on a birthday card for Papa, as Kristin called Gloria's father.

But on this particular afternoon Gloria was astounded to see her father laughing and playing with Kristin, daring her to jump off the edge of the pool into his arms, then spouting water at her like a whale. Gloria couldn't have imagined her father behaving like this with her when she was little; he was always more concerned with his dignity than his daughter, as she remembered it.

"We came home from the pool and I toweled Kristin's hair dry while I tried to cajole her into getting out of her wet bathing suit. My father looked very tired, and I told him he should sit down. His wife was fretting over him, worrying that he'd had too much sun, but he said he was fine, not to fuss so much.

"Suddenly Kristin threw the towel off and ran to my father, jumping into his lap and throwing her arms around his neck.

'Papa,' she cried, 'I love you!' I looked over and saw that he had tears in his eyes. He patted his granddaughter's hair and, after just a moment's hesitation, hugged her fiercely. 'Oh, Kristin, I love you, too,' he sobbed. 'More than you'll ever know.'

"I have to describe this moment as a revelation. I stood there watching them embrace, and I was three people. I was her, when I was little, asking for his love. But this time I was receiving it back, and it made me deliriously happy. And I was also him, older and maybe expecting less emotionally from others, because my daughter had always given less than I really wanted. Here I was getting a bouquet, a whole garden full of flowers from this child who was so precious to me. And most of all I was me, standing between childhood and old age and realizing in a flash what parenting was all about and why I was doing it. I had the chance he had never had to develop the love that filled Kristin. I had the moments to be tender that had slipped away from him, and I had Kristin's passionate impulses, too—the ones I'd always shied away from when I was a kid. I had it all.

"That didn't mean I wasn't a little jealous that my father was capable of this with her but not with me. And it didn't mean that all the worries I had about her melted away. Not at all. It was just that I was aware of how centered being a parent makes you. You can see from both sides: where you came from and where you're going. We all get so caught up in the details and the day-to-day nit-picking junk of why she isn't eating or why she's sucking her thumb or why she hates the play group. And probably the older your kids get the more anxieties there are. But that afternoon I realized that having a daughter, being a parent, being a child yourself is more than the sum of its parts. And God, what a lesson that was!"

You can help your child learn and can nourish him or her with affection, but it's much more subtle than putting a seed in the ground and seeing it grow. Once in a while you'll get a hint that all your worrying is paying off because it's making you pay attention. Anxiety *does* have a place in our lives, and it's a drastic mistake to ignore it or hope that it will just go away.

When you worry, you care, and when you care, you can change

things. With the help of your spouse, the intuitive glimpses you get into yourself, the knowledge of your own past, the willingness to talk to your child and listen to his responses, the good, solid grounding in the facts of the matter, you can be a wonderful parent. You can make a very big difference in your child's life.

This is not to say that some families don't have more troubles than others. If you find that the anxiety you feel about being a parent is overwhelming or that your problems are much more complex than the issues we've covered here, then professional help may be in order. When your life has turned upside-down due to divorce or death or some other major setback, you and your child should have family therapy in order to survive. And this takes a great deal of time and patience.

For most parents, anxiety is a beneficial tool that can be used well and wisely on a daily basis. Children really do grow up before we know it. We have very little time to be part of their lives, to blend with who they are and what they're doing. Our sometimes less-than-objective fix on their feelings and actions may make us a little crazy, but our continuing concern for their well-being keeps us on an even keel as parents. Together as families we can ride out the storms that anxiety provokes and come to a new understanding of where to go from here. When we do that, our horizons will be limitless.

Index

abandonment, 237, 238
  fear of, 19
adulthood, 38–39
aggression, 256–57, 301–2, 311
AIDS, 149
ambivalence, 34, 35
  separation anxiety and, 232
Ames, Louise Bates, 295
Andrew's Bath (MacPhail), 105
annihilation, fear of, 19
antibiotics, 148
antisocial children, 331
anxiety, parental, see parental
  anxiety
Anxiety Questionnaire, 24–26, 68
anxiety spirals, 20, 23, 154
apologies, 266
appliances, hot, 172
asocial children, 331
assertiveness, 256–57
attention-getting, 311

Baby and Child Care (Spock), 147
baby-proofed homes, 160, 171,
  180
Baby Sister for Francis, A (Hoban),
  313
babysitters, 228, 232, 235, 239,
  240, 247
Balaban, Nancy, 243
bathroom language, 219

baths, 102, 171–72
Bedtime for Francis (Hoban), 128
bedtime rituals, 113, 128
bedtime stories, 128
bed wetting, 121, 124–25, 289,
  310
Berenstain, Jan and Stan, 86,
  153, 176, 243
Berenstain Bears and Junk Food,
  The (Berenstain and Berenstain), 86
Berenstain Bears and the Sitter, The
  (Berenstain and Berenstain),
  243
Berenstain Bears Learn About
  Strangers, The (Berenstain
  and Berenstain), 176
Berenstain Bears Visit the Doctor,
  The (Berenstain and Berenstain), 153
Best Friends (Cohen and Hoban),
  335
books, children's:
  on development anxiety, 195,
    198
  on feeding anxiety, 82
  on health anxiety, 147, 153
  on safety anxiety, 176
  on separation anxiety, 243
  on sibling rivalry, 313, 316
  on social relations anxiety, 335

disrupted breathing and, 124
establishing new patterns in,
131–32
events linked to, 123
and fear of dark, 124
of first-time parents, 113–14
grounding thoughts on, 129–
130
infants and, 112, 114–15
lullabies for, 128
nighttime fears and, 124
parental issues over, 118
parents' privacy and, 112
parents' suggestions for, 132–
134
physical needs vs. psychological issues and, 114–15
present-day reactions to, 119
Program for Change, 116–34
questions on, 118–19
"rocking and rolling," 124
separation and, 112
sleep apnea and, 124
toilet training and, 122, 133
too much vs. too little, 112–
113
toys for inducement of, 123
transitional stages of, 115
sleep apnea, 124
sleep walking, 133
snacking, 89
social relations, social relations
anxiety, 318–38
antisocial children and, 331
asocial children and, 331
bad behavior and, 324, 332
books on, 335
child's point of view and, 332–
335
different social settings and,
331
dual-career families and, 323
early sexual behavior and, 325,
332
encouragement and, 320

environment transitions and,
319
equalizing relationships and,
338
establishing new patterns in,
336–37
facts in, 331–32
of first vs. second children,
320
friends' influence and, 324
grounding thoughts on, 335–
336
identification of, 327–29
imagination used in, 336
interference and, 332
introductions between children
and, 322–23
parallel play and, 321
parental concerns in, 328
parents as models and, 321–22
parents' attitudes and, 320,
331–32
parents' past history and, 329–
331
parents' suggestions for, 337–
338
planned social events and,
323–24
play dates for, 322, 323, 332,
337
play groups for, 323
preschoolers and, 325–26
Program for Change, 327–38
restraints for, 323
sexual abuse and, 325
sharing and, 320, 321–22
shyness and, 321, 323
toddlers and, 321
speech, 196–97
Spock, Benjamin, 147
stereotypes, 189
Sudden Infant Death Syndrome
(SIDS), 124
Superbaby Syndrome, 276–95
activities and, 280–81